Glorifying God

Glorifying God

INSPIRATIONAL MESSAGES
OF THOMAS WATSON

Compiled and Updated by
PATTI M. HUMMEL

*Whoever speaks, is to do so as one who is speaking the utterances of God;
whoever serves is to do so as one who is serving by the strength which God
supplies; so that in all things God may be glorified through Jesus Christ,
to whom belongs the glory and dominion forever and ever.*

I PETER 4:11 NASB

THOMAS NELSON
Since 1798

NASHVILLE   DALLAS   MEXICO CITY   RIO DE JANEIRO   BEIJING

Glorifying God
© 2009 by Patti M. Hummel

Published in Nashville, Tennessee, by Thomas Nelson®. Thomas Nelson® is a registered trademark of Thomas Nelson, Inc.

Thomas Nelson, Inc. titles may be purchased in bulk for educational, business, fund-raising, or sales promotional use. For information, please e-mail SpecialMarkets@ThomasNelson.com.

Excerpts were compiled and updated from Thomas Watson's *A Body of Divinity*.

Unless otherwise noted, all Scripture references are from the King James Version.

Other Scripture references are taken from the New American Standard Bible®, (NASB) © The Lockman Foundation 1960, 1962, 1963, 1968, 1971, 1972, 1973, 1975, 1977, 1995.

Managing Editor: Lisa Stilwell

ISBN 978-1-4041-8712-2

Printed and bound in the United States

www.thomasnelson.com

09 10 11 12 WC 6 5 4 3 2 1

Dedicated to the memory of Thomas Watson,
a mighty man of God.

Thomas Watson (1620–1686) was a Puritan minister, an English nonconformist, and an author. Educated at Cambridge's Emmanuel College, Watson pastored St. Stephen's in Walbrook, England. After being imprisoned in 1646 for his involvement in a plot to recall England's Charles II, he was reinstated to St. Stephen's as vicar. Watson enjoyed fame and popularity until the Restoration when his nonconformity to Protestantism gave cause for his ejection from the pastorate. Watson, however, continued to preach privately as opportunities came his way. In 1672, after the Declaration of Indulgence, Watson obtained the required license to preach at the Great Hall in Crosby House of Oundle School. His health suffered after years of ministry there, and he finally retired to Barnston, Essex. He died there while in his private place of prayer. He left a great legacy, much of which can be found on the pages of this book, *Glorifying God.*

Introduction

Thomas Watson's *Body of Divinity* was required reading during my first year of seminary. The assignment left an indelible mark on me—and that was exactly the intended effect.

My professor had grown weary of the seemingly endless procession of graduates falling victim to pragmatism. Dazzled by the innumerable and novel ministry models available to them, they questioned the value of simply applying doctrine to life and ministry. Compared to contemporary strategy, technique, and spin, biblical theology appeared flat and theoretical. The odds were therefore great that, not long after arriving in ministry, these seminarians would leave their doctrine behind in yellowed syllabi and dusty textbooks. Our professor's determination to help us understand the practical value and life-giving power of theology compelled him to introduce us to Thomas Watson.

Upon opening Watson's book, we soon realized that theology is no mere academic pursuit. To think otherwise is to shut oneself off from genuine life change, the kind of change that only transcendent and divine truth can produce. The exercise of the mind in the contemplation of God—and that is a solid definition of *theology*—is actually the heart of true worship. A believer's contemplation of God in his or her devotional life is the spring from which all other devotion flows. The discipline of focusing on God is the aim of, and not merely an aid in, the Christian life. My professor knew full well that what the redeemed most need are not thoughts of self or innovative church programs, but loftier thoughts of God. In fact, when I read Watson, I discovered how ministers most love their people: by giving them a deeper reverence for God's glory.

Furthermore, Thomas Watson's writings enable one to stand strong against the dead orthodoxy that persistently creeps into our doctrine. His works are no stale systematic treatise or dense commentary. They are instead a primary example of what it means to love God with one's mind. Watson's articulations about life and doctrine read like hymns. From his first word to his last, readers are struck by this man's deep devotion to his Maker.

Sadly, we human beings can obscure the practical benefit of

doctrine. As a result, Christians may view doctrine with a certain amount of skepticism. To them, theology has no relevance to everyday life; it is the playground of intellectuals and fodder for academic debate. Too many theologians and preachers inadvertently contribute to this unfortunate stereotype by employing a vocabulary that reeks of elitism. These teachers too often keep theology out of its proper place, which is within the grasp of the average Christian.

In contrast to this kind of teaching—and as evidence of the superiority of the author's intellect—Watson's writings reflect his giftedness in explaining simply and straightforwardly the most transcendent of truths. This one ability separated Watson from his contemporaries whose works were often too dense to be of significant practical use. He made the complex simple; he put eternity's greatest mysteries in the pocket of the ordinary Christian. By reading Watson, any individual is able to engage the loftiest glories and the deepest realities of the Cross.

Watson's ability to explain the complex in simple terms springs from two sources. First, his own devotional life was energized by his love for God. No man can write as Thomas Watson did without having practiced the presence of the Almighty. Watson's constant delight was to know God more fully, and this passion is evident on every page. Second, Thomas Watson was motivated by a pastor's heart. His works are actually sermons he preached to his beloved flock, and readers get the real sense that they are being shepherded in the contemplation of difficult doctrine and guided toward a better understanding of Scripture.

With an amazing economy of words and phrases, Thomas Watson draws the reader's mind upwards. His writings are a unique blend of utility and artistry. Regardless of the topic, he may be depended upon for clarity and precision. Even a brief encounter with Watson's sermons leaves one deeply impacted. For this reason, Patti Hummel's *Glorifying God* is a precious gift to the church. This volume introduces a new generation of believers to Watson's brilliance, and its format makes his insights accessible to any believer. Presenting Watson in this way is a stroke of genius. The reader will emerge transformed after reading the treasures found in these pages.

Byron Forrest Yawn
Senior Pastor of Community Bible Church, Nashville, TN

Watson was one of the most concise, racy, illustrative, and suggestive of those eminent divines who made the Puritan age the Augustan period of evangelical literature. There is a happy union of sound doctrine, heart-searching experience and practical wisdom throughout all his works . . . His writings are his best memorial; perhaps he needed no other, and therefore providence forbade the superfluity.

C. H. SPURGEON

1

SETTLED IN THE FAITH

Continue in the faith grounded and settled,
and be not moved away from the hope of the gospel . . .

COLOSSIANS 1:23

It's a Christian's duty to be settled in the doctrine of faith. The I Peter 5:10 apostle's prayer says that the God of all grace . . . will . . . establish, strengthen, settle you. That is, that settled Christians might not be meteors in the air, but fixed stars. The apostle Jude speaks of "wandering stars" (v. 13). Unsettled Christians are called wandering stars because, as Aristotle says, "They do leap up and down, and wander into several parts of the heaven; and being but dry exhalations, not made of that pure celestial matter as the fixed stars are, they often fall to the earth." Those not settled in their Christian faith will, at one time or other, prove wandering stars; they will lose their former steadfastness and wander from one opinion to another. These wandering stars are like the unsettled tribe of Reuben; like a ship without ballast, overturned with every wind of doctrine. These are not pillars in the temple of God, but reeds shaken every way. To be unsettled in one's Christian faith argues want of judgment. It also argues lightness. Just as feathers will be blown easily everywhere, so will feathery Christians. Therefore such are compared to children: that "we be no more children, tossed to and fro" (Ephesians 4:14). Children are fickle, sometimes of one mind, sometimes of another; nothing pleases them long. So unsettled Christians are childish; the truths they embrace at one time, they reject at another.

2

EXCELLENCE AND HONOR

A gray head is a crown of glory;
it is found in the way of righteousness.

PROVERBS 16:31 NASB

It is the great end of the word preached to bring us Christians to a settlement in our faith. Jeremiah 23:29 refers to the Word of God as a hammer: Every blow of the hammer is to fasten the nails of the building. So the words are to fasten you to Christ; preachers weaken themselves to strengthen and settle you. The grand design of preaching is to both enlighten and establish souls, guiding them in the right way as well as *keeping* them in it. Those not settled in their faith can't suffer for it; religious skeptics rarely prove martyrs. Those not settled do not answer God's end in giving them the ministry.

To be settled in one's faith is both a Christian's *excellence* and *honor*. It is their excellence: when the milk is settled, it turns to cream. Now Christians will be zealous for truth and walk in close communion with God. And it is their honor: it is a blessing to see an old disciple, to see silver hairs adorned with golden virtues.

Those not settled in their faith also cannot suffer for it; Christian skeptics rarely prove martyrs. Those not settled in their Christian faith hang in suspense; when they think of the joys of heaven, they espouse the gospel, but when they think of persecution, they desert it. Unsettled Christians do not consult what is best, but what is safe. Defectors from the gospel weigh God and Satan against each other, accept the devil's ways, and proclaim him the best master, "putting Christ to an open shame" (Hebrews 6:6). These unsettled Christians will never suffer for the truth, but as soldiers defecting to the enemy's side, they will fight on the devil's side for pay.

3

TO ESPOUSE THE TRUTH

They turned aside like a treacherous bow.
For they provoked Him with their high places
And aroused His jealousy with their graven images.
When God heard, He was filled with wrath
And greatly abhorred Israel.

PSALM 78:57–59 NASB

Not being settled in the Christian faith provokes God. To espouse the truth, and then to fall away, brings an ill report upon the gospel, which will not go unpunished. The apostate drops as a windfall into the devil's mouth.

And if you are not settled, you will not grow. Christians are commanded in Ephesians 4:15 to grow up in all aspects into Him who "is the head, even Christ." But if we are unsettled, there is no growing: "the plant which is continually removing never thrives." Christians who are unsettled can no more grow in godliness than a bone that is out of joint can grow in the body.

There is a great need to be settled, for so many things unsettle us. Seducers are abroad, whose work is to draw people away from Christian principles. First John 2:26 says, "These things have I written unto you concerning them that seduce you." They are the devil's factors; they are the greatest felons robbing you of the truth. Seducers have silver tongues that can put off bad wares; they are deceivers. "By good words and fair speeches they deceive the hearts of the simple" (Romans 16:18). They have fine, elegant phrases, flattering language, whereby they work on weak Christians. They possess a pretence of extraordinary piety, so others may admire them and suck in their doctrine. They seem to be men of zeal and sanctity, to be divinely inspired and pretend to new revelations.

4

BEWARE THE FALSE TEACHERS

They eagerly seek you, not commendably,
but they wish to shut you out so that you will seek them.

GALATIANS 4:17 NASB

Another group of seducers labors to vilify and nullify sound orthodox teachers. They would eclipse those who bring the truth, like black vapors that darken the light of heaven; they would defame others, that they themselves may be more admired. Thus the false teachers cried down Paul, that they might be received.

Yet another group of seducers preaches the doctrine of liberty: as though men are freed from the moral law, the rule as well as the curse, and Christ has done all for them, and they need to do nothing. Thus they make the doctrine of free grace a key to open the door to all those lacking legal or moral restraints, especially those who disregard sexual restraints.

Another means to unsettle Christians is by persecution. The gospel is a rose that cannot be plucked without prickles. Christ's legacy is the cross. As long as there is a devil and a wicked man in the world, never expect a charter of exemption from trouble. How many fall away in an hour of persecution! "There appeared . . . a great red dragon, having seven heads and ten horns . . . and his tail drew the third part of the stars of heaven" (Revelation 12:3–4). The red dragon, by his power and subtlety, drew away stars, or eminent professors of the Christian faith, who seemed to shine as stars in the firmament of the church. The children of Zion should be like Mount Zion, which cannot be removed.

5

CHRISTIANS ARE TO BE GROUNDED

Rooted and grounded in love.

EPHESIANS 3:17 NASB

The way for Christians to be settled is to be well grounded. Christians should be grounded in the knowledge of fundamentals of their faith. The apostle spoke of "the first principles of the oracles of God" (Hebrews 5:12). In all arts and sciences, in logic, physics, and mathematics, there are rules and principles that must be known to practice those arts; so in divinity, there must also be first principles laid down. The knowledge of the foundational principles of the Christian faith is exceedingly useful, or we cannot serve God aright. We cannot worship God acceptably unless we worship Him regularly; and how can we do that if we are ignorant of the rules and elements of our faith? We are to give God a "reasonable service" (Romans 12:1). If we do not understand foundational Christian principles, we cannot offer a reasonable service.

Foundational knowledge of Christianity much enriches the mind. It is a lamp to our feet; it directs us in the whole course of living out our Christian faith. Knowledge of fundamentals is the golden key that opens the mysteries of the gospel; it gives us a whole system and body of divinity. It helps us understand those difficult things that occur in the reading of the Word; knowledge of the fundamentals helps. It furnishes us with armor of proof and weapons to fight against adversaries of the truth. Such knowledge is the holy seed of which grace is formed. It is the seed of faith and the root of love. The knowledge of the foundational principles of the faith is key to the making of a complete Christian.

6

GROUNDED AND SETTLED

*You have need again for someone to teach you
the elementary principles of the oracles of God.*

HEBREWS 5:12 NASB

A well-settled tree must first be well rooted; so, if you would be well settled in the Christian faith, you must be rooted in its principles. So that we may stand in difficult times, we must have a principle of knowledge within; first grounded, and then settled. For a ship to be stationary, it must release its anchor. Knowledge of principles is to the soul as the anchor is to the ship, steadying it in the midst of the rolling waves of error or the violent winds of persecution.

Many people are unsettled, ready to embrace every novel opinion, adorning themselves in as many religions as fashions, because they are ungrounded. Peter referred to these as "unlearned and unstable" (2 Peter 3:16). Those unlearned in the main points of divinity are unstable. Christians cannot be strong in their faith if they lack the grounds of knowledge, for those principles are sinews to strengthen and establish them. It is essential to lay down the main foundations of biblical truths so that the weakest believer may be instructed in the knowledge and strengthened in the love of it. Clearly teaching the principles of Christian dogma, discipline, and ethics is the best expedient for the grounding and settling of people. I fear one reason why there has been no more good done by preaching is because the main doctrinal truths of Christianity have not been fully or clearly explained. Therefore, no solid foundations for living out one's Christian faith are being laid.

MAN'S CHIEF END: TO GLORIFY GOD

That God in all things may be glorified.

1 PETER 4:11

Man's chief end is to glorify God and to enjoy Him forever. The glory of God is a silver thread that must run through all our actions: "whatsoever ye do, do all to the glory of God" (1 Corinthians 10:31). Everything works to some end in things natural and artificial. Man, being a rational creature, must propose some end to himself, and that should be that he may lift up God in the world. He had better lose his life than the purpose of his living. The great truth asserted is that the end of each man's living should be to glorify God—to glorify God the Father who gave us life; God the Son, who lost His life for us; and God the Holy Ghost, who produces a new life in us. We must bring glory to the whole Trinity.

And what are we to understand by "God's glory"? There is a twofold glory. First is the glory that God has in Himself, His intrinsic glory. Glory is essential to the Godhead, as light is to the sun: He is called the "God of glory" (Acts 7:2). Second is the glory ascribed to God, that which His children labor to bring to Him. We are to "give unto the Lord the glory due unto his name" (1 Chronicles 16:29). Paul wrote, "Glorify God in your body, and in your spirit" (1 Corinthians 6:20). The glory we give God lifts His name up in the world, magnifying Him in the eyes of others. "Christ shall be magnified in my body" (Philippians 1:20).

8

GOD'S LIFE, HIS GLORY

My glory I will not give to another.

ISAIAH 48:11 NASB

Glory is the sparkling of the Deity: it is so co-natural to the Godhead that God cannot be God without it. The creature's honor, however, is not essential to his being. A king is a man without his regal ornaments when his crown and royal robes are taken away; but God's glory is such an essential part of His being that He cannot be God without it. God's very life lies in His glory. This glory can receive no addition, because it is infinite; it is that which God is most tender of, and which He will not part with: "I will not give my glory unto another" (Isaiah 48:11). God will give temporal blessings to His children, such as wisdom, riches, honor. He will give them spiritual blessings, He will give them grace, He will give them His love, He will give them heaven. But His essential glory He will not give to another. King Pharaoh parted with a ring off his finger to Joseph, and a gold chain, but he would not part with his throne: "Only in the throne will I be greater than thou" (Genesis 41:40). So God will do much for His people: He will give them the inheritance; He will put some of Christ's glory, as Mediator, upon them; but His essential glory He will not part with.

9

GLORY ASCRIBED TO GOD THROUGH APPRECIATION

Ascribe to the LORD the glory due His name;
bring an offering, and come before Him;
worship the LORD in holy array.

1 CHRONICLES 16:29 NASB

We glorify God by showing our appreciation to Him for everything He is to us and for everything He does for us. To glorify God is also to set God highest in our thoughts and to have a venerable esteem of Him. The psalmist did this when he sang, "Thou, LORD, art most high for evermore" (Psalm 92:8) and "Thou art exalted far above all gods" (97:9). There is in God all that may draw forth both wonder and delight; there is a constellation of all beauties; He is the original and springhead of being, who sheds a glory upon His children. We glorify God when we are God-admirers—when we admire His attributes, which are the glistering beams by which the divine nature shines forth; His promises, which are the charter of free grace and the spiritual cabinet where the pearl of price is hid; the noble effects of His power and wisdom in making the world, which is called "the work of [His] fingers" (Psalm 8:3). To glorify God is to have God-admiring thoughts, to esteem Him as most excellent, and to search for diamonds in this Rock only.

GLORY ASCRIBED TO GOD
THROUGH ADORATION OF HIM

Ascribe to the LORD the glory due to His name;
worship the LORD in holy array.

PSALM 29:2 NASB

Glorifying God consists in adoration or worship. There is a twofold worship. First is the civil reverence that we give to persons of honor, as when "Abraham stood up, and bowed himself to . . . the children of Heth" (Genesis 23:7). Piety is no enemy to courtesy. Second is the divine worship that we give to God as His royal prerogative, as when God's people "bowed their heads, and worshiped the LORD with their faces to the ground" (Nehemiah 8:6). This divine worship God is very jealous of; it is the apple of His eye, the pearl of His crown; which He guards, as He did the tree of life, with cherubim and a flaming sword, that no man may come near it to violate it. Divine worship must be such as God Himself has appointed; otherwise it is offering strange fire (Leviticus 10:1). The Lord would have Moses make the tabernacle and its furnishings: "look that thou make them after their pattern, which was shewed thee in the mount" (Exodus 25:40). Moses must not leave out anything in the pattern, nor add to it. If God was so exact and curious about the place of worship, how exact will He be about the matter of His worship! Surely here every thing must be according to the pattern prescribed in His Word.

11

ASCRIBED GLORY TO GOD THROUGH AFFECTION

Let them praise the name of the LORD:
for his name alone is excellent;
his glory is above the earth and heaven.

PSALM 148:13

Affection is part of the glory we give to God, who counts Himself glorified when He is loved: "Thou shalt love the LORD thy God with all thine heart, and with all thy soul, and all thy might" (Deuteronomy 6:5). There is a twofold love. First is a *love of concupiscence*, which is self-love; as when we love another, because that person does us a good turn. A wicked man may be said to love God because He has given him a good harvest or filled his cup with wine. This is rather to love God's blessing than to love God. The second is a *love of delight*, as a man takes delight in a friend. This is to love God indeed: the heart is set upon God as a man's heart is set upon his treasure. This love is exuberant, not a few drops, but a stream. It is superlative: we give God the best of our love, the cream of it. This love is intense and ardent. True saints are seraphims, burning in holy love to God. He who is the chief of our happiness has the chief of our affections.

12

ASCRIBE GLORY TO GOD THROUGH SUBJECTION

Humble yourselves under the mighty hand of God,
that He may exalt you at the proper
time, casting all your anxiety on Him,
because He cares for you.

1 PETER 5:6–7 NASB

Subjection is when we dedicate ourselves to God and stand ready dressed for His service. The angels in heaven glorify Him; they wait on His throne and are ready to take a commission from Him. Therefore the angels are represented by the cherubims with wings displayed, to show how swift they are in their obedience. We glorify God when we are devoted to His service: our head studies for Him, our tongue pleads for Him, and our hands relieve His members. The wise men who came to Christ did not only bow the knee to Him, but presented Him with gold and myrrh. We must not only bow the knee, give God worship, but bring presents of golden obedience. We glorify God when we stick at committed and faithful service, when we fight under the banner of His gospel against an enemy, and say to Him as David to King Saul, "Thy servant will go and fight with this Philistine" (1 Samuel 17:32).

A good Christian is like the sun, which not only sends forth heat, but shines round the world. Those who glorify God have not only their affections heated with love to God, but they go their circuit too: they move vigorously in the sphere of obedience.

CHRISTIANS MUST GLORIFY GOD

It is He who has made us.

PSALM 100:3 NASB

We must glorify God because He gives us our being. We think it a great kindness in a man to spare our life, but what kindness is it in God to give us our life! We draw our breath from Him, and all the comforts of life are from Him. He gives us health to sweeten our life and food that nourishes the lamp of life. If all we receive is from His bounty, isn't it reasonable that we should glorify Him? Shouldn't we live *for* Him since we live *by* Him? "For of him, and through him . . . are all things" (Romans 11:36). All we have is from His fullness; all we have is through His free grace. It follows, therefore, "to him be glory for ever." God is not our benefactor only, but our founder, as rivers that come from the sea empty their silver streams into the sea again.

We must also glorify God because He has made all things for His own Glory. "The Lord hath made all things for himself" (Proverbs 16:4), that is, for His glory. God will have glory out of everything, even the wicked, but He has especially made the godly for His glory. They are the lively organs of His praise, the people He formed for Himself (Isaiah 43:12). They cannot add to His glory, but they may exalt it; they cannot raise Him in heaven, but they may raise Him in the esteem of others here. God has adopted the saints into His family and made them a royal priesthood, that they should show forth the praise of Him who has called them.

14

GOD'S GLORY HAS INTRINSIC VALUE

The heavens declare the glory of God.

PSALM 19:1

God's people must glorify God because His glory has intrinsic value and excellence; God's glory transcends the thoughts of men and the tongues of angels. His glory is His treasure; all His riches lie here. God's glory is worth more than heaven and more than the salvation of all men's souls. Creatures below us, and above us, bring glory to God. Do we think we sit rent free? Shall everything glorify God but man?

The workmanship of heaven sets forth the glory of its Maker; the firmament is beautified and penciled out in blue and azure colors, where the power and wisdom of God may be clearly seen. The heavens declare God's glory, and we see the glory of God blazing in the sun and twinkling in the stars. The birds, with their chirping music, sing hymns of praise to God. Every beast in its own way glorifies God (Isaiah 43:20).

Creatures above us glorify God. Surely man should be much more studious of God's glory than the angels; for God has honored him more than the angels, in that Christ took man's nature upon Him, and not the angels'. Regarding creation, God made man "a little lower than the angels" (Hebrews 2:7); regarding redemption, God has set man higher than the angels. He has married mankind to Himself; the angels are Christ's friends, not His spouse. He covered us with the purple robe of righteousness, which is a better righteousness than the angels have. If, then, the angels bring glory to God, much more should we, being dignified with honor above angelic spirits.

Our Hope Is Christ

My hope is in thee.

PSALM 39:7

We bring glory to God because our hope is in Him. I expect a king-dom from Him. As the psalmist said, "All my springs are in thee" (Psalm 87:7). The silver springs of grace and the golden springs of glory are in God.

And in how many ways may we glorify God? We glorify God when we aim purely at His glory. It is one thing to advance God's glory, another thing to aim at it. God must be the ultimate end of all our actions. "I seek not mine own glory," said Jesus, but the glory of Him who sent Me (John 8:50). A hypocrite looks more to his own glory than God's. Our Savior understands that and gives a warning against them in Matthew 6:2: "When you give to the poor, do not sound a trumpet." Chrysostom calls such vainglory one of the devil's great nets to catch men. Oh, let us not worship self! Rather, let us aim purely at God's glory.

We aim for God's glory when we prefer God's glory above all other things—above credit, wealth, relations—and when the glory of God comes in competition with these things, we prefer His glory before them. If relations lie in our way to heaven, we must either leap over them or tread upon them. A child must forget he is a child; he must know neither father nor mother in God's cause. This is to aim at God's glory.

16

CONTENTMENT IN GOD'S WILL GLORIFIES HIM

Not as I will, but as thou wilt.

MATTHEW 26:39

We aim at God's glory when we are content that God's will take place, though it may cross our own desires. Lord, I am content to be a loser if Thou be a gainer; to have poor health if I have more grace and Thou more glory. Let it be food or bitter physic if Thou givest it to me. Lord, I desire that which may be most for Thy glory. Our blessed Savior said, "Not as I will, but as thou wilt" (Matthew 26:39). If God might have more glory by Jesus' sufferings, He was content to suffer.

We also aim at God's glory when we are content to be outshined by others in gifts and recognition, so that His glory may be increased. A man who has God in his heart and God's glory in his eye desires that God should be exalted; and if this happens, let whoever will be the instrument rejoice. Paul said, "Some preach Christ of envy . . . notwithstanding, Christ is preached, and I therein do rejoice, yea, and will rejoice" (Philippians 1:15–18). They preached Christ of envy, they envied Paul that concourse of people, and they preached that they might outshine him in gifts, and get away some of his hearers. Well, says Paul, Christ is preached, and God is like to have the glory. Therefore I rejoice. Let my candle go out if the Sun of Righteousness may but shine. "Father, glorify thy name" (John 12:28).

17

CONFESSION OF SIN GLORIFIES GOD

I have sinned against heaven, and before thee.

LUKE 15:18

We glorify God by an ingenuous confession of sin. The thief on the cross had dishonored God in his life, but at his death he brought glory to God by confessing his sins. "We indeed [suffer] justly," he said (Luke 23:41). He acknowledged he deserved not only crucifixion, but damnation. "My son, give, I pray thee, glory to the LORD God of Israel, and make confession unto him" (Joshua 7:19). A humble confession exalts God. How is God's free grace magnified in crowning those who deserve condemnation! The excusing and mincing of sin casts a reproach upon God. Adam denied not that he tasted the forbidden fruit, but, instead of a full confession, he blamed God: "The woman whom thou gavest to be with me, she gave me of the tree, and I did eat" (Genesis 3:12). "If Thou hadst not given me the woman to be a tempter, I had not sinned." Our confession glorifies God, because it clears Him; it acknowledges that He is holy and righteous, whatever He does. Nehemiah vindicates God's righteousness: "Thou art just in all that is brought upon us" (Nehemiah 9:33). A confession is ingenuous when it is not forced. The prodigal admitted his sin before his father charged him with it.

18

OUR BELIEF GLORIFIES GOD

[Abraham] grew strong in faith, giving glory to God.

ROMANS 4:20 NASB

Unbelief is an affront to God: "he that believeth not God hath made him a liar" (1 John 5:10). Faith brings glory to God; it asserts that God is true. He who believes flies to God's mercy and truth, as to an altar of refuge; he garrisons himself in the promises and trusts all he has to God. Jesus Himself did the same: "Into thy hands I commit my spirit" (Psalm 31:5).

God honors faith, because faith honors Him. It brings great honor to a man when we trust him with all we have, when we put our lives and treasures into his hand; it is a sign we have a good opinion of him. Shadrach, Meshach, and Abednego glorified God by believing: "Our God whom we serve is able to deliver us . . . and he will deliver us" (Daniel 3:17). Faith knows there are no impossibilities with God and will trust Him where it cannot see Him.

We also glorify God by being sensitive to His glory. God's glory is dear to Him as the apple of His eye. An ingenuous child weeps to see his father disgraced. "The reproaches of them that reproached thee are fallen upon me" (Psalm 69:9). When God is reproached, it is as if we were reproached; when God's glory suffers, it is as if we suffer. This is to be tender toward God's glory.

19

BEARING FRUIT GLORIFIES GOD

Hereby is my Father glorified, that ye bear much fruit.

JOHN 15:8

We glorify God by fruitfulness. We must not be like the fig tree in the gospel, which had nothing but leaves, but like the limon, that is continually either mellowing or blossoming, and is never without fruit. It is not profession, but fruit that glorifies God. God expects to have His glory from us in this way: "Who planteth a vineyard, and eateth not of the fruit of it?" (1 Corinthians 9:7). We must bring forth the fruits of love and good works: "Let your light so shine before men, that they may see your good works, and glorify your Father which is in heaven" (Matthew 5:16). Faith sanctifies our works, and works testify to our faith; to be doing good to others, to be eyes to the blind, feet to the lame, glorifies God. Thus Christ glorified His Father: He "went about doing good" (Acts 10:38). By being fruitful, we are fair in God's eyes. "The Lord called thy name a green olive tree, fair and of goodly fruit" (Jeremiah 11:16). We must bear much fruit; it is much fruit that glorifies God. Though the smallest amount of grace may bring salvation to you, yet it will not bring much glory to God. It was not a spark of love Christ commended in Mary, but much love: "for she loved much" (Luke 7:47).

20

CONTENTMENT GLORIFIES GOD

I can do all things through Him who strengthens me.

PHILIPPIANS 4:13 NASB

We glorify God by being content in that state in which His providence has placed us. We give God glory for His wisdom when we rest satisfied with what He carves out for us. Paul glorified God even when the Lord cast him into a great variety of circumstances, yet he had learned to be content. Paul could sail in a storm or the calm; he could be anything that God would have him; he could either want or abound. Many Christians contend that it is God who has put them in difficult conditions and He could have raised them higher if He pleased, but that might have been a snare to them. God has allowed us in wisdom and love; therefore we are to rest satisfied with our circumstances. God counts Himself much honored when Christians in difficult circumstances glorify Him. A Christian who will let God have His way, without murmuring, shows abundance of grace. When grace is abundant, it is easy to be content; but when grace is conflicting with inconveniences, then contentment is a glorious thing indeed. To be content under the cross means bringing glory to God; for a Christian shows to all the world that though he has little food to eat, he has enough in God to make him content. He says as David said in Psalm 16:5–6, "The LORD is the portion of mine inheritance . . . The lines are fallen unto me in pleasant places."

21

OUR WITNESS GLORIFIES GOD

Let your light so shine before men that they may see your
good works, and glorify your Father which is in heaven.

MATTHEW 5:16

We glorify God by working out our own salvation. God has twisted together His glory and our good. We glorify Him by promoting our own salvation. It is a glory to God to have multitudes of converts; now, His design of free grace takes, and God has the glory of His mercy; so that, while we are endeavoring our salvation, we are honoring God. What an encouragement is this to the service of God: to think, while I am hearing and praying, I am glorifying God; while I am furthering my own glory in heaven, I am increasing God's glory. Would it not be an encouragement to a subject to hear his prince say to him, "You will honor and please me very much if you will go to the gold mine and dig as much gold for yourself as you can carry away"? So, for God to say, "Go to the biblical ordinances, get as much grace as you can, dig out as much salvation as you can; and the more happiness you have, the more I shall count myself glorified."

22

LIVING FOR GOD GLORIFIES HIM

*That they which live should not live to
themselves, but unto him who died for them.*

2 CORINTHIANS 5:15

We glorify God by living for God. "Whether we live, we live unto the Lord" (Romans 14:8). The rich live to their money, the gourmet lives to his belly: the design of a sinner's life is to gratify lust, but we glorify God when we live to God. We live to God when we live to His service and lay ourselves out wholly for God. The Lord has sent us into the world as a merchant sends his representatives beyond the seas to trade for him. We live to God when we trade for His interest and propagate His gospel. God has given every man a talent; and when a man does not hide it in a napkin, but improves it for God, he lives to God. When the head of a family, by counsel and good example, labors to bring his family to Christ; when a minister spends himself that he may win souls to Christ and make the crown flourish upon Christ's head; when the magistrate labors to cut down sin and to suppress vice—this is to live for God, and this is glorifying God. "That Christ might be magnified . . . whether by life or by death" (Philippians 1:20). Paul had three wishes, and they were all about Christ: that he might be found in Christ, be with Christ, and magnify Christ.

23

CHEERFULNESS GLORIFIES GOD

Serve the LORD with gladness.

PSALM 100:2

It brings glory to God when the world sees a Christian who is cheerful in the worst times; who, with the nightingale, can sing with a thorn at his breast. The people of God have many reasons to be cheerful. They are justified and adopted, and this creates inward peace; it makes music within their hearts, whatever storms are without. If we consider what Christ has done for us by His blood and wrought in us by His Spirit, it is a reason for great cheerfulness, and this cheerfulness glorifies God. It reflects upon a master when the servant is always drooping and sad. Sure he is kept to hard commons, his master does not give him what is fitting. When God's people hang their heads, it looks as if they did not serve a good master, or have fallen from their choice to follow Him, which reflects dishonor on God. As the gross sins of the wicked bring a scandal on the gospel, so do the uncheerful lives of the godly. Our service to God does not glorify Him unless we do so with gladness. A Christian's cheerful looks glorify God; our Christian faith does not take away our joy, but refines it; it does not break our violin, but tunes it and makes the music sweeter.

24

ADVOCATING TRUTH BRINGS GLORY TO GOD

*It was needful for me to write unto you, and exhort
you that ye should earnestly contend for the faith.*

JUDE 3

We glorify God by standing up for His truths. Much of God's glory lies in His truth. God has entrusted us with His truth as a master entrusts his servant with his checkbook. We have no richer jewel to trust God with than our souls, nor has God a richer jewel to trust us with than His truth. Truth is a beam that shines upon us from God. Much of His glory lies in His truth. When we are advocates for truth, we glorify God: "ye should earnestly contend for the faith" (Jude 3). The Greek word *contend* signifies great contending, as one would contend for his land and not suffer it to be taken from him; so we should contend for the truth. Were there more of this holy contention, God would have more glory. Some contend earnestly for trifles and ceremonies, but not for the truth. We should count him indiscreet who would contend more for a picture than for his eternal inheritance; for a box of items that can be stacked and counted rather than for something that actually gives a deed of ownership . . . the promise of heaven.

25

PRAISE GLORIFIES GOD

Whoso offereth praise glorifieth me.

PSALM 50:23

We glorify God by praising Him. Doxology, or praise, is a God-exalting work. The Hebrew words *bara*, "to create," and *barak*, "to praise," are little different, because the end of creation is to praise God. David was called the sweet singer of Israel, and his praising God was called glorifying God. Though nothing can add to God's essential glory, yet praise exalts Him in the eyes of others. When we praise God, we spread His fame and renown; we display the trophies of His excellency. In this manner the angels glorify Him; they are the choristers of heaven and do trumpet forth His praise. Praising God is one of the highest and purest acts of the Christian faith. In prayer we act like men; in praise we act like angels. Believers are called "temple[s] of God" (1 Corinthians 3:16). When our tongues praise, then the organs in God's spiritual temple are sounding. How sad that God receives so little glory from us in this way! Many Christians are full of murmuring and discontent, but seldom bring glory to God by giving Him praise due to His name. We read of the saints having harps in their hands, the emblems of praise. Many Christians today have tears in their eyes and complaints in their mouths, but few have harps in their hand, blessing and glorifying God. Let us honor God this way. Praise is the quit-rent we pay to God: while God renews our lease, we must renew our rent.

26

ZEALOUS CHRISTIANS GLORIFY GOD

*For I testify about them that they have a zeal
for God, but not in accordance with knowledge.*

ROMANS 10:2 NASB

We glorify God by being zealous for his name. "[Phinehas] hath turned my wrath away . . . while he was zealous for my sake" (Numbers 25:11). Zeal is a mixed affection, a compound of love and anger; it carries forth both our love to God and our anger against sin in an intense degree. Zeal is impatient of God's dishonor; a Christian fired with zeal takes a dishonor done to God worse than an injury done to himself: "thou canst not bear them which are evil" (Revelation 2:2).

Our Savior Christ thus glorified His Father; He, being baptized with a spirit of zeal, drove the money-changers out of the temple and fulfilled the prophecy that "the zeal of thine house has eaten me up" (John 2:17).

27

OUR ACTIONS GLORIFY GOD

Whether therefore ye eat or drink or whatsoever
ye do, do all to the glory of God.

1 CORINTHIANS 10:31

We glorify God when we have an eye to God in our natural and in our civil actions. In our natural actions, a gracious person holds the golden bridle of temperance. He takes his meat as a medicine to heal the decays of nature that he may be the fitter by the strength he receives for the service of God. He makes his food not fuel for lust, but help to duty. In buying and selling we do all to the glory of God. The wicked live upon unjust gain by falsifying the balances, as in Hosea 12:7, "The balances of deceit are in his hand." Thus while men make their weights lighter, they make their sins heavier when by exacting more than the commodity is worth, when they exact double the price that a thing is worth. We buy and sell to the glory of God when we observe that golden maxim, "To do to others as we would have them do to us," so that when we sell our commodities, we do not sell our consciences also. "Herein do I exercise myself, to have always a conscience void of offence toward God, and toward men" (Acts 24:16). We glorify God when we do nothing that may reflect any blemish on the Christian faith.

28

GLORIFY GOD IN SUFFERING

For to you it has been granted for Christ's sake,
not only to believe in Him, but also to suffer for His sake.

PHILIPPIANS 1:29 NASB

We glorify God by seeking to convert others and so make them instruments of glorifying God. We should be diamonds and loadstones—diamonds for the beautiful luster of grace and loadstones for attractive virtue in drawing others to Christ.

We glorify God in a high degree when we suffer for God and seal the gospel with our blood. "When thou shalt be old . . . another shall gird thee, and carry thee whither thou wouldest not. This spake [Jesus], signifying by what death [Peter] should glorify God" (John 21:18–19). God's glory shines in the ashes of His martyrs: Isaiah was sawn asunder, Paul beheaded, Luke hanged on an olive tree; thus did they, by their death, glorify God. The sufferings of primitive saints honored God and made the gospel famous in the world. The glory of Christ's kingdom does not stand in worldly pomp and grandeur, as other kings'; but it is seen in the cheerful sufferings of His people. The saints of old "loved not their lives to the death" (Revelation 12:11). They embraced torments as so many crowns. God grant we may thus glorify Him if He calls us to it. Many pray, "Let this cup pass away," but few, "Thy will be done."

29

GLORIFY GOD IN YOUR LIFE

I have been crucified with Christ; and it is
no longer I who live, but Christ lives in me.

GALATIANS 2:20 NASB

We glorify God when we give God the glory of all that we do. When Herod had made an oration, and the people gave a shout, saying, "It is the voice of a god, not of a man," he took the glory to himself. The text says, "Immediately the angel of the Lord smote him, because he gave not God the glory, and he was eaten of worms" (Acts 12:23).

We glorify God when we sacrifice the praise and glory of all to God. Paul said, "I labored more abundantly than they all," a speech, one would think, of pride. But the apostle pulls the crown from his own head and sets it upon the head of free grace: "yet not I, but the grace of God which was with me" (1 Corinthians 15:10). As Joab, when he fought against Rabbah, sent for King David, that he might carry away the crown of the victory (2 Samuel 12:27–30), so a Christian, when he has gotten power over any corruption or temptation, sends for Christ, that He may carry away the crown of the victory. As the silkworm, when weaving her curious work, hides herself under the silk and is not seen, so when we do anything praiseworthy, we must hide ourselves under the veil of humility and transfer the glory of all we have done to God. Let Him wear the garland of praise.

30

HOLY LIVING GLORIFIES GOD

Ye are . . . a holy nation . . . that ye should show forth the praises
of him who hath called you out of darkness into his marvelous light.

1 PETER 2:9

We glorify God by a holy life. A bad life dishonors God. As Paul testifies, "The name of God is blasphemed among the Gentiles through you [Christians who dishonor God]" (Romans 2:24). Epiphanius says that the looseness of some Christians in his time made many of the heathens shun their company, and these heathens would not be drawn to hear their sermons. By our exact Bible-conversation, we glorify God. Though the main work of Christianity lies in the heart, our light must so shine that others may see it. So the beauty of our Christian faith is in our conversation. When the saints, who are called jewels, cast a sparkling luster of holiness in the world, they walk as Christ walked (1 John 2:6). When Christians live as if they had actually seen the Lord and been with Him upon the mount, they adorn Christianity, bringing revenues of glory to the crown of heaven.

Our chief end shouldn't be to get great wealth or to lay up treasures on earth. Sometimes people never get wealth, nor do they get the venison they hunt for; or if they do, what have they? Something that won't fill the heart any more than the mariner's breath will fill the sails of a ship. They spend their time gathering straw, not remembering that the end of living is to glorify God.

31

THE CAPACITY TO GLORIFY GOD

O LORD, thou art my God; I will
exalt thee, I will praise thy name.

ISAIAH 25:1

God has put in everyone on earth some capacity of glorifying Him. The health He has given you, abilities, wealth, seasons of grace, all are opportunities to glorify Him. And, be assured, He will call you to account, to know what you have done with the mercies He has entrusted to you, what glory you have brought to Him. The parable of the talents, where the men with the five talents and the two talents are brought to a reckoning, shows that God will call you to a strict account, to know how you have traded your talents and what glory you have brought to Him. How sad for those who hide their talents, who bring God no glory at all! "Cast ye the unprofitable servant into outer darkness" (Matthew 25:30). It is not enough for you to say that you have not dishonored God by not living in gross sin. But what good have you done? What glory have you brought to God? It is not enough for the servant of the vineyard to do no wrong in the vineyard, that he does not break the trees or destroy the hedges. If he does not do service in the vineyard, he loses his pay. So, if you do not good in your place, if you do not glorify God, you will lose your pay, you will miss of salvation. Think of this, all you who do not serve the Lord: Christ cursed the barren fig tree.

1

GLORY ROBBERS

Will a man rob God? Yet ye have robbed me.

MALACHI 3:8

They rob God who take the glory due to God for themselves. They ascribe their wealth to their own wisdom, they set the crown upon their own head, not considering that "it is he that giveth thee power to get wealth" (Deuteronomy 8:18). If they do any Christian service, they look to their own glory "that they may be seen of men" (Matthew 6:5) for others to admire them. The oil of vainglory feeds their lamp. Those Satan cannot destroy by indulgence he does by vainglory. [The holy life] reproves those who fight against God's glory, "lest ye be found even to fight against God" (Acts 5:39).

God's glory is promoted by the preaching of the Word, which is His engine whereby He converts souls. Those who hinder the preaching of the Word fight against God's glory, "forbidding us to speak to the Gentiles that they might be saved" (1 Thessalonians 2:16). Those who hinder preaching stop the well of the water of life. They take away physicians who should heal sin-sick souls. Ministers are lights, and who but thieves hate the light? They directly strike at God's glory; and what an account will they have to give to God when He shall charge the blood of men's souls upon them! "Ye have taken away the key of knowledge: ye entered not in yourselves, and them that were entering in ye hindered" (Luke 11:52). If there be either justice in heaven or fire in hell, they shall not go unpunished.

2

CHRISTIANS EXHORTED TO GLORIFY GOD

*Whoever speaks, is to do so as one who is speaking the utterances of God;
whoever serves is to do so as one who is serving by the strength which
God supplies; so that in all things God may be glorified through Jesus Christ,
to whom belongs the glory and dominion forever and ever. Amen.*

I PETER 4:11 NASB

Let us make it our chief end and design to glorify God. Let me speak
to magistrates. God has put much glory upon them. "I have said, Ye
are gods" (Psalm 82:6); and will they not glorify Him who has put
much glory upon them? Ministers should also study to promote
God's glory. God has entrusted them with two of the most precious
things: His truth and the souls of His people. Ministers, by virtue of
their office, are to glorify God. They must glorify God by laboring
in the Word and doctrine. "I charge thee before God, and the Lord
Jesus Christ, who shall judge the quick and the dead . . . : preach
the Word . . . reprove, rebuke, exhort" (2 Timothy 4:1–2). It was
Augustine's wish "that Christ, at his coming, might find him either
praying or preaching." Ministers must glorify God by their zeal and
sanctity. It is matter of grief and shame to think how many, who call
themselves ministers, instead of bringing glory to God, dishonor
Him. Their lives and their doctrines are not holy; they are not free
from the sins which they reprove in others. Finally, masters of fami-
lies must glorify God, must train their children and servants with
the knowledge of the Lord; their houses should be little churches.
You that are masters have a charge of souls. For want of the bridle of
family discipline, youth runs wild.

3

GLORIFY GOD IN DEATH

I have glorified thee on the earth.

JOHN 17:4

It will be a great comfort in our dying hour to think we have glorified God in our lives. It was Christ's comfort before His death. . . . At the hour of death, all your earthly comforts will vanish: if you think how rich you have been, what pleasures you have had on earth, this will be so far from comforting you that it will torment you even more. What is one the better for an estate that is spent? But to have conscience telling you that you have glorified God on the earth will be sweet comfort and peace to your soul and will make you long for death! The servant that has been all day working in the vineyard longs for evening to come, when he shall receive his pay. How can they who have lived, and brought no glory to God, think of dying with comfort? They cannot expect a harvest where they sowed no seed. How can they expect glory from God, who never brought any glory to Him? Oh, in what horror will they be at death! The worm of conscience will gnaw their souls, before the worms can gnaw their bodies. If we glorify God, He will glorify our souls forever. By raising God's glory, we increase our own: by glorifying God, we come at last to the blessed enjoyment of Him.

4

GLORIFY GOD BY ENJOYING HIM

Whom have I in heaven but thee?

PSALM 73:25

It is a great matter to enjoy God's ordinances, but to enjoy God's presence in the ordinances is what a gracious heart aspires after. "To see thy power and thy glory, so as I have seen thee in the sanctuary" (Psalm 63:2). This sweet enjoyment of God is when we feel His Spirit cooperating with the ordinance and distilling grace upon our hearts. When in the Word the Spirit quickens and raises affections: "Did not our heart burn within us?" (Luke 24:32). When the Spirit transforms the heart, He leaves an imprint of holiness upon it: "We are changed into the same image, from glory to glory" (2 Corinthians 3:18). When the Spirit revives the heart with comfort, He comes not only with anointing but with His seal; He sheds God's love abroad in the heart. In the Word we hear God's voice; in the sacrament we have His kiss. The heart being warmed and inflamed in our work is God's answering by fire. The sweet communications of God's Spirit are the first fruits of glory. Now Christ has pulled off His veil and showed His smiling face; now He has led a believer into the banquet house . . . and He has touched the heart and made it leap for joy. How sweet is it thus to enjoy God!

GLORIFY GOD WITH SPIRITUAL COMMUNION

My soul thirsteth for God, for the living God.

PSALM 42:2

Is the enjoyment of God in this life so sweet? How wicked are they who prefer the enjoyment of their lusts before the enjoyment of God! "The lust of the flesh, and the lust of the eyes, and the pride of life" is the Trinity they worship (1 John 2:16). Lust is an inordinate desire or impulse, provoking the soul to that which is evil. There is the revengeful lust, and the wanton lust. Lust, like a feverish heat, puts the soul into a flame. How many make it their chief end not to enjoy God, but to enjoy their lusts? Lust first bewitches with pleasure, and then comes the fatal dart. Who, for a drop of pleasure, would drink a sea of wrath?

Let it be our great care to enjoy God's sweet presence in His ordinances. Enjoying spiritual communion with God is a riddle and mystery to most people. Everyone that hangs about the court does not speak with the king. We may approach God in ordinances and hang about the court of heaven, yet not enjoy communion with God. We may have the letter without the Spirit, the visible sign without the invisible grace. It is the enjoyment of God that we should chiefly look at.

6

GLORIFY GOD BY ENJOYING HIS ORDINANCES

For as often as you eat this bread and drink this cup,
you proclaim the Lord's death till He comes.

1 CORINTHIANS 11:26 NASB

What are all our worldly enjoyments worth without the enjoyment of
God! What is it to enjoy good health, and a brave estate, but to not
enjoy God? "I went mourning without the sun" (Job 30:28). So
may thou say in the enjoyment of all creatures without God, "I went
mourning without the sun." I have the starlight of outward enjoyments, but I want the Sun of Righteousness. It should be our great
design not only to have the ordinances of God, but the God of the
ordinances. The enjoyment of God's sweet presence here on earth
is the most contented life: He is a hive of sweetness, a magazine of
riches, and a fountain of delight. The higher the lark flies, the
sweeter it sings; and the higher we fly by the wings of faith, the more
we enjoy of God. How is the heart inflamed in prayer and meditation! What joy and peace is there in believing! Is it not comfortable
being in heaven? He that enjoys much of God in this life carries
heaven about him. Oh, let this be the thing we are chiefly ambitious
of, the enjoyment of God in His ordinances! The enjoyment of
God's sweet presence here is a promise of our enjoying Him in
heaven.

7

GLORIFY GOD BY ENJOYING HIM FOREVER

Blessed are the pure in heart: for they shall see God.

MATTHEW 5:8

There is to be the enjoyment of God in the life to come. Man's chief end is to enjoy God forever. Before meeting God in heaven, there must be something previous and antecedent; and that is our being in a state of grace. We must have conformity to Him in grace before we can have communion with Him in glory. Grace and glory are linked and chained together. Grace precedes glory, as the morning star ushers in the sun. God will have us qualified and fitted for a state of blessedness. Drunkards and swearers are not fit to enjoy God in glory; the Lord will not lay such vipers in His bosom. Only the pure in heart shall see God. We must first be daughter, . . . glorious within, before we are clothed with the robes of glory. We must have the anointing of God and be perfumed with the graces of the Spirit . . . and then we shall stand before the king of heaven. Being thus divinely qualified by grace, we shall be taken up to the mount of vision and enjoy God forever. And what is enjoying God forever but to be put in a state of happiness? Just as the body cannot have life without communion with the soul, so the soul cannot have blessedness without having immediate communion with God. God is the chief good; therefore the enjoyment of Him is the highest pleasure.

8

GLORIFY GOD BY DESIRING HIM

I shall be satisfied . . . with thy likeness.

PSALM 17:15

God is a *universal* good; "a good, in which are all goods." The excellencies of the creature are limited. A man may have health, not beauty, learning, not parentage, riches, not wisdom; but in God are contained all excellencies . . . . God is an *unmixed* good. There is no condition in this life that does not have its mixture; for every drop of honey there is a drop of gall. Solomon, who gave himself to find out the philosopher's stone, to search out for happiness here below, found nothing except vanity and vexation (Ecclesiastes 1:2). God is perfect, the quintessence of good. He is sweetness in the flower. God is a *satisfying* good. The soul cries out, "I have enough." Let a man who is thirsty be brought to an ocean of pure water, and he has enough. If there be enough in God to satisfy the angels, then surely there is enough to satisfy us. The soul is finite, but God is infinite. Fresh joys spring continually from His face; and He is as much to be desired after millions of years by glorified souls as at the first moment. There is a fullness in God that satisfies, and yet so much sweetness that the soul still desires more of Him.

9

GLORIFY GOD BY DELIGHTING IN HIM

Whom having not seen, ye love.

1 PETER 1:8

God is a *delicious* good. That which is the chief good must ravish the soul with pleasure; there must be in it rapturous delight and quintessence of joy. There is certain sweetness about God's person which delights, even ravishes, the soul. God's love drops such infinite suavity into the soul that is unspeakable and full of glory. When we delight in God when we see Him only by faith, what will our joy be when we see Him *face to face*? If the saints found so much delight in God while they were suffering, oh, what joy and delight will they have when they are being crowned! If flames are beds of roses, what will it be to lean on the bosom of Jesus! What a bed of roses that will be! God is a *superlative* good. He is better than anything you can put in competition with Him: He is better than health, riches, and honor. Other things maintain life; He *gives* life. Who would weigh anything opposite the Deity? Who would weigh a feather against a mountain of gold? God excels in all things more infinitely than the sun outshines the light of a taper. God is an *eternal* good. He is the Ancient of days, yet never decays, nor grows old (Daniel 7:9). The joy He gives is eternal, the crown does not fade away. The glorified soul shall forever comfort itself in God, feasting on His love, and sunning itself in the light of His countenance. God is the chief good, and the enjoyment of God is the highest contentment of which the soul is capable.

10

GLORIFY GOD BY LOVING HIS LIFE

With thee is the fountain of life.

PSALM 36:9

We read of the river of pleasure at God's right hand; but will not this in time be dried up? No. There is a fountain of life at the bottom which feeds it. Let it be the chief end of our living to enjoy God, this chief good, forever. The highest elevation of a reasonable soul is to enjoy God forever. It is the enjoyment of God that makes heaven. The soul trembles as the needle in the compass, and is never at rest until it comes to God. To understand this excellent state of a glorified soul's enjoyment of God, it must not be understood in a sensual manner: we must not conceive any carnal pleasures in heaven. Though the state of glory is compared to a feast, and is set out by pearls and precious stones, yet these metaphors are only helps to our faith, and show us that there is superabundant joy and contentment in the highest heaven; but they are not carnal but spiritual delights. Our enjoyment will be in the perfection of holiness, in seeing the pure face of Christ, in feeling the love of God, in conversing with heavenly spirits; which will be proper for the soul, and infinitely exceed all carnal voluptuous delights.

11

GLORIFY GOD BY PARTAKING OF HIS GLORY

Glory . . . shall be revealed in us.

ROMANS 8:18

A man in a state of lethargy, though alive, is as good as dead, because he is not sensible, nor does he take any pleasure in his life; but we shall have a quick and lively sense of the infinite pleasure which arises from the enjoyment of God: we shall know ourselves to be happy; we shall reflect with joy upon our dignity and contentment; we shall taste every crumb of that sweetness, every drop of that pleasure which flows from God. We shall be made able to bear a sight of His glory. We could not now bear that glory; it would overwhelm us. But God will make us fit for His glory; our souls shall be so heavenly, and perfected with holiness, that they may be able to enjoy the blessed vision of God. From our blessed Rock Christ, we shall behold the beatific sight of God. This enjoyment of God shall be more than a bare contemplation of Him. That is something, but it is one half of heaven only; there shall be a loving of God, an acquiescence in Him, a tasting of His sweetness; not only inspection but possession. There is inspection: "That they may behold my glory" (John 17:24); and there is possession: "And the glory which thou gavest me I have given them" (v. 22), glory not only revealed to us, but in us. To behold God's glory, there is glory revealed *to* us; but, to partake of His glory, there is glory revealed *in* us. As the sponge sucks in the wine, so shall we suck in glory.

12

GLORIFY GOD BY PRACTICING HIS PRESENCE

So shall we ever be with the Lord.

1 THESSALONIANS 4:17

We shall not only have God's glorious presence at certain special seasons, but we shall be continually in His presence, continually under divine raptures of joy. There shall not be one minute in heaven wherein a glorified soul may say, "I do not enjoy happiness." The streams of glory are not like the water of a conduit, often stopped, so that we cannot have one drop of water; but those heavenly streams of joy are continually running. We should hate this valley of tears where we are now, for the mount of transfiguration instead! How we should long for the full enjoyment of God in Paradise! If we could see that land of promise, we should need patience to be content to live here any longer.

Let this be a spur to duty. How diligent and zealous should we be in glorifying God, that we may come at last to enjoy Him? If anything can make us rise off our bed of sloth and serve God with all our might, it should be this, the hope of our near enjoyment of God forever . . . .

Let this comfort the godly in all the present miseries they feel. You complain, Christian, you do not enjoy yourself, fears disquiet you, wants perplex you. In the day you can not enjoy ease, in the night you can not enjoy sleep; and you do not enjoy the comforts of your life. Let this encourage you: soon you shall enjoy God, and then you shall have more than you can ask or think; you shall have angels' joy, glory without intermission or expiration. We shall never enjoy ourselves fully until we enjoy God eternally.

13

THE SCRIPTURES

All scripture is given by inspiration of God.
2 TIMOTHY 3:16

The Word of God, which is contained in the Old and New Testaments, is the only rule to direct us how we may glorify and enjoy Him. It is given by divine inspiration; the Scripture is not the work of man's brain, but is divine in its origin. The Holy Scripture is to be reverenced and esteemed, *because we are sure it came from heaven.* The two Testaments are the two lips by which God has spoken to us.

The Old and New Testaments are the foundation of all religion. If their divinity cannot be proved, the foundation on which we build our faith is gone. One shall therefore endeavor to prove this great truth, that the Scriptures are the very Word of God. One shall wonder whence the Scriptures should come, if not from God. Bad men could not be the authors of it. Would they declare so fiercely against sin? Good men could not be the authors of it. Could it stand with their grace to counterfeit God's name, and put, "Thus saith the Lord" to a book of their own devising? Nor could any angel in heaven be the author, because the angels pry and search into the abyss of gospel mysteries, which implies their ignorance of some parts of Scripture; and sure they cannot be the authors of that book which they themselves do not fully understand. Besides, what angel would be so arrogant as to impersonate God and say, "I create" (Isaiah 65:17), and, "I the Lord have said" (Numbers 14:35)? It is evident, the pedigree of Scripture is sacred, and it could come from none but God Himself.

14

THE SACRED PRESERVATION OF SCRIPTURE

Sanctify them through thy truth.

JOHN 17:17

The Word of God is of ancient standing. The grey hairs of Scripture make it venerable. No human histories extant reach further than Noah's flood: but the holy Scripture relates matters of fact that have been from the beginning of the world; it writes of things before time.

We may know the Scripture to be the Word of God by its miraculous preservation in all ages. The holy Scriptures are the richest jewel that Christ has left us; and the church of God has so kept these public records of heaven that they have not been lost. The Word of God has never wanted enemies to oppose and, if possible, to destroy it. They have given out a law concerning Scripture, as Pharaoh did the midwives, concerning the Hebrew women's children, to strangle it in the birth; but God has preserved this blessed Book inviolable to this day. The devil and his agents have been blowing at Scripture light, but could never blow it out; a clear sign that it was lighted from heaven. Nor has the church of God, in all revolutions and changes, kept the Scripture that it should not be lost only, but that it should not be depraved. The letter of Scripture has been preserved, without any corruption, in the original tongue. The Scriptures were not corrupted before Christ's time, for then Christ would not have sent the Jews to them. He said, "Search the Scriptures" (John 5:39). He knew these sacred springs were not muddied with human fancies.

15

SCRIPTURE

Thy word is very pure.

PSALM 119:140

The Scriptures appear to be the Word of God by the matter contained in them. The mystery of Scripture is so abstruse and profound that no man or angel could have known it had it not been divinely revealed. That eternity should be born; that He who thunders in the heavens should cry in the cradle; that He who rules the stars should suck the breasts; that the Prince of Life should die; that the Lord of Glory should be put to shame; that sin should be punished to the full, yet pardoned to the full. Who could ever have conceived such a mystery had not the Scripture revealed it to us? So for the doctrine of the resurrection; that the same body, which is crumbled into a thousand pieces, should rise again, the same individual body, else it were a creation, not a resurrection. How could such a sacred riddle, above all human inquiry, be known had not the Scripture made a discovery of it? The matter of Scripture is so full of goodness, justice, and sanctity that it could be breathed from none but God; the holiness of it shows it to be of God. The Book of God is a crystal stream flowing from the fountain of life. It is so pure that it purifies everything else. The Scripture presses holiness as no other book ever has: it bids us live "soberly, righteously, and godly" (Titus 2:12); soberly, in acts of temperance; righteously, in acts of justice; godly, in acts of zeal and devotion.

16

SCRIPTURE COMMANDS US

*Whatsoever things are just . . . lovely . . .
of good report . . . think on these things.*

PHILIPPIANS 4:8

The Scripture is the royal law which commands not only our actions, but affections; it binds the heart to good behavior. Where is there such holiness to be found as is dug out of this sacred mine? Who could be the author of such a book but God Himself?

That the Scripture is the Word of God is evident by its predictions. It prophesies of things to come, which shows the voice of God speaking in it. It was foretold by the prophet, "A virgin shall conceive" (Isaiah 7:14) and the "Messiah [shall] be cut off" (Daniel 9:26). The Scripture foretells things that would occur many centuries later; as how long Israel should serve in the iron furnace and the very day of their deliverance. "And it came to pass at the end of the four hundred and thirty years, even the selfsame day it came to pass, that all the hosts of the LORD went out from the land of Egypt" (Exodus 12:41). This prediction of future things, merely contingent and not depending upon natural causes, is a demonstration of Scripture's divine origin.

Consider the impartiality of those men of God who wrote the Scriptures, who do not spare to set down their own failings. What man who writes a history would black his own face by recording those things of self that might stain his reputation? Surely had their pen not been guided by God's own hand, they would never have written that which reflects dishonor upon themselves. Men rather hide their blemishes than publish them to the world; but the penmen of holy Scripture eclipse their own name; they take away all glory from themselves and give the glory to God.

17

THE WORD GLORIFIES GOD

Ye are manifestly declared to be the epistle of Christ,
written not with ink, but with the Spirit of the living God.

2 CORINTHIANS 3:3

The mighty power that the Word has had upon the souls and consciences of men shows it to be God. It changes their hearts. Some, by
reading Scripture, have been turned into other men; they have been
made holy and gracious. By reading other books the heart may be
warmed, but by reading this Book it is transformed. The Word was
copied out into their hearts, and they became Christ's epistles, so
that others might read Christ in them. God's Word has comforted
their hearts. When Christians have sat by the rivers weeping, the
Word has dropped as honey and sweetly revived them. A Christian's
chief comfort is drawn out of these wells of salvation: "that we
through patience and comfort of the Scriptures might have hope"
(Romans 15:4). "Our light affliction, which is but for a moment,
worketh for us a far more exceeding and eternal weight of glory"
(2 Corinthians 4:17). God may change His providence, not His purpose; He may have the look of an enemy, but He has the heart of a
father. Thus the Word has a power in it to comfort the heart: "This
is my comfort in mine affliction: for thy word has quickened me"
(Psalm 119:50). Divine comforts are conveyed through the promises
of the Word. The Scriptures have such an exhilarating, heart-com-
forting power in them, clearly showing that they are of God, and it is
He that has put the milk of consolation into these breasts.

18

GLORIFY GOD IN TRUTH

Built upon the foundation of the apostles and prophets.

EPHESIANS 2:20

Miracles were used by Moses, Elijah, and Christ, and were continued, many years after, by the apostles, to confirm the truth of the holy Scriptures. As props are set under weak vines, so these miracles were set under the weak faith of men, that if they would not believe the writings of the Word, they might believe the miracles. We read of God's dividing the waters, making a pathway in the sea for His people to go over to the other side, the iron swimming, the oil increasing by pouring out, Christ's making wine of water, His curing the blind, and raising the dead. Thus God has set a seal to the truth and divinity of the Scriptures by miracles.

Critics cannot deny that the Scripture is divine and sacred; but they affirm it receives divine authority from the church; and in proof of it they bring 1 Timothy 3:15, where the church is said to be the ground and pillar of truth.

It is true, the church is the pillar of truth; but it does not therefore follow that the Scripture has its authority from the church. If the Word of God be divine merely because the church holds it forth, then our faith is to be built upon the church, and not upon the Word. God forbid!

The king's proclamation is fixed on the pillar, the pillar holds it out that all may read, but the proclamation does not receive its authority from the pillar, but from the king; so the church holds forth the Scriptures, but they do not receive their authority from the church, but from God.

19

GLORIFY GOD BY KNOWING SCRIPTURE

From a child thou hast known the holy Scriptures, which are able to make thee wise unto salvation through faith which is in Christ Jesus.

2 TIMOTHY 3:15

The Word is a rule of faith, a canon to direct our lives. The Word is the judge of controversies, the rock of infallibility that only is to be received as truth which agrees with Scripture, as the transcript with the original. All maxims in divinity are to be brought to the touchstone of Scripture, as all measures are brought to the standard.

The Scripture is a full and perfect canon, containing all things necessary to salvation. Scripture shows what we are to believe and what we are to practice. It gives us an exact model of religion and perfectly instructs us in the deep things of God. "If any man shall add unto these things, God shall add unto him the plagues that are written in this book" (Revelation 22:18).

The main scope and end of Scripture is to reveal a way of salvation. It makes a clear discovery of Christ in John 20:31: "These things are written, that ye might believe that Jesus is the Christ, the Son of God; and that believing ye might have life through his name." The design of the Word is to be a test whereby our grace is tried; a sea-mark to show us what rocks are to be avoided. The Word is to quicken our affections; it is to be our directory and source of comfort; it is to waft us over to the land of promise.

20

GLORIFY GOD BY UNDERSTANDING SCRIPTURES

All scripture is given by inspiration of God, and is profitable for doctrine,
for reproof, for correction, for instruction in righteousness.

2 TIMOTHY 3:16

The Scripture is to be its own interpreter, or rather the Spirit speaking in it. Nothing can cut the diamond but the diamond; nothing can interpret Scripture but Scripture. The sun discovers itself by its own beams; the Scripture interprets itself to the understanding. But the question is concerning hard places of Scripture, where the weak Christian is ready to wade beyond his depth. Who shall interpret here?

The church of God has appointed some to expound and interpret Scripture; therefore God has given gifts to men. Pastors of churches, like bright constellations, give light to dark Scriptures. "The priest's lips should keep knowledge, and they should seek the law at his mouth" (Malachi 2:7).

We are to receive nothing for truth, however, but what is agreeable to the Word. As God has given to His ministers gifts for interpreting obscure places, so He has given to His people so much of the spirit of discernment that they can tell (at least in things necessary to salvation) what is in agreement with Scripture, and what is not (1 Corinthians 12:10). God has provided His people with such a measure of wisdom and discretion that they can discern between truth and error and judge what is sound and what is false. They weighed the doctrine they heard, whether it was agreeable to Scripture.

21

GLORIFY GOD BY OBEYING THE WORD

*Lord, how is it thou wilt manifest thyself
unto us, and not unto the world?*

JOHN 14:22

See the wonderful goodness of God, who has committed to us the sacred Scriptures. The heathen are enveloped in ignorance. "As for his judgments, they have not known them" (Psalm 147:20). They have the oracles of false prophets, but not the writings of Moses and the apostles. How many live in the region of death, where this bright star of Scripture never appeared! We have this blessed Book of God to resolve all our doubts, to point out a way of life to us.

God, having given us His written Word to be our directory, takes away all excuses from men. No man can say, "I went wrong for want of light." God has given you His Word as a lamp to your feet; therefore, if you go wrong, you do so willfully. No man can say, "If I had known the will of God, I would have obeyed it." There are no excuses, for God has given the rule to go by; He has written His law with His own finger. Therefore, if you do not obey, you have no apology left. If a master leaves instructions in writing with his servant and tells him what work to do, and the servant neglects the work, that servant is left without excuse. "Now they have no cloak for their sins" (John 15:22). Thanks be to God that we are clothed in the righteousness of His Son.

22

GLORIFY GOD BY PROTECTING HIS WORD

If any man shall take away from the words of the book of this prophecy, God shall take away his part out of the book of life.

REVELATION 22:19

All Scripture is of divine inspiration. It reproves those who take away part of Scripture, those who, if they meet with anything in Scripture which they dislike, either put a false gloss over it or pretend it is corrupted. They are like Ananias, who kept back part of the money (Acts 5:2). They keep back part of the Scripture from the people. It is a high affront to God to deface and obliterate any part of His Word. God has stamped a divine majesty upon both Testaments; and until it can be proven that God has repealed the Old, it stands in force. The two Testaments are the two wells of salvation. There is much gospel in the Old Testament. The comforts of the gospel in the New Testament rise from the Old. The great promise of the Messiah is in the Old Testament, "A virgin shall conceive and bear a son" (Isaiah 7:14). Nay, I say more. The moral law, in some parts of it, speaks gospel—"I am the Lord thy God" (Isaiah 43:2); here is the pure-wine of the gospel. The saint's great charter, where God promises to "sprinkle clean water upon them, and put His Spirit within them" is to be found primarily in the Old Testament (Ezekiel 36:25–26). So those who take away the Old Testament, as Samson pulled down the pillars, would take away the pillars of a Christian's comfort.

23

GLORIFY GOD BY DESIRING TO KNOW THE SCRIPTURES

For the word of the LORD is right.

PSALM 33:4

What impudence it is when people, pretending to have the Spirit, lay aside the whole Bible and say the Scripture is a dead letter and they live above it. Until we are above sin, we shall not be above Scripture. Let not men talk of a revelation from the Spirit, but suspect it to be an imposture. The Spirit of God acts regularly; it works in and by the Word; and he that pretends to a new light, which is either above the Word or contrary to it, abuses both himself and the Spirit: his light is borrowed from him who transforms himself into an angel of light. The truths of God's Word also condemn the backsliders of Scripture; such as those who can go whole weeks and months and never read the Word. They lay it aside as rusty armor; they prefer a play or romance before Scripture. The weighty matters of the law are to them insignificant. Oh, how many can be looking at their faces in a glass all morning, but their eyes begin to be sore when they look upon a Bible! Heathens die for want of Scripture, and these in contempt of it. Surely they will go astray who slight their guide. Such as lay the reins upon the neck of their lusts, and never use the curbing bit of Scripture to check them, they are carried to hell, and never stop.

24

GLORIFY GOD BY NOT ABUSING SCRIPTURE

And the Word became flesh, and dwelt
among us, and we saw His glory.

JOHN 1:14 NASB

God sees no sin in His people with an eye of revenge, but He sees it with an eye of observation. He sees not sin in them, so as to damn them; but He sees it, so as to be angry, and severely to punish them. Did not David find it so when he cried out of his broken bones? In like manner the Arminians twist the Scripture in John 5:40: "Ye will not come to me;" where they bring in free will. This text shows how willing God is for us to have life, and that sinners may improve upon the gifts God has given them; but it does not prove the power of free will, for it is contrary to that Scripture, "No man can come to me, except the Father which has sent me draw him" (John 6:44). These Arminians wring out the text so hard that they make the blood come out; they do not compare Scripture with Scripture. Some make a joke of Scripture. When they are sad, they take the Scripture as their lute or minstrel to play upon, and so drive away the sad spirit. In the fear of God, take heed of this. One man took a part of the Scripture to make a joke of it, but was presently struck with a frenzy and ran mad. Martin Luther proclaimed, "Whom God intends to destroy, He gives them leave to play with Scripture."

25

GLORIFY GOD BY SEARCHING THE SCRIPTURES

They received the word with all readiness of mind,
and searched the scriptures daily, . . .

ACTS 17:11

If the Scripture be of divine inspiration, then be exhorted to study the Scripture. It is a copy of God's will. Be Scripture-men, Bible-Christians! In the Book of God are scattered many truths like so many pearls. Search as you search for a vein of silver. This blessed Book will fill your head with knowledge and your heart with grace. God wrote two tables with His own fingers; and if He took pains to write, we should take pains to read. The Word is our Magna Charta for heaven; shall we be so ignorant of our charter? "Let the word of Christ dwell in you richly" (Colossians 3:16). The memory must be a tablebook where the Word is written. There is majesty sparkling in every line of Scripture. Many are converted by reading one verse of the Word, beholding a majesty in it beyond all human rhetoric. There is a melody in Scripture, that blessed harp which drives away sadness of spirit. Hear the sounding of this harp a little: "This is a faithful saying, and worthy of all acceptation, that Christ Jesus came into the world to save sinners" (1 Timothy 1:15). He took not only our flesh upon Him but our sins. And Matthew 11:28 says, "Come unto me, all ye that are heavy laden, and I will give you rest." How sweetly does this harp of Scripture sound. What heavenly music does it make in the ears of a distressed sinner, especially when the finger of God's Spirit touches this instrument!

26

GLORIFY GOD BY BEHOLDING GOD'S GLORY IN SCRIPTURE

He who gives attention to the word will find good,
and blessed is he who trusts in the LORD.

PROVERBS 16:20 NASB

There is divinity in Scripture. It contains the marrow and quintessence of religion. It is a rock of diamonds, a mystery of piety. The lips of Scripture have grace poured into them. The Scripture speaks of faith, self-denial, and all the graces which, as a chain of pearls, adorn a Christian. The Scripture leads to holiness, it tells of another world, it gives a prospect of eternity! Search the Scripture! Make the Word familiar to you. Had I the tongue of angels, I could not sufficiently set forth the excellency of Scripture. It is a spiritual reflection, in which we behold God's glory; it is the tree of life, the oracle of wisdom, the rule of manners, the heavenly seed of which the new creature is formed . . . . The leaves of the tree of life were for healing. So these holy leaves of Scripture are for the healing of our souls. Scripture is profitable for all things. If we are deserted, here is spiced wine that cheers the heavy heart; if we are pursued by Satan, here is the sword of the Spirit to resist him; if we are diseased with sin's leprosy, here are the waters of the sanctuary, both to cleanse and to cure. There is no danger in plucking from this tree of holy Scripture; if we do not eat of this tree of knowledge, we shall surely die. Oh, then, read the Scriptures!

27

GLORIFY GOD BY REVERENCING HIS WORD

*Let the word of Christ dwell in you richly in all wisdom; teaching
and admonishing one another in psalms and hymns and
spiritual songs, singing with grace in your hearts to the Lord.*

COLOSSIANS 3:16

Read the Bible with reverence. Think in every line you read that
God is speaking to you. The ark where the law was put was overlaid
with pure gold and was carried on bars, that the Levites might not
touch it (Exodus 25:14). Why was this, but to give reverence to the
law? Read with seriousness. It is matter of life and death; by this
Word you must be tried; conscience and Scripture is the jury God
will proceed by in judging you. Read the Word with affection. Get
your hearts quickened with the Word; go to it to fetch fire. Labor
so the Word may not only be a lamp to direct, but a fire to warm.
Read the Scripture, not only as a history, but as a love letter sent to
you from God, which may affect your hearts. Pray that the same
Spirit that wrote the Word may assist you in reading it; that God's
Spirit would show you the wonderful things of His law. "Then the
Spirit said unto Philip, 'Go near, and join thyself to this chariot'"
(Acts 8:29). Likewise, when God's Spirit joins Himself with the
chariot of His Word, it becomes effectual.

28

GLORIFY GOD BY MEDITATING ON HIS WORD

The commandment is a lamp; and the law is light.

PROVERBS 6:23

Be exhorted to prize the written Word. David valued the Word more than gold. What would the martyrs have given for one page of the Bible! The Word is the field where Christ, the pearl of price, is hid. In this sacred mine we dig, not for a wedge of gold, but for a weight of glory. The Scripture is a sacred eye—salve to illuminate us. It is the chart and compass by which we sail to the New Jerusalem. It is a sovereign cordial in all distresses. What are the promises but the water of life to renew fainting spirits? Is it sin that troubles? Here is a Scripture cordial: "Iniquities prevail against me: as for our transgressions, thou shalt purge them away" (Psalm 65:3). Do outward afflictions disquiet you? Here is a Scripture cordial: "I will be with him in trouble" (Psalm 91:15), not only to behold, but to uphold. Thus, as in the ark manna was laid up, so promises are laid up in the ark of Scripture. The Scripture will make us wise. Wisdom is above rubies. "Through thy precepts I get understanding" (Psalm 119:104). What made Eve desire the tree of knowledge? It was a tree "to make one wise" (Genesis 3:6). The Scriptures teach a man to know himself. They reveal Satan's snares and schemes. God's Word makes you "wise unto salvation" (2 Timothy 3:15). Oh, then, highly prize the Scriptures.

1

GLORIFY GOD BY BELIEVING HIS WORD

If they hear not Moses and the prophets, neither
will they be persuaded, though one arose from the dead.

LUKE 16:31

The Scripture is divinely inspired, so believe it. Give credence to the Word. It is breathed from God's own mouth. Hence the profaneness of men, that they do not believe the Scripture. "Who hath believed our report?" (Isaiah 53:1). If you believe the glorious rewards the Scripture speaks of, would you not persist in making your election sure? If you believe the infernal torments the Scripture speaks of, would it not put you into a cold sweat and cause your heart to tremble for sin? But people are in part atheists: they give but little credit to the Word. Therefore they are irreverent, drawing dark shadows in their lives. Learn to understand and appreciate Scripture with a firm belief of it. Some think that if God should send an angel from heaven and declare His mind, they would believe Him; or if He sent one from the damned to preach the torments of hell, all in flames, they would believe. But God is wise, and He is to make His mind known to us by writing; and those not convinced by the Word shall be judged by the Word. The belief of Scripture is of high importance, enabling us to resist temptation. If the written Word is not believed, it is like writing on water, which makes no impression.

GLORIFY GOD BY LOVING THE SCRIPTURES

O how I love Your law!

PSALM 119:97 NASB

We are to love the written Word. Augustine said, "Let the Holy Scriptures be my chaste delight." Chrysostom compares the Scripture to a garden where every truth is a fragrant flower, which we should wear, not on our bosom, but in our heart. David counted the Word "sweeter than honey and the honeycomb" (Psalm 19:10). There is in Scripture that which may breed delight. It shows us the way to riches (Deuteronomy: 25:8 and Proverbs 3:9–10); to long life (Psalm 34:11–14; and to a kingdom (Hebrews 12:28). Well then may we count those the sweetest hours that are spent in reading and meditating on the Holy Scriptures, so that we may say with the prophet Jeremiah, "Thy words were found, and I did eat them; and they were the joy and rejoicing of my heart" (15:16).

3

GLORIFY GOD BY CONFORMING TO THE SCRIPTURES

Establish my footsteps in Your word.

PSALM 119:133 NASB

Conform to Scripture. Let us lead scriptural lives that the Bible might be seen printed in our lives. We are to do what the Word commands. Obedience is an excellent way of commenting upon the Bible. "I will walk in thy truth" (Psalm 86:11). Let the Word be the sundial by which you set your life. Are we better off having the Scripture available to us if all our words and actions are not aligned with it? What is a carpenter without his ruler if he hides it behind his back, never making use of his ruler to measure and square his work? Are Christians better off having the rule of the Word of God if we do not make use of it to guide us and to regulate our lives, living by it? How many swerve and deviate from the rule! The Word teaches believers to be sober and temperate, but they are drunk; to be chaste and holy, but they are profane. They go quite from the rule! What a dishonor it is to the Christian faith for men to live in such contradiction to Scripture. The Word is called a "light to our feet" (Psalm 119:105). It is not only a light to our eyes to mend our sight, but to our feet to mend our walk. Oh, let us lead Bible conversations with our words and with our lives!

4

Glorify God by Contending for His Word

*In the beginning was the Word, and the Word was with God,
and the Word was God. The same was in the beginning with God.
In him was life; and the life was the light of men.*

JOHN 1:1–2, 4

Contend by making a statement, for "all Scripture is inspired by God and profitable for teaching, for reproof, for correction, for training in righteousness; so that the man of God may be adequate, equipped for every good work" (2 Timothy 3:16). Though we should not possess argumentative attitudes and hearts, we ought to be willing to stand firm and contend for the Word of God. This jewel, God's Word, is too precious to be parted with. "Keep her; for she is thy life" (Proverbs 4:13). The Scripture is surrounded by enemies; heretics fight against it. We must therefore "contend for the faith which was once delivered to the saints" (Jude 3). The Scripture is our book of evidences for heaven. Shall we part with our proof? The saints of old were both advocates and martyrs for truth; they would hold fast to the Scripture, even though they knew they could lose their lives for that stand.

5

GLORIFY GOD BY BEING THANKFUL FOR HIS WORD

For the Word of the LORD is upright:
and all His work is done in faithfulness.

PSALM 33:4 NASB

What mercy is it that God has not only acquainted us what His will is, but that He has made it known by writing! In old times God revealed His mind by visions, but the Word written is a more sure way of knowing God's mind. "This voice which came from heaven we heard . . . We have also a more sure word of prophecy" (2 Peter 1:18–19). The devil can transform himself into an angel of light. We know how Satan does his evil work, deceiving people with delusion instead of divine revelations. We are to thank God for revealing His mind to us through the written Word. We are not left in doubtful suspense, not knowing what to believe, but we have an infallible rule to go by. The Scripture is our polestar to direct us to heaven. It shows us every step we are to take: when we go wrong, it instructs us; when we go right, it comforts us. It is a matter of thankfulness that the translated Scriptures are made intelligible.

GLORIFY GOD BY ADORING HIS GRACE

But grow in the grace and knowledge of our Lord and Savior Jesus Christ.
To Him be the Glory, both now and to the day of eternity. Amen.

2 PETER 3:18 NASB

Adore God's distinguishing grace, particularly if you have felt the power and authority of the Word upon your conscience and if you can say, as David did, "Thy word hath quickened me" (Psalm 119:50). Christian, bless God that He has not only given you His Word to be a rule of holiness, but He has given you His grace to be a principle of holiness. Bless God that He has not only written His Word, but that He has sealed it upon your heart and made it effectual. Can you not say it is of divine inspiration, because you have felt it to carry out its functional operations in your life? Oh, free grace! That God should send out His Word and heal you; that He should heal thee and not others! The same Scripture that to them is a dead letter should be to thee something you savor and relish in your life for life eternal! In the same way then, there has come to be at the present time a remnant according to God's gracious choice. But if it is by grace, it is no longer on the basis of works. Otherwise grace is no longer grace (Romans 3:24).

GLORIFY THE SPIRIT OF GOD

*"I will give them a heart to know Me, for I am the LORD;
and they will be My people, and I will be their God,
for they will return to Me with their whole heart."*

JEREMIAH 24:7 NASB

The Scriptures principally teach what man is to believe concerning God and what responsibility and accountability God requires of man. God is a Spirit, infinite, eternal, and unchangeable, in His being, His wisdom, His power, His Holiness, His justice, His goodness, and His truth. There is a God, and He speaks to our spirit. Belief in God's essence is the foundation of all Christian worship: "He that cometh to God must believe that he is" (Hebrews 11:6). There must be a first cause of existence, which gives being to all things. We know that there is a God by the book of nature. The notion of a deity is engraved upon man's heart; it is demonstrated by the light of its intrinsic and essential qualities. I think it is hard for a man to be a natural atheist. He may wish there were no God, and he may not agree with the fact that there is a deity. But he cannot, no matter how much he tries in his judgment, believe there is no God, unless, by his accumulated sin, his conscience be so seared, and he has such a lethargy upon him, that he has sinned away his very power of being able to think in a logical and rational manner.

8

GLORIFY GOD BY LOVING HIS CREATION

God . . . made the world, and all things therein.

ACTS 17:24

We know that there is a God by His works, as is demonstrated in the Godhead. The most atheistical spirits, when they have considered these works, have been forced to acknowledge some wise and supreme Maker of these things. Considering the creation of the heaven and earth, there must be some Architect or First Cause. The world could not make itself. Who could hang the earth on nothing but the great God? Who could provide such rich furniture for the heavens, the glorious constellations, and the firmament bespangled with such glittering lights? We see God's glory blazing in the sun and twinkling in the stars. Who could give the earth its clothing, cover it with grass and corn, adorn it with flowers, and enrich it with gold? Only God! Who but God could make the sweet music in the heavens, cause the angels to join in concert, and sound forth the praises of their Maker? "The morning stars sang together, and all the sons of God shouted for joy" (Job 38:7). To imagine that the work of the creation was not framed by God is like believing that a curious landscape was drawn by a pencil without the hand of an artist. To create is proper to the Deity. God is the great Superintendent of the world. He holds the golden reins of government in His hand and guides all things harmoniously to their proper end.

GLORIFY GOD BY ACKNOWLEDGING HIS PROVIDENCE

As God has called each, in this manner let
him walk. And so I direct in all the churches.

I CORINTHIANS 7:17 NASB

Providence is the governess of the world. It is the hand that turns the wheel of the whole creation; it sets the sun its race, the sea, its bounds. If God did not guide the world, things would run into disorder and confusion. When one looks on a clock and sees the motion of the wheels, the striking of the hammer, the hanging of the plummets, he would say, "Some artificer made it." So, when we see the excellent order and harmony in the universe, the sun, that great luminary, dispensing its light and heat to the world, without which the world would be a grave; the rivers sending forth their silver streams to refresh the bodies of men and prevent a drought; and every creature acting within its sphere, keeping its due bounds, we must acknowledge there is a God, who wisely orders and governs all these things. Who could set this great army of creatures in their ranks and squadrons, keeping them in unified march, but He, whose name is the Lord of Hosts? God is all wise in His plans for His children, so by His power, He supports them. All motion is from something that is immoveable. Who moves that highest sphere and is the first mover of the planets? It can be no other than God Himself.

GLORIFY GOD BY EMULATING HIM

It is He who has made us, and not we ourselves.

PSALM 100:3 NASB

Man is a microcosm, a miniature copy of our heavenly Father. The excellent makeup and frame of his body is fashioned curiously as with needlework: "I was curiously wrought in the lowest parts of the earth" (Psalm 139:15). This body is endowed with desirable qualities, abilities, and a noble soul. Who but God could make such a union of different substances into flesh and spirit? In Him we "live, and move, and have our being" (Acts 17:28). The quick motion of every part of the body shows there is a God. We may see something of Him in the sparkling of the eye. If the frame of the body be so uniquely shaped, what is the jewel? The soul has a celestial brightness in it; as one old saint said, "It is a diamond set in a ring of clay." What noble faculties is the soul endowed with: understanding, a will, and affections are a mirror of the Trinity. The matter of the soul is a spiritual one: it is a divine spark illuminated from heaven. Being spiritual means being able to be immortal: the soul does not grow old, it lives forever. Who could create a soul ennobled with such rare and angelic properties but God? "God created man in his own image, in the image of God created he him; male and female created he them" (Genesis 1:27).

GLORIFY GOD FROM THE DEPTHS OF OUR CONSCIENCE

Blessed are those who mourn, for they shall be comforted.

MATTHEW 5:4 NASB

We may prove a Deity by our conscience. Conscience is God's deputy or administrative deputy. Conscience is a witness of a Deity. If there were no Bible to tell us there is a God, yet conscience might. Conscience, as the apostle says, "either accuseth" or "excuseth" (Romans 2:15). It is accountable to a higher judicatory. Natural conscience, being kept free from gross sin, excuses. When a man does virtuous actions, lives soberly and righteously, observes the golden rule, then conscience approves and says, "Well done." Like a bee, it gives honey. Natural conscience in the wicked accuses. When men go against its light, they feel the worm of conscience. Alas! What scorpion lurks within? Conscience, being sinned against, spits fire in men's faces, fills them with shame and horror. When the sinner sees the handwriting on the wall of conscience, his countenance changes. What could put a man's conscience into such agony except the impression of a Deity and the thoughts of coming before His tribunal? Those who are above human laws are subject to the checks of their own conscience. It is observable: the nearer the wicked approach death, the more they are terrified. This comes from the apprehension of judgment approaching. The soul, being sensible of its immortal nature, trembles at Him who never ceases to live and therefore will never cease to punish.

GLORIFY GOD THROUGH HIS PROPHETIC WORD

Declare the things that are going to come afterward,
That we may know that you are gods.

ISAIAH 41:23 NASB

That there is a God appears by the consent of nations, by the universal vote and suffrage of all men. Though the heathen did not worship the true God, they did worship *a* god. They set up an altar "To the unknown God" (Acts 17:23). They knew a God should be worshipped, though they knew not the God whom they ought to worship. Some worshipped Jupiter; some, Neptune; and some, Mars. Rather than not worship something, they would worship anything.

That there is a God also appears by His prediction of future things. He who can prophesy future events that shall surely come to pass is the true God. God foretold that a virgin should conceive and prefixed the time when the Messiah should be crucified. God foretold the captivity of the Jews in Babylon and who would be their deliverer. Isaiah 45:1 explains that God Himself uses this argument to prove that He is the true God and that all the gods of the heathens are fictitious and legally invalid. To foretell things dependent on or resulting from a future and as yet unknown event or circumstance, and things that depend upon no natural causes, is peculiar to Deity.

GLORIFY GOD BY ACKNOWLEDGING HIS SOVEREIGNTY

Who is like You among the gods, O LORD?
Who is like You, majestic in holiness,
Awesome in praise, working wonders?

EXODUS 15:11 NASB

The God who can work, and none can hinder, is the *true* God; nothing can hinder action except some superior authority; but there is no authority above God. All authority that is, is by Him; therefore all authority is under Him. He has a "mighty arm" (Psalm 89:13). He sees the plans men devise against Him, and He plucks off their chariot wheels. He makes the diviners angry and cuts off the spirit of princes. He calms the sea, gives check to the large beast, and binds the devil in chains. He acts according to His pleasure; He does what He will.

There are devils; therefore there is a God. Atheists cannot deny that there are devils, for then they must admit that there is a God. We read of many possessed by the devil. An old saint tells that Satan appeared to a holy man in a most glorious manner and professed himself to be Christ. The old man answered, "I desire not to see my Savior here in this desert. It shall suffice me to see Him in heaven." Now, if there be a devil, there is a God. God is real! God has unlimited authority and sovereignty. "Who is like You among the gods, O LORD?"

14

GLORIFY GOD BY RECOGNIZING HIS EXISTENCE

The fool has said in his heart, "There is no God."

PSALM 14:1 NASB

Seeing there is a God, it reproves such atheistical fools who deny it. Some deny that there is a Providence, saying that all things occur by chance. An atheist who says there is no God is the wickedest creature alive and worse than a thief, for the thief takes away our goods, but the atheist would take away our God from us. He dare not speak it with his tongue, but he says it in his heart; he wishes it. None can be speculative atheists: "the devils . . . believe, and tremble" (James 2:19). I have read about a professing atheist who, when faced with death, cried out that he was damned. Though there are few who say, "There is no God," yet many deny Him in their lives. "In works they deny him" (Titus 1:16). Some deny the existence of the gods, but He permits them to remain. The world is full of practical atheism; most people live as if they do not believe there is a God. Do they lie or defraud? Are they unclean? Would they do so if they believed there was a God who would call them to account? If a heathen never having seen God should come among us, and we had no other means to convince him of a Deity except the lives of men in our age, surely he would question whether there were a God.

15

GLORIFY GOD FOR RIGHTEOUSNESS SAKE

Say ye to the righteous, that it shall be well with him . . .
Woe unto the wicked! It shall be ill with him:
for the reward of his hands shall be given him.

ISAIAH 3:10–11

God will deal righteously and give just rewards to all men. Things seem to be carried in the world very unequally; the wicked flourish (Psalm 73:3). They who tempt God are delivered. The ripe cluster of grapes is squeezed into their cup while the godly, who wept for sin and served God, are afflicted. "I have eaten ashes like bread, and mingled my drink with weeping" (Psalm 102:9). It appears that evil men enjoy all the good, and good men endure all the evil, but because there is a God, He will deal righteously with men. "Shall not the Judge of all the earth do right?" (Genesis 18:25). Offenders must come to punishment. The sinner's day of death and dooms-day is coming. "The LORD . . . seeth that his day is coming" (Psalm 37:13). While there is a hell, the wicked shall be scourged enough; and while there is eternity, they shall lie there long enough; and God will abundantly compensate the faithful service of His people. They shall have their white robes and crowns. "Verily there is a reward for the righteous: verily he is a God that judgeth in the earth" (Psalm 58:11). Because God is God, He will give glorious rewards to His people.

Glorify God Through Obedience

God shall judge the righteous and the wicked;
for there is a time for every purpose and for every work.

ECCLESIASTES 3:17

Woe to all who have God against them. He lives forever to be avenged upon them. "Can thine heart endure, or can thine hands be strong, in the days that I shall deal with thee?" (Ezekiel 22:14). Those who pollute God's Sabbath, oppose His saints, trample these jewels in the dust, those who live in contradiction to God's Word, engage the Infinite Majesty of heaven against them; and how dismal will their case be! "If I whet my glittering sword, and mine hand take hold on judgment, I will render vengeance to mine enemies . . . I will make mine arrows drunk with blood" (Deuteronomy 32:41–42). The lion's roar is loud, so what must the tearing of his prey sound like? "Consider this, ye that forget God, lest I tear you in pieces" (Psalm 50:22). Oh, that those men would think of this, who continue on in sin! Shall we engage the great God against us? God strikes slow, but heavy. "Hast thou an arm like God?" (Job 40:9). Cannot thou strike such a blow? *God is the best friend but the worst enemy.* If He can look men into their grave, how far can He throw them? "Who knows the power of his wrath?" (Psalm 90:11). What fools are they, who, for a moment of pleasure, drink a sea of wrath!

17

GLORIFY GOD BY BELIEVING THAT HE IS ALL-SUFFICIENT

I have set the LORD always before me.

PSALM 16:8

To worship God, pray to Him, but not believe there is a God, puts a high scorn and contempt upon Him. Believe that God is the only true God, such a God as He has revealed Himself in His Word, a lover of righteousness, and hater of wickedness (Psalm 45:7).

The real belief in a Deity gives life to all Christian worship. The more we believe the truth and infiniteness of God, the more holy and angelic we are in our lives. God sees us; He is the heart-searcher; and this truth would make us live always under God's eye. The belief of a Deity would be a bridle to sin and a spur to duty; it would add wings to prayer and oil to the lamp of our devotion. Belief in a Deity would cause dependence upon God in all our difficulties and earthly demands. God can supply all your wants, scatter all your fears, resolve all your doubts, conquer all your temptations. The arm of God's power can never be shrunk; He can create mercy for us and therefore can help, and not be in debt to us. If we believe there is a God, we should so depend on His providence and not use any indirect means; we should not run ourselves into sin to rid ourselves from trouble. We need to run to Him believing that He is the all-sufficient One.

GLORIFY THE GREAT "I AM!"

"I, even I, am the LORD, And there is no savior besides Me.
"It is I who have declared and saved and proclaimed, And there was
no strange god among you; So you are My witnesses," declares the
LORD, "And I am God. Even from eternity I am He, And there is none
who can deliver out of My hand; I act and who can reverse it?"

ISAIAH 43:11–13 NASB

Let us labor to learn about God: "This God is our God" (Psalm
48:14). Since the Fall, we have lost our likeness of God and our
communion with God. Let us labor to recover this lost interest and
proclaim, "My God" (Psalm 43:5). It is little comfort to know there
is a God unless He is ours and we are His. God offers Himself to
be our God: "I will be their God" (Jeremiah 31:33). Faith catches
hold of the offer: it appropriates God and makes all that is in Him
to be ours. His wisdom is ours, and He is our teacher; His Holiness
is ours, to sanctify us; His Spirit is ours, to comfort us; His mercy
is ours, to save us. To be able to say, "God is mine," is more than
to have all the mines of gold and silver in the world.

19

GLORIFY HIM AS GOD THROUGH OUR WORSHIP

Come, let us worship and bow down;
let us kneel before the LORD our Maker.

PSALM 95:6

Let us serve and worship the true and living God. It was an indict-ment brought against some in that "they glorified him not as God" (Romans 1:21). Let us pray to Him as the only true God. Pray with fervency. "The effectual fervent prayer . . . availeth much" (James 5:16). This is both the fire and the incense; without fervency, it is no prayer. Let us love Him as God. "Thou shalt love the LORD thy God with all thy heart" (Deuteronomy 6:5). To love Him with all the heart is to give Him precedence in our love, to let Him have the cream of our affections; to love Him not only appreciatively, but intensely, as much as we can. As sunbeams that are united in a burn-ing glass burn even hotter, so our affections should be united: that our love of God may be more passionate. Let us obey Him as God. All the creatures obey Him, the stars fight His battles, the wind and sea obey Him, and man should even more because God has endued him with a principle of reason. He is God and has sovereignty over us. Therefore, as we received life from Him, so we must receive a law from Him and submit to His will in all things. This is to kiss Him with a kiss of loyalty, and it is to glorify Him as God.

GLORIFY THE OMNIPRESENT SPIRIT OF GOD

God is a Spirit.

JOHN 4:24

God is an immaterial substance, of pure and unmixed essence, not compounded of body and soul. The more spiritual God's essence in our life, the more noble and excellent our life is.

God differs from other spirits, and we must distinguish between the spirits. The angels are created spirits; God is a Spirit uncreated. The angels are finite and capable of being annihilated; the same power that made them is able to reduce them to nothing; but God is an infinite Spirit. The angels are confined spirits, confined to a place; but God is an immense Spirit; He is omnipresent. The angels, though spirits, are but ministering spirits (Hebrews 1:14). Though they are spirits, they are servants. God is the Father of spirits (Hebrews 12:9).

The soul is a spirit: "The spirit shall return unto God who gave it" (Ecclesiastes 12:7). The essence of God is incommunicable. Thus, that the soul is a spirit means that God has made it intelligible and stamped upon it His likeness, not His essence.

By divine nature is meant divine qualities (2 Peter 1:4). We are made partakers of the divine nature, not by identity or union with the divine essence, but by a transformation into the divine likeness. Thus you see how God differs from other spirits, angels, and souls of men. He is a Spirit of transcendent excellence, the Father of spirits.

21

Glorify God by Embracing Him

But will God indeed dwell on the earth? behold,
the heaven and heaven of heavens cannot contain thee;
how much less this house that I have builded?

1 Kings 8:27

In Scripture, a human shape and figure is given to God; He is said to have eyes and hands. It is contrary to the nature of a spirit to have a physical body. "Handle me, and see: for a spirit hath not flesh and bones, as ye see me have" (Luke 24:39). Bodily members are ascribed to God, not properly, but metaphorically, and in a borrowed sense. The right hand of the Lord refers to His power, and the eyes of the Lord refer to His wisdom. That God is a Spirit, not capable of bodily shape or substance, is clear, for a body is visible, but God is invisible; therefore He is a Spirit "whom no man has seen, nor can see" (1 Timothy 6:16), not by an eye of sense. A human body cannot be in two places at once, but God is everywhere, in all places at once; therefore He is a Spirit (Psalm 139:7–8). God's center is everywhere. A body being compounded of integral parts may be dissolved, but the Godhead is not capable of dissolution: He can have no end. So, clearly, God is a Spirit, which adds to the perfection of His nature.

Glorify God by Acknowledging His Spirit

This is the word of the L<small>ORD</small> . . . saying,
Not by might, nor by power, but by
my spirit, saith the L<small>ORD</small> of hosts.

Z<small>ECHARIAH</small> 4:6

Because God is a Spirit, He is not susceptible to and not capable of feeling physical pain or injury. Wicked men set up their banners and bend their forces against God; they are said to fight against God (Acts 5:39). But how will this fighting help in achieving anything good? What hurt can they do to the Deity? God is a Spirit and therefore cannot receive any hurtful impression. Wicked men may imagine evil against the Lord. "What do ye imagine against the Lord?" (Nahum 1:9). But God, being a Spirit, is impenetrable. The wicked may eclipse His glory, but they cannot touch His essence. God can hurt His enemies, but they cannot hurt Him. God is a Spirit and therefore invisible. How can the wicked with all their forces hurt Him when they cannot see Him? Hence all the attempts of the wicked against God are foolish and prove abortive. "The kings of the earth set themselves . . . against the L<small>ORD</small> and against his anointed . . . He that sitteth in the heavens shall laugh" (Psalm 2:2, 4). He is a Spirit, He can hold them accountable, but they cannot touch the Lord God!

WORSHIP GOD IN TRUTH AND SPIRIT

Do not I fill heaven and earth? saith the LORD.

JEREMIAH 23:24

As God is a spirit, we are not to make graven images to represent Him. "The LORD spake to you out of the midst of the fire: ye heard the voice of the words, but saw no similitude" (Deuteronomy 4:12). God being a Spirit is imperceptible, so cannot be discerned. How then can there be any resemblance made of Him? "To whom then will ye liken God? or what likeness will ye compare unto him?" (Isaiah 40:18). How can you paint the Deity? Can we make an image of that which we never saw? Ye saw no similitude. It is folly to endeavor to make a picture of the soul, because it is a spiritual thing, or to paint the angels, because they are spirits.

Are not angels in Scripture represented by the cherubim? The cherubim did not represent the persons of the angels, but their office. The cherubims were made with wings, to show the swiftness of the angels in discharge of their office. If we cannot picture the souls nor the persons of angels because they are spirits, much less can we make an image or picture of God, who is infinite and the Father of spirits.

God is also an omnipresent Spirit, present in all places. Therefore, being everywhere present, it is abuse to worship Him by an image. Is it not a foolish thing to bow down to the king's picture when the king is present? So it is to worship God's image when God Himself is present.

24

Do Others See Christ in You?

We have the mind of Christ.

1 Corinthians 2:16

We must form an idea of God spiritually based on His attributes, by His holiness, His justice, and His goodness, which are the beams by which His divine nature shines forth. We must imagine Him as He is in Christ. Christ is "the image of the invisible God" (Colossians 1:15). Set your faith on Christ as God-man. In Christ we see some sparklings of the divine glory; in Him is the exact resemblance of all His Father's excellencies. The wisdom, love, and holiness of God the Father shine forth in Christ. "He that hath seen me hath seen the Father" (John 14:9).

God being a Spirit shows us that the more spiritual we grow, the more we grow to be like God. But how do earth and spirit agree? What resemblance is there between an earthly heart and Him who is a Spirit? The more spiritual anyone is, the more like God.

To be spiritual is to be refined and sublimated, to have the heart still in heaven, to be thinking of God and glory, and to be carried up in a fiery chariot of love to God. "Whom have I in heaven but thee?" (Psalm 73:25). A Christian, who is taken off from these earthly things as the spirits are taken off from the lees, has a noble spiritual soul and most resembles Him who is a Spirit.

25

GOD REQUIRES SPIRIT-WORSHIP

At the name of Jesus every knee should bow.

PHILIPPIANS 2:10

That God is a Spirit shows that the worship that God requires of us, and that is most acceptable to Him, is spiritual worship. "They that worship him must worship him in spirit and in truth" (John 4:24). Spiritual worship is virgin worship. Though God will have the service of our bodies, our eyes and hands lifted up, to testify to others that reverence we have of His glory and His majesty, yet He will have the worship of the soul chiefly. "Glorify God in your body, and in your spirit" (1 Corinthians 6:20). God prizes Spirit-worship, because it comes near to His own nature, which is a Spirit.

To worship God in spirit is to worship Him without ceremonies. The ceremonies of the law, that God Himself ordained, are now done away with. Christ the substance is come, shadows fly away, and the apostle calls the legal ceremonial "procedures." If we are not to use those Old Testament ceremonies that God once appointed, then we are not to use those He never appointed.

To worship God in Spirit is to worship Him with faith in the blood of the Messiah and with the utmost zeal and intenseness of soul. "Our twelve tribes, instantly serving God day and night" (Acts 26:7) with intenseness of spirit; not only constantly, but earnestly. The more spiritual any service is, the nearer it comes to God, who is a Spirit.

26

GLORIFY GOD THROUGH SPIRIT-WORSHIP

[Make] melody in your heart to the Lord.

EPHESIANS 5:19

God is a Spirit, and He will be worshipped in spirit. It is not pomp of worship, but purity that God accepts. Repentance is not in the outward severities used to the body, as penance, fasting, and chastising the body, but repentance consists in the sacrifice of a broken heart. Thanksgiving does not stand in church music, the melody of an organ, but rather in making melody in the heart to the Lord. Prayer is not tuning the voice into a heartless confession or talking over a few beads, but it consists in sighs and groans. When the fire of fervency is put to the incense of prayer, it ascends as a sweet aroma. Spirit-worship acknowledges God who is a Spirit. "The Father seeketh such to worship him" (John 4:23); God is delighted with spiritual worship. This is the savory meat that God loves. Some disagree and give Him more sediment than spirits, bringing their tasks, not their hearts, which makes God disclaim the very services He Himself appointed. Let us then give God spirit-worship, which best suits His nature. A little prayer, given with the heart and spirit, may have much virtue and efficacy in it. The publican made but a short prayer, "God, be merciful to me a sinner" (Luke 18:13), but it was full of life and spirit. It came from the heart, therefore it was accepted.

GOD'S SPIRIT WITHIN US

*I will put my Spirit within you and cause you to walk in
my statutes, and ye shall keep my judgments, and do them.*

EZEKIEL 36:27

Let us pray to God, that as He is a Spirit, so He will give us of His
Spirit. The essence of God is incommunicable, but not the motions,
the presence, or the influences of His Spirit. When the sun shines
in a room, the actual sun is not there, but the light, heat, and influence of the sun. God has made a promise of His Spirit: "I will put
my Spirit within you." Turn promises into prayers: *O Lord, Thou who
art a Spirit, give me of Thy Spirit. I, flesh, beg Thy Spirit, Thy enlightening, sanctifying,
quickening Spirit.* How needful is His Spirit! Without Him, we cannot
do any task in an effective manner. When this wind of God's Spirit
blows upon our sails, we move swiftly toward heaven. Let us pray,
therefore, that God would give us the residue of His Spirit: "Yet had
he the residue of the spirit, and wherefore one? That he might seek
a godly seed" (Malachi 2:15), that we may move more vigorously in
the sphere of our Christian faith and our worship of God.

28

A Crown of Glory for the Saints

Blessed be the God and Father of our Lord Jesus Christ, who hath blessed us with all spiritual blessings in heavenly places in Christ.

EPHESIANS 1:3

As God is a Spirit, so the rewards that He gives His children are spiritual, and the chief blessings He gives us in this life are spiritual blessings, not gold and silver. He gives Christ, His love, and He fills us with grace. So the main rewards He gives us after this life are spiritual, "a crown of glory that fadeth not away" (1 Peter 5:4). Earthly crowns fade, but the believer's crown, because it is spiritual, is immortal; it is a crown that never fades away. "It is impossible," says Joseph Scaliger, "for that which is spiritual to be subject to change or corruption." This truth may comfort a Christian in all his labors and sufferings here on earth; he gives of himself to the service of God and has little or no reward here. But remember, God, who is a Spirit, will give spiritual rewards in heaven: the very sight of the face of God, white robes, and a weight of glory. Be not then weary of God's service here on earth. Think of the spiritual rewards that await His children in heaven, a crown of glory that will not fade away.

29

GOD IS INFINITE

It is he that sitteth upon the circle of the earth.

ISAIAH 40:22

God is infinite. All created beings are finite. But infinite may be applied to all God's attributes: He is infinitely merciful, infinitely wise, infinitely holy. Yet, if we take infinity, it implies God's omnipresence. The Greek word for *infinite* signifies "without bounds or limits." God is not confined to any place: He is infinite, and so is present in all places at once. Augustine reminds us that "His center is everywhere; in no place is God's Being either confined or excluded." That truth is grounded in Scripture: "Behold, the heaven and heaven of heavens cannot contain thee" (1 Kings 8:27). God's essence is not limited to the regions above, or to the terrestrial globe, but is everywhere. As philosophers say of the soul, the soul is in every part of the body, in the eye, heart, foot, so we may say of God, He is here and everywhere; His essence is everywhere; His circuit is in heaven, and in earth, and sea; and He is in all places of His circuit at once. God, who binds everything else, is Himself without bounds. He sets bounds to the sea. He sets bounds to the angels; they, like the cherubim, move and stand at his appointment (Ezekiel 10:16), but He is infinite, without bounds. He who can span the heavens, and weigh the earth in scales, forever and ever will be infinite.

30

THE GLORIOUS PRESENCE OF GOD

Do not I fill heaven and earth?

JEREMIAH 23:24

God is in all places at once, but not in regard to His essence, but by His virtue and influence, as a king, who is in all places of his kingdom authoritatively, by his power and authority, but he is personally on his throne.

God, who is infinite, is in all places at once, not only by His influence, but by His essence; for, if His essence fills all places, then He must be there in person.

But does not God say in Isaiah 66:1 that heaven is His throne and, in 57:15, that a humble heart is His throne? The humble heart is His throne in regard to His gracious presence; and heaven is His throne in regard to His glorious presence. Yet neither of these thrones will hold Him, for the heaven of heavens cannot contain Him.

Though God be in all places, even in the heart of a sinner by His inspection, and in hell by His justice, yet He does not mingle with the impurity or receive the least hint of evil. Augustine stated, "The divine nature does not intermix with created matter, nor is contaminated by its impurities." No more than the sun shining on a dunghill is defiled or its beauty tarnished, neither was Christ, when He was among sinners, defiled, because His Godhead was a sufficient antidote against infection.

GOD HAS NO BOUNDARIES

*Neither is there any creature that is not manifest
in his sight: but all things are naked and opened
unto the eyes of him with whom we have to do.*

HEBREWS 4:13

God is infinite in all places at once, not only in regard to the simplicity and purity of His nature, but in regard to His power, which being so glorious, who can set boundaries for Him or prescribe Him a trail to walk in? It is as if the drop should limit the ocean or a star set bounds to the sun.

Some people would make more things infinite than the Godhead. They hold that Christ's body is in many places at once, that it is in heaven and in the bread and wine in the sacrament. Christ as He is God is infinite and in all places at once, yet as man He is not. When on earth, God's manhood was not in heaven, though His Godhead was; in heaven, His manhood is not on earth, though His Godhead is. Hebrews 10:5 speaks of Christ as "a body thou hast prepared me."

Since God is infinite, then it is certain He governs all things in His own person; He needs no proxies to help Him to carry on His government. He is in all places in an instant, and He manages all affairs, both in the earth and in heaven. He sees all with His own eyes, and He hears all with His own ears. He is everywhere in His own person. He is therefore capable of being Judge of the world, and He will do everyone right.

1

GOD IS MAJESTIC

O LORD, our Lord, how excellent is thy name in all the earth!
who hast set thy glory above the heavens. . . .
O LORD, our Lord, how excellent is thy name in all the earth!

PSALM 8:1, 9

Since God is infinite by His omnipresence, see the greatness and
immenseness of the divine majesty! What a great God do we serve!
"Thine, O LORD, is the greatness, and the glory, and the majesty . . .
and thou art exalted as head above all" (1 Chronicles 29:11). Well
may the Scripture display the greatness of His glory, who is infinite
in all places. He transcends our weak conceptions. How can our
finite understanding comprehend Him who is infinite? He is infinitely above all our praises. "Blessed be thy glorious name, which is
exalted above all blessing and praise" (Nehemiah 9:5). Oh, what a
poor nothing is man when we think of God's infiniteness! As the
stars disappear at the rising of the sun, oh, how does a man shrink
into nothing when infinite majesty shines forth in its glory! "The
nations are as a drop of the bucket, and are counted as the small dust
of the balance!" (Isaiah 40:15). On what a little of that drop are we!
The heathens thought they had sufficiently praised Jupiter when
they called him "Great Jupiter." Of what immense majesty is God,
who fills all places at once! (Psalm 150:2).

2

GOD IS OUR PORTION

Unto me, who am less than the least of all saints, is this grace given.

EPHESIANS 3:8

Christians have God, who is infinite, for their portion. His fullness is an infinite fullness; and He is infinitely sweet and infinitely full. A pipe filled with wine has a sweet fullness, but still it is finite; but God is a sweet fullness, and He is infinite. He is infinitely full of beauty and of love. His riches are called unsearchable because they are infinite. Expand your thinking to understand that there is that in God which exceeds; it is an infinite fullness. He blesses us abundantly, above all that we can ask or even imagine (Ephesians 3:20). God can give more than we can ask, nay, or imagine, because He is infinite. We can think, "What if all the dust were turned to silver, if every flower were a ruby, every sand in the sea a diamond?" Yet God can give more than we can think, because He is infinite. Oh, how rich are they who have the infinite God for their portion! Well might David say, "The Lord is the portion of mine inheritance. The lines are fallen unto me in pleasant places, and I have a goodly heritage" (Psalm 16:5–6). Jacob said, "I have enough" (Genesis 33:11); in the Hebrew, "I have all," because he had the infinite God for his portion.

3

GLORIFY GOD'S INFINITE PRESENCE

Whither shall I flee from thy presence?

PSALM 139:7

God being an infinite fullness, there is no fear of want for any of the heirs of heaven. Though there be millions of saints and angels who have a share in God's riches, yet He has enough for each of them, because He is infinite. Though a thousand men behold the sun, there is light enough for them all, and there is water enough in the sea to fill every bucket. Though an innumerable company of saints and angels are to be filled out of God's fullness, yet God, being infinite, has enough to satisfy them. God has land enough to give to all His heirs. There can be no want in that which is infinite.

God being infinite is sad to the wicked. God is their enemy, and they cannot escape Him, nor flee from Him, for He is everywhere present. They are never out of His eye nor out of His reach. "Thine hand shall find out all thine enemies" (Psalm 21:8). What caves or thickets can men hide in that God cannot find them? Go where they may, He is present. If a man owes a debt to another, he may make his escape and flee into another land, where the creditor cannot find him. But "whither shall I flee from thy presence?" Sinners can neither go from an accusing conscience, nor from a revenging God.

4

GLORIFY GOD BY WALKING WITH HIM

Enoch walked with God.

GENESIS 5:22

God is present everywhere, therefore it is not impossible to walk with Him. God is in heaven and in earth too. Heaven is His throne; there He sits. Earth is His footstool; there He stands. He is present everywhere. Therefore we may walk with God.

If God were confined to heaven, trembling souls might wonder how they can converse with God, how they can walk with Him who lives above the upper region. God is not confined to heaven; He is omnipresent. He is above us, but He is near to us. Though He is not far from the assembly of the saints, "He standeth in the congregation of the mighty" (Psalm 82:1). He is present with us: God is in every one of us, so that here on earth we may walk with God.

In heaven the saints rest with Him; on earth they walk with Him. To walk with God is to walk by faith. We are said to draw nigh to God and to see Him, "as seeing him who is invisible" (Hebrews 1:27), and to fellowship with Him: "Our fellowship is with the Father" (1 John 1:3). We walk with Him in fellowship daily by faith. We slight God when we refuse to walk with Him. There is no walk in the world so sweet as to walk with God. It is like walking among beds of spices, which send forth a fragrant perfume.

5

GLORIFY GOD, THE INFINITE ONE

Canst thou by searching find out God?

JOB 11:7

God is infinite in His glorious essence. The angels wear a veil, adoring His majesty. Admire where you cannot fathom. Here on earth we see some beams of His glory: we see Him in creation. We also see Him in His picture: His image shines in the saints.

Who can search out all His essential glory? What angel can measure these pyramids? God is infinite. We can no more search out His infinite perfections than a man upon the top of the highest mountain can reach the firmament or take a star in his hand. Oh, have God-admiring thoughts! Adore where you cannot fathom. There are many mysteries in nature that we cannot fathom; the sea should be higher than the earth, yet not drown it; why the Nile should overflow in summer when, by the course of nature, the waters are lowest; how the bones grow in the womb. If these things concern us, how may the infinite mystery of the Deity transcend our most raised intellectuals!

In heaven we shall see God clearly, but not fully, for He is infinite. He will communicate Himself to us according to the largeness of our heart, but not the immenseness of His nature. Adore then where you cannot fathom.

6

GLORIFY GOD BY NOT LIMITING HIM

"Where can I go from Thy Spirit?
Or where can I flee your presence?
If I take the wings of the dawn,
If I dwell in the remotest part of the sea,
Even there Your hand will lead me,
And Your right hand will lay hold of me."

PSALM 139:7, 9–10 NASB

God is infinite in all places, so let us not limit Him as our forefathers did: they "limited the Holy One of Israel" (Psalm 78:41). We limit God when we confine Him within the narrow compass of our reason. Reason thinks God must go such a way to do His work, or the business will never be effected. This action does limit God to our reasoning, whereas He is infinite, and His ways are past finding out (Romans 11:33). In the deliverance of the church, it is limiting God either to set Him a time or to prescribe Him a method for deliverance. God will deliver Zion, but He will be left to His own liberty. He will not be tied to a place, to a time, or to an instrument, which were to limit Him, and then He should not be infinite. God will go His own way. He will baffle those who do not accept His omnipresence, and He will nonplus reason. He orchestrates our lives for good even when we think He is destroying them. *He acts like Himself, like an infinite, wonder-working God.*

7

THE KNOWLEDGE OF GOD

The LORD is a God of knowledge,
and by him actions are weighed.

1 SAMUEL 2:3

Glorious things are spoken of God. He transcends both our thoughts and the praises of angels. God's glory lies chiefly in His attributes, the beams by which the divine nature shines forth. Among other of His excellencies, the Lord is a God of knowledge. Through the bright mirror of His own essence, He is cognizant of all things: the world is to Him a transparent body. "I am he which searcheth the reins and the heart" (Revelation 2:23). The clouds are no canopy, the night is no curtain to draw between us and His sight. "The darkness hideth not from thee" (Psalm 139:12). He hears every whisper: "There is not a word in my tongue, but lo, O LORD, thou knowest it altogether" (Psalm 139:4). He perceives our every thought: "I know . . . their thoughts" (Isaiah 66:18). Our actions, though never so subtly contrived and secretly conveyed, are visible to the eye of Omniscience: "I know their works" (Isaiah 66:18). God's eye is always upon us. God knows whatever is knowable, and He knows future contingencies. The perfection of God's knowledge is primary. He is the original, the pattern, and the prototype of all knowledge. Others borrow their knowledge from Him, and the angels light their lamps at this glorious sun.

8

GOD IS ALL KNOWING

*Dost thou know the balancing of the clouds,
the wondrous works of him which is perfect in knowledge?*

JOB 37:16

God's knowledge is *pure*. Though God knows sin, yet it is to hate and punish it. No evil can mix or incorporate with His knowledge, any more than the sun can be defiled with the vapors that arise from the earth.

God's knowledge is *without any difficulty*. We study and search for knowledge: "thou seekest her as silver" (Proverbs 2:4). The lamp of God's knowledge is so infinitely bright that all things are intelligible to Him.

God's knowledge is *infallible*. Human knowledge is subject to error. A physician may mistake the cause of a disease, but God's knowledge is unerring. He can neither deceive nor be deceived. He cannot deceive, because He is truth, nor be deceived, because He is wisdom.

God's knowledge is *instantaneous*. Our knowledge is successive, one thing after another. We argue from the effect to the cause. God knows things past, present, and to come all at once; they are all before Him in one entire prospect.

God's knowledge is *retentive*: He never loses any of His knowledge. He remembers as well as understands. Many things pass out of our minds, but God's knowledge is *eternal*. Things transacted a thousand years ago are as fresh to Him as if they were done at the last minute. Thus He is perfect in knowledge.

9

GOD, THE JUST JUDGE

*I will go down now, and see whether they have
done altogether according to the cry of it,
which is come unto me; and if not, I will know.*

GENESIS 18:21

The Lord speaks in the manner of a judge, who will first examine the
cause before he passes the sentence. Not that Ephraim's sin is hid
from God, but his sin is hid; that is, it is recorded, and it is laid up
for a day of reckoning. The meaning is clear: his iniquity is bound
up. As the inquest clerk binds up indictments and reads them aloud
at the hearing, so God binds up men's sins in a bundle, and, at judgment, all their sins are brought to light before men and angels.

God is *infinite in knowledge*. He who gives being to things must have
a clear understanding of them. "He that planted the ear, shall he
not hear? he that formed the eye, shall he not see?" (Psalm 94:9).
He who makes a watch or engine knows all the workmanship in it.
God, who made the heart, knows all its movements. He is full of
eyes, and it ought to be so, for He is to be "Judge of all the world"
(Genesis 18:25). There are so many causes brought before Him
and so many persons to be tried that He must have a perfect knowledge, or He could not do justice. God can judge without a jury. He
knows all things in and of Himself, and He needs no witnesses to
inform Him. A judge judges only matters of fact, but God judges
the heart. He not only judges wicked actions, but wicked designs.
He sees the treason of the heart and punishes it, because He is a
God of justice.

10

GOD IS LIGHT IN A DARK WORLD

I beseech you therefore, brethren, by the mercies
of God, that ye present your bodies a living sacrifice,
holy, acceptable unto God, which is your reasonable service.

ROMANS 12:1

Is God infinite in knowledge? Is He light, and in Him is there no darkness? How are they to God who are darkness, in whom is no light, who are destitute of knowledge, such as the heathen who never heard of God? Are there not many among us who are no better than baptized heathens, who need to seek the first principles of the oracles of God? Sadly, after the sun of the gospel has shined so long in our horizon, to this day the veil should be upon their hearts. Those enveloped in ignorance cannot give God a reasonable service. Ignorance is the lack of religious respect. "They proceed from evil to evil, and know not me, saith the LORD" (Jeremiah 9:3). Where ignorance reigns in the understanding, lust rages in the affections. "That the soul be without knowledge, it is not good" (Proverbs 19:2). Such have neither faith nor fear, for knowledge carries the torch before faith. "They that know thy name will put their trust in thee" (Psalm 9:10). Without knowledge, a man cannot believe. He can have no fear of God, for how can they fear Him whom they do not know? An ignorant mind is a covering of the face that is a fatal forerunner of destruction.

SEEING THROUGH HYPOCRISY

And when thou prayest, thou shalt not be as the hypocrites.

MATTHEW 6:4

God is a God of knowledge, and He sees the folly of hypocrisy. Hypocrites don't actually do well, they merely make a show of it. They are seemingly good, but they are actually false and care not how bad their hearts are, living in secret sin. They say, "How doth God know?" (Psalm 73:11), but "His understanding is infinite" (Psalm 147:5). He looks into men's hearts; He has a key for the heart. He beholds the sinful workings of men's spirits, and He sees in secret. As a merchant enters debts in his book, so God has His daybook, in which He enters every sin. The hypocrite tries to get out of telling the truth and rearranges data, but God will unmask him. "God shall bring every work into judgment, with every secret thing" (Ecclesiastes 12:14). "They have committed villainy in . . . I know, and am a witness, saith the LORD" (Jeremiah 29:23). Ay, the hypocrite hopes to color over his sin and make it look true when actually false, but God sees through these fig leaves. You may see a jade under his gilt trappings. "Neither is their iniquity hid from mine eyes" (Jeremiah 16:17). He that has an eye to see will find a hand to punish.

GOD KNOWS

Apply your mind to my knowledge.

PROVERBS 22:17 NASB

God being infinite in knowledge should make us want to be under His omniscient eye, living as if always in full view. David said, "I have set the LORD always before me" (Psalm 16:8). Consideration of God's omniscience would help to prevent much sin. The eye of man will restrain us from sin. And will not God's eyes much more? Will we sin when our Judge looks on? Would men speak so vainly if they considered God overheard them? What care would persons have of their words if they remembered that God hears and the pen is going on in heaven? Would men go after strange flesh if they believed God was a spectator of their wickedness and would make them do penance in hell for it? Would they defraud in business, and use false weights, if they thought God saw them and, for making their weights lighter, would make their damnation heavier? Viewing ourselves as under the eye of God's omniscience would cause reverence in worship of God. He sees the frame and carriage of our hearts when we come before Him. How would this call in our straggling thoughts? How would it animate and spirit duty? It would make us put fire to the incense. To think God is in this place would add wings to prayer and oil to the flame of our devotion.

13

THE HEART MUST BE RIGHT WITH GOD

*The refining pot is for silver, and the furnace
for gold: but the LORD trieth the hearts.*

PROVERBS 17:3

Is God's knowledge infinite? Study sincerity; be what you seem. "The LORD looketh upon the heart" (1 Samuel 16:7). Men judge the heart by actions; God judges actions by the heart. If the heart is sincere, God will see the faith and bear with the failing. Asa had his blemishes, but his heart was right with God (2 Chronicles 15:17). God saw his sincerity and pardoned his infirmity. Sincerity in a Christian is like chastity in a wife, which excuses many failings. Sincerity makes our duties acceptable, like musk among linen that perfumes it. If God sees our heart is right, that we love Him, and desire His glory, "Now," says He, "give me your prayers and tears. Now you shall come up with Me into the chariot of glory." Sincerity makes our services to be golden, and God will not cast away the gold though it may want some weight. Is God omniscient, and His eye chiefly upon the heart? Wear the girdle of truth about you—and never leave it off.

GOD SEES THE GOOD

In him there is found some good thing
toward the LORD God of Israel.

1 KINGS 14:13

God is infinite knowledge: He provides comfort to saints in particular in private devotion. Christian, you set hours apart for God, your thoughts treasured thoughts of Him, and God takes notice. He has a book of remembrance written for them "that thought upon his name" (Malachi 3:16). He hears every sigh and groan when you enter your closet to pray: "My groaning is not hid from thee" (Psalm 38:9). God bottles every tear you water the seed of prayer with: "Put thou my tears into thy bottle" (Psalm 56:8). When the secrets of hearts are opened, God will make honorable mention of the zeal and devotion of His people, and He will be the herald of their praises. "Then shall every man have praise of God" (1 Corinthians 4:5).

God's infinite knowledge is a comfort when saints have no clear knowledge of themselves. They find so much corruption within, believing they have no grace with a heart that is dead and in an earthly state. But God sees grace where we cannot, hidden under corruption as the stars are hidden behind clouds. God sees holiness in us that we can't discern in ourselves; He sees the flower of grace, though overtaken with weeds. God sees some good thing in His people when they can see no good in themselves; and though they judge themselves, He will give them forgiveness.

15

GOD IS OUR COMFORT

I know their sorrows.

EXODUS 3:7

It is the saints' lot to suffer. The head crowned with thorns, the feet must not tread upon roses. If saints find this life painful, their comfort is that God sees what wrong is done to them; He sees the apple of His eye is touched. Paul was scourged by cruel hands: "Thrice was I beaten with rods" (2 Corinthians 11:25). God beholds it. The wicked make wounds on the backs of the saints and then pour it in vinegar, but God writes down their cruelty. Believers are a part of Christ's body; and for every drop of a saint's blood spilt, God puts a drop of wrath in His vial.

God being a God of knowledge sees all the plots of the enemies against Zion and can abort them. The wicked are subtle, having borrowed their skill from the old serpent. They dig deep to hide their counsels from God, but He sees them and can easily counter them. The dragon is described with seven heads to show how he plots against the church (Revelation 12:3); but God is described with seven eyes to show that He sees all the plots and schemes of the enemies and that He is above them (Zechariah 3:9). The Lord sees and knows all the plans of the enemy. He sees their sequence and can destroy their plans.

16

GOD'S ETERNAL NATURE

From everlasting to everlasting thou art God.

PSALM 90:2

Learned men explain the notion of eternity. First, such as had a beginning and shall have an end: as all sensitive creatures, the beasts, fowls, fishes, which at death are destroyed and return to dust, their being ends with their life. Second, such as had a beginning, but shall have no end. Angels and the souls of men, which are eternal, abide forever. Only God is without beginning and without end, and that is proper only to God. He is from everlasting to everlasting. This is God's title, a jewel of His crown: He is called "the King eternal" (I Timothy 1:17). *Jehovah* is a word that properly sets forth God's eternity, a word so dreadful that the Jews trembled to name or read it and used *Adonai, Lord,* in its place. *Jehovah* contains past, present, and future. "Which is, and which was, and which is to come" (Revelation 1:8) interprets the word *Jehovah*: (which is) He subsists of Himself, having a pure and independent being; (which was) only God was before time; there is no searching into the records of eternity; (which is to come) His kingdom has no end; His crown has no successors. "Thy throne, O God, is for ever and ever" (Hebrews 1:8). He is Alpha and Omega, the First and the Last. God exists from eternity to eternity: "I AM THAT I AM" (Exodus 3:14).

SOME WILL HAVE NO REST IN ETERNITY

That he may dip the tip of his finger in water, and
cool my tongue; for I am tormented in this flame.

LUKE 16:23

The sinner takes liberty to sin. He breaks God's laws like a wild beast that breaks over the hedge and leaps into forbidden pasture. He sins with greediness, as if he thought he could not sin fast enough (Ephesians 4:19). But remember, one of God's names is *Eternal*, and as long as God is eternal He has time enough to reckon with all His enemies. To make sinners tremble, let them think of this truth: the torments of the damned are without intermission. Their pains shall be acute and sharp, and there will be no rest; the fire shall not be slackened or abated. "They have no rest day nor night" (Revelation 14:11), like one who has his joints stretched continually on a rack, unable to move about to find a more comfortable position. The wrath of God is compared to a stream of brimstone (Isaiah 30:33). A stream runs without intermission; so God's wrath runs like a stream and pours continuously without a break. In the pains of this life, there is some abatement and intermission: the fever abates; after a fit of the stone, the patient has some ease. But the pains of hell are intense and violent. The damned soul never says, "I am now more at ease."

18

HELL IS WITHOUT MIXTURE

[If any man worships the beast and his image] . . . the same
shall drink of the wine of the wrath of God, which is
poured out without mixture into the cup of his indignation.

REVELATION 14:10

Hell is a place of pure justice. In this life, God in anger remembers mercy, He mixes compassion with suffering. Asher's shoe was of iron, but his foot was dipped in oil (Deuteronomy 33:25). Affliction is the iron shoe, but mercy is mixed with it; the foot is dipped in oil. But the torments of the damned are not mixed with mercy. No mixture of mercy. So how is the cup of wrath said to be full of mixture? "For in the hand of the LORD there is a cup, and the wine is red; it is full of mixture: and he poureth out of the same: but the dregs thereof all the wicked of the earth shall wring them out, and drink them" (Psalm 75:8). Yet in the Revelation it is said to be without mixture. It is full of mixture: that is, it is full of all the ingredients that may make it bitter: the worm, the fire, the curse of God, all these are bitter ingredients. It is a cup mixed, yet it is without mixture; there shall be nothing to afford the least comfort, no mixture of mercy, and so without mixture. In the sacrifice of jealousy (Numbers 5:15), in the torments of the damned, there is no oil of mercy to abate their sufferings.

19

Torment Without End

The smoke of their torment ascendeth for ever and ever.

REVELATION 14:11

Sin's pleasures are for a season, but the torments of the wicked are forever. Sinners have a short feast, but a long reckoning. The worm, the fire, and the prison are all eternal, and the torments of hell keep on punishing, and never end. Eternity is a sea without bottom or banks. After millions of years, there is not one minute in eternity wasted; the damned will burn forever, never consumed; always dying, but never dead. "They shall seek death, but shall not find it" (Revelation 9:6). The fire of hell is such that multitudes of tears will not quench it; length of time will not finish it. As long as God is eternal, He lives to be avenged upon the wicked. Who can fathom eternity? The Lord's breath kindles the infernal lake, and where shall we have engines or buckets to quench that fire? If the earth and sea turned to sand, and all the air up to heaven were nothing but sand, and a little bird should come every thousand years and fetch in her bill but the tenth part of a grain of all that heap of sand, what numberless years would be spent before that vast heap of sand would be taken away! Yet, if at the end of all that time, the sinner might come out of hell, there would be some hope; but that word *ever* breaks the heart.

20

EVER WITH THE LORD

*To them who by patient continuance in well doing
seek for glory and honor and immortality, eternal life.*

ROMANS 2:7

God is eternal. Therefore He lives forever to reward the godly,
which is a comfort to them. People of God are in a suffering condition: "Bonds and afflictions abide me" (Acts 20:23). The wicked
are clad in purple, and fare deliciously, while the godly suffer. Goats
climb upon high mountains, while Christ's sheep are in the valley of
slaughter. But here is the comfort: God is eternal, and He has
appointed eternal recompenses for the saints. In heaven are fresh
delights, sweetness without becoming sickening; and that which is
the crown and the high point of heaven's happiness, is, that it is
eternal. Were there but the least suspicion that this glory must cease,
it would much obscure, yea, embitter it; *but* it is eternal. What angel
can span eternity? Bearing "an eternal weight of glory" (2 Corinthians
4:17), the saints shall bathe themselves in the rivers of divine pleasure; and these rivers can never be dried up. "At thy right hand are
pleasures for evermore" (Psalm 16:11). This is the highest strain in
the apostle's rhetoric: "ever with the Lord" (1 Thessalonians 4:17).
That there is peace without trouble, ease without pain, glory without
end is comfort to the saints in their troubles; their sufferings are
short, but their reward is eternal. Eternity makes heaven to be
heaven; it is the diamond in the ring.

21

GRACE, COMFORT, AND GLORY

Ye shall receive a crown of glory that fadeth not away.

1 PETER 5:4

Oh, blessed day that shall have no night! The sunlight of glory shall rise upon the soul and never set! Oh, blessed spring that shall have no autumn or fall of the leaf. The Roman emperors have three crowns set upon their heads: the first of iron, the second of silver, the third of gold. So the Lord sets three eternal crowns on His children: grace, comfort, and glory. The wicked have a never-dying worm, and the godly, a never-fading crown. Oh, how should this be an incentive to virtue! How willing should we be to work for God! Though we had nothing here, God has time enough to reward His people. The crown of eternity shall be set upon their head.

MY SOUL, NOW BLESS THY MAKER

"He shows to man His treasure.
Of judgment, truth, and righteousness,
His love beyond all measure,
His yearning pity o'er distress,
Nor treats us as we merit,
But lays His anger by,
The humble, contrite spirit
Finds His compassion nigh;
And high as heaven above us,
As break from close of day,
So far, since He doth love us,
He puts our sins away."

JOHANN GRAMANN, 1487–1541

GLORIFY GOD BY STUDYING ETERNITY

The Ancient of Days . . .

DANIEL 7:9

Our thoughts should be upon eternity. We wish for the present, something that may delight the senses. If we could have lived, as Augustine says, from the infancy of the world to the world's old age, what were this? What is time, measured with eternity? The earth is but a small point to the heaven, and time is scarcely a minute to eternity. What is this poor life that crumbles away so fast? Oh, think of eternity! We are traveling every day toward eternity; and whether we wake or sleep, we are making the journey. Some of us are upon the borders of eternity. Oh, study the shortness of life and the length of eternity! Particularly think of God's eternity and the soul's eternity. He is the *Ancient of Days*, who was before all time: "The Ancient of Days did sit, whose garment was white as snow, and the hair of his head like the pure wool" (Daniel 7:9). His white garment, wherewith He was clothed, signified His majesty; His hair, like the pure wool, His holiness; and the Ancient of Days, His eternity. The thought of God's eternity should make us have high adoring thoughts of God. When all our power ceases, He is King eternal, and His crown flourishes forever.

23

GLORIFY GOD BY BOWING BEFORE HIM

O come, let us worship and bow down:
let us kneel before the LORD our Maker;
for he is our God;
and we are the people of his pasture.

PSALM 95:6–7

"The four and twenty elders fall down before him that sat upon the throne, and worship him that liveth for ever and ever; and cast their crowns before the throne" (Revelation 4:10). The saints fall down to signify by that humble posture that they are not worthy to sit in God's presence. They fall down and they worship Him who liveth forever and ever; they do as it were to kiss His feet. They cast their crowns before the throne, they lay all their honor at His feet and thus they show humble adoration to the Eternal Essence. Study God's eternity: it will make us adore where we cannot fathom. Think of the soul's eternity. As God is eternal, so He has made us eternal. We are never-dying creatures; we are shortly entering upon an eternal state, either of happiness or misery. Have serious thoughts of this. Say, "O my soul, which of these two eternities is likely to be thy portion? I must shortly depart from here, and whither then shall I go, to which of these eternities, either of glory or misery?" The serious meditation of the eternal state we are to pass into would work strongly with us.

ETERNAL TORMENT, ETERNAL HAPPINESS

"Come now, and let us reason together," saith the LORD.

ISAIAH 1:18

Thoughts of eternal torments are a good antidote against sin. Sin tempts with its pleasure; but when we think of eternity, it may cool the intemperate heat of lust. Shall I, for the pleasure of sin for a season, endure eternal pain? Sin, like locusts mentioned in Revelation 9:7–10, seems to have on its head a crown like gold, but it has in it a tail like a scorpion and a sting in its tail that can never be plucked out. Shall I venture eternal wrath? Is sin committed so sweet as lying in hell forever is pungent? This thought should make us flee from sin, as Moses fled from the serpent.

The serious thoughts of eternal happiness should hinder our worldly thoughts. We are to enter upon an everlasting estate. If I hope to live with Him who is eternal, what is the world to me? To those who stand upon the top of the Alps, the great cities below are small things in their eyes; so to him who has his thoughts fixed on his eternal state after this life, all these things seem as nothing in his eye. The world's glory is poor and contemptible compared with an eternal weight of glory!

THE UNCHANGEABLENESS OF GOD

I am the LORD, I change not.

MALACHI 3:6

God is unchangeable in His nature. There is no shadow to His brightness; His essence shines with a fixed luster. "With whom is no variableness, neither shadow of turning" (James 1:17). "Thou art the same" (Psalm 102:2). All created things are full of unexpected changes. Though kingdoms have a head of gold, they have feet of clay. The heavens change: "As a vesture shalt thou change them, and they shall be changed" (Psalm 102:26). The heavens are the most ancient records, yet these shall change. Their qualities change; they shall melt with fervent heat and be more refined and purified. The heavens shall be changed, but not He who dwells in heaven. Though the seed of grace does not die, yet its beauty and activity often wither. What Christian can say that he does not find a change in his graces, that the bow of his faith never unbends, that the strings of his violin never weaken? Surely we shall never meet with such Christians till we meet them in heaven. But God is without any shadow of turning: God's glory shines with a fixed brightness. In God there is nothing that looks like a change, for better or worse; not better, because then He were not perfect; not worse, for then He would cease to be perfect. He is unchangeably holy, unchangeably good. There is no shadow of change in Him.

26

GOD CANNOT DIE

The same, yesterday, and today, and for ever.
HEBREWS 13:8

If divine nature had been converted into the human or the human into the divine, there would have been a change, but that did not occur. The human nature was distinct from the divine. Therefore there was no change. A cloud over the sun makes no change in the body of the sun; so, though the divine nature is covered with the human, it makes no change in the divine nature.

There is no period put to His being, to Him "who only has immortality" (1 Timothy 6:16). The Godhead cannot die. An infinite essence cannot be changed into finite; but God is infinite. He is eternal; He is not mortal. To be eternal and mortal is a contradiction.

This is the glory of the Godhead. Changeable denotes weakness, and is not in God. Men are fickle and can change, "unstable as water" (Genesis 49:4). They are changeable in their principles. If their faces altered as fast as their opinions, we should not know them. Changeable in their resolutions as the wind that blows in the east presently turns about to the west. They resolve to be virtuous, but quickly change their resolutions. An apostle compares them to waves of the sea and wandering stars (Jude 13). They are not pillars in God's temple, but reeds, changing in their friendship: quickly loving and quickly hating. They change as the chameleon into several colors, but God is unchangeable.

THE UNCHANGEABLE GOD

Thy throne is established of old:
thou art from everlasting.

PSALM 93:2

See the vanity of the creature. There are changes in everything but in God. "Men of high degree are vanity, and men of low degree are a lie" (Psalm 62:9). We look for more from the creature than God has put in it. It has two evils in it: it promises more than we find, and it fails us when we most need it. A man desires to have his corn ground, and the water fails; the mariner is on a voyage, and the wind does not blow, or it blows in the opposite direction; one depends upon another for the payment of a promise, and he fails. Who would look for a fixed stability in the vain creature? It is as if one should build houses on the sand, where the sea comes in and washes the house away. The creature is true to nothing but deceit, and is constant only in its disappointments. It is no more wonderful to see changes fall out here below than to see the moon dressing itself in a new shape and figure. Christians can expect changes in everything, in people and everything around them, in everything but God.

28

God Comforts the Godly

God is the strength of my heart, and my portion for ever.

PSALM 73:26

God comforts the godly in their losses. If you lose wealth to a burning fire, if you lose friends by death, there is a double shadow over your life; but the comfort is that God is unchangeable. I may lose many things, but I cannot lose my God; He never dies. When the fig tree and olive tree failed, God did not fail. "I will joy in the God of my salvation" (Habakkuk 3:18). Flowers in the garden die, but a man's portion remains. So outward things die and change, but not God!

In the case of a broken spirit, God seems to cast off the soul in desertion, yet He is unchangeable. He is unchangeable in His love; He may change His countenance, but not His heart. "I have loved thee with an everlasting love" (Jeremiah 31:3). If once God's electing love rises upon the soul, it never sets. "The mountains shall depart, and the hills be removed, but my kindness shall not depart from thee, neither shall the covenant of my peace be removed" (Isaiah 54:10). God's love is more steadfast than the mountains. His love to Christ is unchangeable; and He will no more cease loving believers than He will cease loving Christ.

GOD WILL NEVER LEAVE HIS CHILDREN

They that trust in the LORD shall be like
mount Zion, which cannot be removed.

PSALM 125:1

When we get interested in the unchangeable God, we become like a rock in the sea, immoveable in the midst of all circumstances. How shall we get a part in the unchangeable God? By having a change wrought in us: "ye are washed, but ye are sanctified" (1 Corinthians 6:11), from darkness to light, and we become interested in the unchangeable God.

Trust Him only. Trust to the Rock of ages! One secure in God is safe in all circumstances; he is like a boat tied to an immoveable rock. He who trusts in God trusts in that which cannot fail him; He is unchangeable. Health, riches, friends may leave us, but God who will not leave us has power to support us. His Spirit shall sanctify thee, His mercy shall save thee, but He will never leave thee. Trust in this unchangeable God! God is jealous of our love, lest we love self more than Him, and jealous of our trust, lest we should place more confidence in it than in Him. Outward comforts are given us to refresh us, not as crutches to lean on. If we make self an idol, then whatever we make our trust, God will make our shame. Oh, trust in the immortal God! Like Noah's dove, we have no footing for our souls till we get into the ark of God's unchangeableness.

30

GOD'S UNCHANGEABLE DECREE

My counsel shall stand.

ISAIAH 46:10

What God has decreed from eternity is unalterable: His eternal counsel or decree is immutable. Men change their opinions and purposes; they see something they did not see before. But this cannot be the cause why God should alter His decree, because His knowledge is perfect. He sees all things in their entirety all the time.

In Jonah 3:10, there seems to be a change in His decree: "God repented of the evil, that he said he would do unto them." This repentance is attributed to God figuratively: He "is not a man . . . that he should repent" (Numbers 23:19). There may be a change in God's work, but not in His will. He may will a change, but not change His will. *God may change His sentence, but not His decree.* A king may cause sentence to be passed upon a criminal whom he intends to pardon, so God threatened destruction to Nineveh, but the people of Nineveh did repent and God spared them (Jonah 3:10). Here God changed His sentence, but not His decree; it was what had lain hidden in the womb of His heart's purpose from eternity. God's purpose and plans for His children were established before the beginning of time and will not change throughout eternity. The children of God make choices that alter life for them, but God's decree for His children remains the same.

1

GOD'S DECREE OF ELECTION

*And that he might make known the riches of his glory on
the vessels of mercy, which he had afore prepared unto glory.*

ROMANS 9:23

God's decree is unchangeable, therefore our endeavors toward salvation cannot alter His decree. God's decree does not affect my attempts toward salvation. He who decreed my salvation decreed it by means, and if I neglect those means, I reprobate myself. God decreed how long I shall live; therefore I will not use means, like starvation or suicide, to end my life. And God has decreed my salvation in the use of the Word and prayer. As a man refusing food murders himself, so he who refuses to work out his salvation destroys himself. The vessels of mercy are prepared for glory by being sanctified. That can only be in the use of means; therefore let not God's decree take thee off from holy endeavors. If we have a heart to pray to God, that is a sign that no decree of wrath has passed against us.

God's decree is eternal and unchangeable and God does not elect upon our faith foreseen. We are not elected for holiness, but to holiness (Ephesians 1:4). We are neither justified nor elected for our faith. We are justified through faith as an instrument, not for faith as a cause; if not justified for faith, then much less elected. God's decree of election depends not upon faith foreseen. "As many as were ordained to eternal life believed" (Acts 13:48). They were not elected because they believed, but they believed because they were elected.

2

God's Decree Gives Comfort

For an angel went down at a certain season into the pool, and
troubled the water: whosoever then first after the troubling of
the water stepped in was made whole of whatsoever disease he had.

JOHN 5:4

God's decree is unchangeable, therefore gives comfort to His church. "For I am the LORD, I change not" (Malachi 3:6). Concerning God's providence toward His church, we are ready to argue with God's providence if everything in life does not agree with our own desires. Remember, God's work goes on, and nothing falls out except what He has decreed from eternity. God has decreed troubles for the church's good. The trouble in God's church is like the angels troubling the water, which made way for healing His people. God has decreed troubles in the church. His "fire is in Zion, and his furnace in Jerusalem" (Isaiah 31:9). The wheels in a watch move over one another, but they all carry on the motion of the watch; so the wheels of providence often cross our desires, but still they carry on God's unchangeable decree, that He declared for all eternity. "Many shall be . . . made white" (Daniel 12:10). God lets the waters of affliction be poured on His people to make them white. Therefore murmur not at God's dealings. His work goes on, and nothing falls out except what He has wisely decreed from eternity. Everything shall promote God's design and fulfill His decree.

3

COMFORT THE GODLY

The foundation of God standeth sure, having this seal,
The Lord knoweth them that are his.

2 TIMOTHY 2:19

God's decree is unchangeable, therefore gives comfort to the godly in regard to their salvation. "I will not blot his name out of the book of life" (Revelation 3:5). God's decree book is without error or stain. Once justified, never unjustified. "Repentance shall be hid from mine eyes" (Hosea 13:14): God never repents of His electing love. "He loved them unto the end" (John 13:1). If thou art a believer, comfort thyself with this: the immutability of God's decree.

The wicked march furiously against God and His people, but God's decree is unchangeable. God will not alter it, nor can they break it. While they resist God's will, they fulfill it. God's will is precept and decree. The wicked resist the will of God's precept; they fulfill the will of His permissive decree. Christ was betrayed, condemned, and crucified: while the will of God's precepts were resisted, the will of His permissive decree was fulfilled. God commands one thing, they do the opposite: to keep the Sabbath, and they profane it. While disobeying His command, they fulfill His permissive decree. A man sets up one net of silk, the other of iron, the silken net may be broken, not the iron. While men break the silken net of God's command, they are taken in the iron net of His decree. While rowing against God's precepts, they row forward to His decrees—to His decrees to permit their sin and to punish them for their sin permitted.

4

THE WISDOM OF GOD

[He is] the only wise God.

God's wisdom is one of the brightest beams of the Godhead. "He is wise in heart" (Job 9:4), and the heart is the seat of wisdom. Among the Hebrews, the heart is put for wisdom. "Let men of understanding tell me" (Job 34:34) is, in the Hebrew, "Let men of heart tell me." God is wise in heart; that is, He is most wise. Not only is God wise, but He solely and wholly possesses *all* wisdom. Therefore, the treasures of wisdom are in Him, and no one has wisdom other than what God gives them from His treasury of wisdom. Perfectly wise, there is no defect in God's wisdom. Men may be wise in some things, but in others they betray imprudence and weakness. God is the standard and pattern of wisdom, which is perfect.

God's wisdom appears in His infinite intelligence: He knows profound secrets and thoughts and the most intricate, subtle things. Let sin be contrived ever so politically, but God will remove disguises exposing the heart. He knows future contingencies: all things are before Him in clear prospect.

He is wise in heart, and His wisdom lies in His precise works. These works of God are bound up in the work of creation, in the work of redemption, and in the work of His providence.

5

THE WORK OF CREATION

O LORD, how manifold are thy works!
In wisdom hast thou made them all.

PSALM 104:24

Creation is both a monument of God's power and a mirror in which we see His wisdom. Only a wise God could so intricately contrive the world. Behold the earth decked with a variety of flowers, which are both for beauty and fragrance. Behold the heaven bespangled with lights. We see God's wisdom blazing in the sun and twinkling in the stars; we see it in His marshalling and ordering everything in its proper place and sphere. God's wisdom is seen in appointing the seasons of the year: "Thou hast made summer and winter" (Psalm 74:17). God's wisdom is seen in the balance of dark and light providing time for labor and rest; in mixing the elements, as the earth with the sea; in preparing and ripening the fruits of the earth; in wind and frost that prepare the fruits; in the sun and rain that ripen the fruits; and in setting bounds to the sea, and so wisely contriving it, though the sea be higher than many parts of the earth, yet it won't overflow. There is nothing to be seen but miracles of wisdom.

God's wisdom is seen in ordering things in the body politic, that one shall have need of another. The poor need the rich man's money, and the rich need the poor man's labor. God makes one trade depend upon another, that one may be helpful to another, and that mutual love may be preserved.

6

GOD'S WORK OF REDEMPTION

God manifest in the flesh.

1 TIMOTHY 3:16

The masterpiece of divine wisdom is to contrive a way to joy between man's sin and God's justice. The apostle cried, "O the depth of the riches both of the wisdom and knowledge of God" (Romans 11:33). This astonished men and angels. If God had made the lost find a way to salvation, we could neither have had a head to devise, nor a heart to desire, what God's infinite wisdom had found out for us. Mercy saved sinners, yet was loath that the justice of God should be wronged. "It is a pity," says Mercy, "that man should be made to be unfastened, yet God's justice must not be a loser. Angels cannot satisfy the wrong done to God's justice, nor should one nature sin and another nature suffer. Shall man be forever lost?" While Mercy debated itself, how to recover fallen man, God's wisdom stepped in; and the oracle spoke: "Let God become man: let the Second Person in the Trinity be incarnate and suffer. For fitness, He shall be man; for ability, He shall be God. Justice may be satisfied, and man saved." O the depth of the riches of God's wisdom, to make justice and mercy kiss each other! Great is this mystery that Christ be made sin, yet know no sin; that God should condemn the sin, yet save the sinner! Here was wisdom, to find the way of salvation.

GOD'S FREE GRACE

Faith comes by hearing.

ROMANS 10:17

The means by which salvation is applied sets forth God's wisdom: that salvation should be by faith, not by works. Faith is a humble grace, in that it gives all to Christ. Faith is an adorer of free grace; and free grace being advanced here, God has His glory. And faith is His highest wisdom to exalt His own glory.

The way of working faith declares God's wisdom. It is wrought by the Word preached. What is the weak breath of a man to convert a soul? It is like whispering in the ears of a dead man. This is foolishness in the eyes of the world; but the Lord loves to show His wisdom by that which seems folly. God has "chosen the foolish things of the world to confound the wise" (1 Corinthians 1:27). Why so? "That no flesh should glory in his presence" (v. 29). If God converted by the ministry of angels, then we should be ready to glory in angels and give that honor to them which is due to God. But when God works by weak tools, when He makes use of men who are of like passions with ourselves and, by them, converts, then the power is plainly seen to be of God. "We have this treasure in earthen vessels, that the excellency of the power may be of God and not of us" (2 Corinthians 4:7). Herein is God's wisdom seen, that no flesh may glory in His presence (1 Corinthians 1:29).

8

GOD'S PERFECT DESIGN

The things which happened unto me have fallen out
rather unto the furtherance of the gospel.

PHILIPPIANS 1:12

God's wisdom appears in the works of His providence, where mercy is wrapped up in it effecting great things by small contemptible means. He cured the stung Israelites by a brazen serpent. If some sovereign antidote had been used, if the balm of Gilead had been brought, there had been some likelihood of a cure; but what was there in a brazen serpent? It was a mere image, and not applied to him who was wounded; he was to look upon it only, yet this brought a cure. The less probability in the instrument, the more is God's wisdom seen.

The wisdom of God is also seen in doing His work by that which to the eye of flesh seems quite contrary. God had a mind to save Jonah when he was cast into the sea; He let the fish swallow him up, and so brought him to the shore. God would save Paul and all that were in the ship with him, but the ship must break, bringing them all safely to land upon the broken pieces.

In the church, God often goes by contrary means and makes the enemy do His work. He has often made His church grow and flourish by persecution: "Come on, let us deal wisely with them; lest they multiply" (Exodus 1:10). The way the Egyptians suppressed them made them multiply: "The more they afflicted them, the more they multiplied" (v.12), and the more the ground was harrowed, the better crop it yielded. The apostles were scattered by persecution, and their scattering was like the scattering of seed; they went up and down, preaching the gospel, bringing daily converts. Paul was put in prison, but his bonds were the means of spreading the gospel.

9

GOOD FROM EVIL

For our light affliction, which is but for a moment,
worketh for us a far more exceeding and eternal weight of glory.

2 CORINTHIANS 4:17

God's wisdom is seen when He turns desperate evils to good for His children. God makes deadly afflictions work together for the good of His children. He purifies them, preparing them for heaven. God, by divine chemistry, turns afflictions into cordials. His people gain by losing, and He turns crosses into blessings.

God's wisdom is seen when the sins of men carry on God's work, yet He has no hand in their sin. He has a hand in the action in which sin is, but not in the sin of the action. As in crucifying Christ, it was a natural action, and God concurred. If He had not given the Jews life and breath, they could not have done it; but it was a sinful action, so God abhorred it. A musician creates sound coming from an out-of-tune stringed instrument, but the discord is from the instrument itself. In the same way, men's natural motion is from God, but their sinful motion is from themselves. When a man rides on a lame horse, his riding is the cause why the horse goes, but the lameness is from the horse itself. Herein is God's wisdom: that the sins of men carry on His work, yet He has no hand in them.

ADORE THE WISDOM OF GOD

God taketh the wise in their own craftiness.

JOB 5:13

God's wisdom fools wise men and makes their wisdom the means of their overthrow. "The counsel of Ahithophel, which [Absalom] counseled, was as if [he] had enquired at the oracle of God" (2 Samuel 16:23), but he consulted his own shame. "The Lord turned [Ahithophel's] counsel into foolishness," as David had prayed (2 Samuel 15:31). That is, when they think to deal wisely, God not only disappoints them, but ensnares them. The snares they lay for others catch themselves. God loves to counterplot politicians; He makes use of their own wit to undo them and hangs Haman upon His own gallows.

God's wisdom is infinitely deep; the angels cannot search into it. "His ways [are] past finding out" (Romans 11:33). As we adore, so we should rest in the wisdom of God: He knows what is best for us. Believing God's wisdom would keep us from murmuring. God is wise, believing that sometimes it is good for us to be without comfort. Perhaps we should be lifted up with spiritual enlargements. Not so easy to have the heart low when comfort is high. God sees humility to be better for us than joy. It is better to want comfort, and be humble, than to have it, and be proud. In want of bodily strength, rest in God's wisdom. He sees what is best. Perhaps the less health, the more grace; weaker in body, the stronger in faith.

GOD KNOWS WHAT WE NEED

Though our outward man perish,
yet the inward man is renewed day by day.

2 CORINTHIANS 4:16

When we wonder what God is doing with us, and find ourselves worrying and carrying the load of the world's care on our shoulders and in our heart, we should learn to rest in God's wisdom. He knows best what is necessary to make things in life right for His children. His "footsteps are not known" (Psalm 77:19). Trust Him where you cannot see Him. God is most in His way when we think He is most out of the way.

When God shakes the tree of the body, He is gathering the fruits of righteousness. Sickness is God's spear, to let out sin in the case of God's providences to His church. When we think God's church is, as it were, in the grave and there is a tombstone laid upon her, His wisdom can roll away the stone from the sepulcher. Either His power can remove the mountain, or His wisdom knows how to leap over it.

When we are brought low in the world, or have little strength left in us, let us rest in God's wisdom. He sees things best and knows what we need to renew us day by day for His kingdom and for our good.

GOD CURES SELFISH PRIDE

*But they that will be rich fall into temptation
and a snare, and into many foolish and hurtful lusts,
which drown men in destruction and perdition.*

1 TIMOTHY 6:9

God knew if wealth not be lost, our soul had been lost. He knew riches would be a snare for us. Are you troubled that God has prevented a snare? God will make you rich in faith. What you lack in things shall be made up in spirituals. God will give you more of His love. You are weak in wealth, but God will make you strong in assurance. He will carve the best piece for you.

God takes away these because He would have more of our love; He breaks these crutches, that we depend upon Him by faith.

Since God be infinitely wise, let us go to Him for wisdom. "'Give thy servant an understanding heart' . . . and the speech pleased the LORD" (1 Kings 3:9–10). Here is encouragement for us: "If any of you lack wisdom, let him ask of God, that giveth to all men liberally, and upbraideth not" (James 1:5). Wisdom is in God, His wisdom is imparted, not impaired; His stock is not spent by giving.

Lord, do Thou light my lamp; in Thy light shall I see light. Give me wisdom to know the fallacy of my heart, the subtleties of the old serpent; and wisdom to walk jealously toward myself, religiously toward Thee, prudently toward others. Guide me by Thy counsel, and afterward receive me to glory.

THE POWER OF GOD

If I speak of strength, lo, he is strong.

JOB 9:19

God's attribute of power is described in the verse, "Lo, he is strong." The Hebrew word for *strong* signifies a conquering, prevailing strength: "He is strong." The superlative degree is intended: "He is *most strong*." He is called El-Shaddai, God Almighty. His almightiness lies in the fact that He has a sovereign right and authority over man. Who shall ask Him a reason why He does what He does? "He doeth according to his will in the army of heaven, and among the inhabitants of the earth: and none can stay his hand, or say unto him, What doest thou?" (Daniel 4:35). God sits judge in the highest court; He calls the monarchs of the earth to the bar, and is not bound to give a reason of His proceedings. Salvation and damnation are in His power, and the key of justice in His hand. He has the key of mercy in His hand, to open heaven's gate to whomever He pleases. Engraved upon His vesture is "KING OF KINGS, AND LORD OF LORDS" (Revelation 19:16).

God has ultimate authority, so He has infinite power. He is "mighty in strength" (Job 9:4). God's power is evident in creation, which requires infinite power but no instruments to work with. He creates matter, and then works upon it; and because He works without labor: "He spake, and it was done" (Psalm 33:9).

GOD'S SOVEREIGN POWER

And what is the surpassing greatness of His power toward us who believe.
These are in accordance with the working of the strength of His might

EPHESIANS 1:19 NASB

The power of God is seen in the conversion of souls. The same power draws a sinner to God that drew Christ out of the grave to heaven. Greater power is put forth in conversion than in creation. When God made the world, He met with no opposition; He had no help yet nothing to hinder Him. But when He converts a sinner, Satan opposes Him, and the heart opposes Him: a sinner is angry with converting grace. The world was the "work of [God's] fingers" (Psalm 8:3). Conversion is the "work of God's arm" (Luke 1:51). In the creation, God wrought but one miracle: He spoke the word. But in conversion, God works many miracles: the blind is made to see, the dead is raised, the deaf hears the voice of the Son of God.

Oh, the infinite power of Jehovah! Angels fall prostrate before Him, and kings cast their crowns at His feet. He "toucheth the land, and it shall melt" (Amos 9:5). He "shaketh the earth out of her place" (Job 9:6). An earthquake makes the earth tremble upon her pillars, but God shakes it out of its place. He can do "more than we can think" (Ephesians 3:20). He can suspend natural agents. He sealed up the lions' mouths, made the fire not to burn, made the waters to stand up on a heap, and caused the sun to go ten degrees backward in the dial of Ahaz. What can stop Omnipotence?

GOD THE GREAT COMMANDER

*Thy right hand, O LORD, is become glorious in power:
thy right hand, O LORD, hath dashed in pieces the enemy.*

EXODUS 15:6

God counters His enemies; He pulls down their flags and banners of pride, infatuates their counsels, breaks their forces; and He does it with ease, with the turning of His hand; "by the breath of his mouth" (Psalm 33:6). One glance of His can destroy His enemies: "The Lord looked unto the host of the Egyptians through the pillar of fire . . . and troubled their host" (Exodus 14:24). Who shall stop Him in His march? God commands and all creatures in heaven and earth obey Him. When God speaks, the wind and sea obey Him. What can't omnipotent power do? "The Lord is a man of war" (Exodus 15:3). He has "a mighty arm" (Psalm 89:13). It is an irresistible power: "Who hath resisted his will?" (Romans 9:19).

God's power is inexhaustible; it is never spent or wasted. Men, while exercising their strength, weaken it; but God has an everlasting spring of strength in Himself (Isaiah 26:4). Though He uses His arrows on His enemies, He does not exhaust His strength. "The LORD . . . fainteth not, neither is weary" (Isaiah 40:28).

16

POWER IN THE WORD

Where the word of a king is, there is power . . .

ECCLESIASTES 8:4

God is infinite in power, so let us fear Him. "Fear ye not me? saith the LORD: will ye not tremble at my presence?" (Jeremiah 5:22). He has power to cast souls and bodies into hell. "Who knoweth the power of [God's] anger?" (Psalm 90:11). The same breath that made us can dissolve us. "His fury is poured out like fire, the rocks are thrown down by him" (Nahum 1:6). Solomon says, "Where the word of a king is, there is power," much more where the word of God is. The fear of God will drive out all other base fear.

God's power is not for the deplorable condition of wicked men who have no union with Him; they have no warrant to claim His power. God's power forgives sins, but He will not force His power upon unrepentant sinners. God's power is an eagle's wing carrying saints to heaven; but what privilege is that to the wicked? Succumbed by miseries, the wicked have none to help them; they are like a ship in a storm without a pilot, driven upon the rocks.

God's power will not be the sinner's shield to defend him, but a sword to wound him. His power serves to revenge the wrong done to His mercy. God's power is engaged against him, and "it is a fearful thing to fall into the hands of the living God" (Hebrews 10:31).

THE LORD'S ARM IS NOT SHORT

Is anything too hard for [God]?

JEREMIAH 32:27

We say we do not doubt God's power, but His will. But it is His power that we question. We stagger through unbelief, as if the arm of God's power were shrunk. Take away a king's power, and we un-king him; take away the Lord's power, and we un-god Him. And we are guilty! Did not Israel question God's power? They asked, "Can he prepare a table in the wilderness?" (Psalm 78:19). They thought the wilderness was a better place for making graves than spreading a table. Did not Martha doubt Christ's power? "He hath been dead four days" (John 11:39). If Christ had been there while Lazarus was sick, or when he was close to death, Martha would not question that Christ could have raised him; but he had lain in the grave four days, and now she seemed to question His power. Christ had as much to do to raise her faith as to raise her dead brother. Moses, though a holy man, limited God's power through unbelief. Denying God His power is a great affront to Him; Men doubt God's power by taking other courses; by using false weights. If men believed the power of God could provide for them, they would trust what He said to Moses: "And the LORD said unto Moses, Is the LORD's hand waxed short?" (Numbers 11:23).

GOD, THE ALMIGHTY!

The LORD of hosts is the God of Israel, even a God to Israel.

1 CHRONICLES 17:24

God is infinite in power so let us not harden our hearts against Him. "Who hath hardened himself against [God] and prospered?" (Job 9:4). To continue in any sin is to harden the heart against God and to raise a war against heaven. Let him remember God is El-Shaddai, Almighty! "Hast thou an arm like God?" (Job 40:9). Those unwilling to bow to His golden scepter will be broken with His iron rod. Will folly contend with wisdom; weakness with power; finite with infinite? God can send legions of angels to avenge His quarrel. It is better to meet God with tears in your eyes than weapons in your hand. You may overcome Him sooner by repentance than by resistance.

Know God, and this glorious power will be engaged for you. He will put forth the whole power of His Godhead for the good of His people. The almightiness of God's power is a wonderful support and comfort to the believer. It was Samson's riddle: "Out of the strong came forth sweetness" (Judges 14:14). So out of the attribute of God's power, out of this strong, comes forth comforting sweetness.

19

GOD'S POWER IN OUR WEAKNESS

Is any thing too hard for the LORD?

GENESIS 18:14

"My sins," says a child of God, "are potent. I have no power against this army that comes against me. I pray and humble my soul by fasting, but my sins return to me." Do you believe the power of God? The *strong* God can conquer strong corruption. Sin is too hard for you, but not for Him; He can soften hard hearts and quicken the dead. Set His power to work by faith and prayer. *Lord! It is not for Thy honor that the devil should have strength within me. Break the head of this devil! Abba, Father, all things are possible with Thee.*

In case of strong temptation, Satan is called the strong man; but remember the power of God that broke the serpent's head upon the cross. Satan is chained and a conquered enemy.

God is a comfort in case of weakness of grace and the fear of falling away. We pray, but we cannot send out strong cries; we believe, but our faith shakes and trembles. "My strength is made perfect in weakness. Most gladly therefore will I rather glory in my infirmities, that the power of Christ may rest upon me" (2 Corinthians 12:9). We are "kept by the power of God" (1Peter 1:5). God's mercy pardons us, His power preserves us, and He keeps our grace so that it does not fail.

GOD'S COMFORT IN OUR DEFICIENCY

With God all things are possible.

MATTHEW 19:26

God's power is comfort in case of deficiency in thy wealth. God *can* multiply the oil in the cruse; miraculously He can rise up supplies. Cannot He who provides the birds of the air provide for His children? Cannot He who clothes the lilies clothe His lambs?

God's power is comfort in regard of the resurrection. It seems difficult to believe that the bodies of men, when eaten up by worms, devoured by beasts and fishes, or consumed to ashes, should be raised the same numerical bodies; but if we believe the power of God, it is no great wonder. Which is harder, to create or to raise the dead? He who can make a body from nothing can restore its parts when mingled and confounded. If we believe the first article of the creed, that God is Almighty, we may quickly believe the other article, the resurrection of the body. God can raise the dead because of His power, and He cannot but raise them because of His truth.

God can also save and deliver the church when it hurts. He can confine the enemy's power or confound it. "If God be for us, who can be against us?" (Romans 8:31) The church in Ezekiel is compared to dry bones, but God made breath to enter into them, and they lived (Ezekiel 37:3–5). The ship of the church may be tossed, because sin is in it, but it shall not be overwhelmed, because Christ is in it.

21

THE HOLINESS OF GOD

Glorious in holiness . . .

EXODUS 15:11

Holiness is the most sparkling jewel of God's crown; it is the name by which He is known. "Holy and reverend is his name" (Psalm 111:9). He is "the Holy One" (Job 6:10). Seraphim cry, "Holy, holy, holy is the LORD of hosts: the whole earth is full of his glory" (Isaiah 6:3). His power makes Him mighty; His holiness makes Him glorious. God's holiness consists in His perfect love of righteousness and abhorrence of evil. He is "of purer eyes than to behold evil, and canst not look on iniquity" (Habakkuk 1:13).

God is holy intrinsically. He is holy in His nature; His very being is made up of holiness, as light is the essence of the sun. He is holy in His Word. The Word bears a stamp of His holiness upon it, as the wax bears an impression of the seal. "Thy word is very pure" (Psalm 119:140). It is compared to silver refined seven times. Every line in the Word breathes sanctity; it encourages nothing but holiness. God is holy in His operations; all He does is holy. God cannot act but like Himself; He can no more do an unrighteous action than the sun can darken. "The LORD is . . . holy in all his works" (Psalm 145:17). He is the original and pattern of holiness. Holiness began with Him who is the Ancient of Days.

GOD'S PURE HOLINESS

Every good and perfect gift is from above.

JAMES 1:17

God is the cause of all that is holiness in others. He made the angels holy. He infused all holiness into Christ's human nature. All the holiness we have is but a crystal stream from this fountain. We borrow all our holiness from God. "I am the LORD which sanctify you" (Leviticus 20:8). God is a pattern of holiness, a principle of holiness: His spring feeds our cisterns; He drops His holy oil of grace upon us.

God is holy transcendently. "There is none holy as the LORD" (1 Samuel 2:2). No angel in heaven can take the just dimensions of God's holiness. God's holiness is far above holiness in saints or angels. The saints' holiness is like gold in ore, imperfect; humility stained with pride; the holiness of God is pure, with not the least dash or tincture of impurity mixed with it. It is a more unchangeable holiness. Though the saints cannot lose the habit of holiness (for the seed of God remains), yet they may lose some degrees of their holiness. "Thou hast left thy first love" (Revelation 2:4). Grace cannot die, yet the flame of it may go out. Holiness in the saints is subject to ebbing, but holiness in God is unchangeable. He has never lost a drop of His holiness. As He cannot have more holiness, because He is perfectly holy, so He cannot have less holiness, because He is unchangeably holy.

23

Holiness in God

*Israel hath sinned, and they have also transgressed
my covenant which I commanded them . . .*

JOSHUA 7:11

The holiness of God is above the holiness of angels. Holiness in the angels is only a quality, which may be lost, as we see in the fallen angels; but holiness in God is His essence, He is all over holy, and He can as well lose His Godhead as His holiness.

But is He not privy to all the sins of men? How can He behold their impurities and not be defiled? God sees all the sins of men, but He is no more defiled with them than the sun is defiled by the vapors that rise from the earth. God sees sin, not as a patron to approve it, but as a judge to punish it.

Is God so infinitely holy? Then see how unlike to God sin is. Sin is an unclean thing; it is hyperbolically evil. It is called an abomination. God has no mixture of evil in Him; sin has no mixture of good. Sin is the spirit and quintessence of evil: it turns good into evil; it has deflowered the virgin soul, made it red with guilt and black with filth; it is called the accursed thing. No wonder, therefore, that God hates sin, being so unlike to Him, nay, so contrary to Him. Sin strikes at His Holiness; it does all it can to spite God. If sin could help it, God should be God no longer.

24

Infinitely Holy

Be ye holy, for I am holy.

1 Peter 1:16

God is the Holy One, and holiness is His glory. How irreverent are they who are haters of holiness! They hate the sweet perfume of holiness in the saints; their hearts rise against holiness as a man's stomach at a dish he has an aversion for. There is no greater sign of a person devoted to hell than to hate one who is most like God. Others despise the glory of the Godhead. Despising holiness is seen as contempt for it, and is it not sad that men should ridicule that which should save them? Sure that patient will die who shows contempt for the physician. Ridiculing the grace of the Spirit comes close to despising the Spirit of grace. Those who scoff at holiness will be cast out of heaven.

Then let us endeavor to imitate God in His infinite holiness. There is a holiness of equality and a holiness of similitude. A holiness of equality no man or angel can reach. Who can be equally holy with God? Who can parallel Him in sanctity? But there is a holiness of similitude, and after that we must aspire to have some analogy and resemblance of God's holiness in us, to be as like Him in holiness as we can. Though a taper does not give so much light as the sun, yet it resembles it. We must imitate God in holiness.

25

LIKE GOD IN HOLINESS

*Put on the new man, which after God
is created in righteousness and true holiness.*

EPHESIANS 4:24

To be like God in holiness, our holiness consists in God's nature and in our subjection to His will. Hence the saints are said to partake of the divine nature, which is not partaking of His essence, but His image (2 Peter 1:4). The saints' holiness is manifest when they bear the image of God's meekness, mercifulness, heavenliness; they are of the same judgment with God, of the same disposition; loving what He loves, hating what He hates.

Our holiness consists also in our subjection to the will of God. As God's nature is the pattern of holiness, so His will is the rule of holiness. It is our holiness when we do His will (Acts 13:22); when we bear His will (Micah 7:9); when what He inflicts wisely, we suffer willingly. Our concern should be to be like God in holiness. Our holiness should be qualified: as His is a real holiness, ours should be.

Resemble God in holiness like a fair glass in which some of the beams of God's holiness shine forth. When we wear the embroidered garment of holiness, it is for glory and beauty. A good Christian is glowing, being sprinkled with Christ's blood, and white, being adorned with holiness. As the diamond to a ring, so is holiness to the soul; that, even when some oppose it, they also admire it.

26

REFLECTING GOD'S HOLINESS

He [chastened us] for our profit,
that we might be partakers of his holiness.

HEBREWS 12:10

It is the great design God carries on in the world to make a people like Himself in holiness. What are all the showers of ordinances for, but to rain down righteousness upon us and make us holy? What are the promises for, but to encourage holiness? What is the sending of the Spirit into the world for, but to anoint us with the holy unction? (1 John 2:20). All afflictions are to make us partakers of God's holiness. His mercies are to draw us to holiness. What is the end of Christ's dying, but that His blood might wash away our unholiness? Jesus "gave himself for us, to purify unto himself a peculiar people" (Titus 2:14). So that if we are not holy, we thwart God's great design in the world.

Our holiness draws God's heart to us. Holiness is God's image, and God cannot choose but to love His image where He sees it. "Thou lovest righteousness" (Psalm 45:7). And where does righteousness grow, but in a holy heart? "Thou shalt be called Hephzibah . . . for the LORD delighteth in thee" (Isaiah 62:4). It was her holiness that drew God's love to her. "They shall call them, The holy people" (v. 12). God values not any by their prominent birth, but by their holiness.

27

GOD'S HOLINESS IS OUR HONOR

*Every one of you should know how to possess
his vessel in sanctification and honor.*

1 THESSALONIANS 4:4

Holiness is the only thing that distinguishes us from the reprobate part of the world. God's people have His seal upon them. "The foundation of God standeth sure, having this seal, The Lord knoweth them that are his. And, let every one that nameth the name of Christ depart from iniquity" (2 Timothy 2:19). The people of God are sealed with a double seal: election, "The Lord knows who are his"; and sanctification, "Let every one . . . depart from iniquity." As a nobleman is distinguished from another by his silver star; as a virtuous woman is distinguished from a harlot by her chastity; so holiness distinguishes between the two seeds. All who are of God have Christ for their captain, and holiness is the white color they wear (Hebrews 2:10).

Holiness is our honor. Holiness and honor are put together. Dignity goes along with sanctification. Christ has "washed us from our sins in his own blood, and hath made us kings and priests unto God" (Revelation 1:5–6). When we are washed and made holy, then we are kings and priests to God. The saints are called vessels of honor; they are called jewels, for the sparkling of their holiness. Filled with wine of the Spirit, they are then earthly angels.

28

HOLINESS IS GOD'S IMAGE

*Thou shalt put away iniquity far from thy
tabernacles . . ., and shalt lift up thy face unto God.*

JOB 22:23, 26

Holiness gives us boldness with God. Lifting up the face is an emblem of boldness. When Adam had lost his holiness, he lost his confidence; he hid himself. But the holy person goes to God as a child to his father. His conscience does not upbraid him with allowing any sin, so he can go boldly to the throne of grace and have mercy to help in time of need (Hebrews 4:16).

Holiness gives peace. Sin raises a storm in the conscience: where there is sin, there is tumult. "There is no peace . . . to the wicked" (Isaiah 57:21). Righteousness and peace are put together. Holiness is the root that bears this sweet fruit of peace; righteousness and peace kiss each other (Psalm 85:10).

Holiness leads to heaven. It is the King of heaven's highway. "An highway shall be there . . . and it shall be called The way of holiness" (Isaiah 35:8). At Rome there were temples of virtue and honor, and all were to go through the temple of virtue to the temple of honor. In the same way, we must go through the temple of holiness to the temple of heaven. Glory begins in virtue, and God "has called us to glory and virtue" (2 Peter 1:3). Joy is the personification of holiness: holiness is glory militant, and joy, holiness triumphant. Joy is the quintessence of holiness.

29

Union with God and the Saints

Create in me a clean heart, O God.

PSALM 51:10

What shall we do to resemble God in holiness? Have recourse to Christ's blood by faith. This is the washing of the soul. Legal purifications were types and emblems of it. The Word of God is a glass to show us our dirty spots, and Christ's blood is a fountain to wash them away, cleansing us from all unrighteousness. Pray for a holy heart. "Create in me a clean heart, O God" (Psalm 51:10). Lay thy heart before the Lord, and say, "Lord, my heart is full of leprosy; it defiles all it touches. Lord, I am not fit to live with such a heart, for I cannot honor Thee; nor die with such a heart, for I cannot see Thee. Oh, create in me a clean heart. Send thy Spirit into me, to refine and purify me, that I may be a temple fit for Thee, the holy God, to inhabit.

Walk with them who are holy: "He that walketh with the wise shall be wise" (Proverbs 13:20). Be among the spices and you will smell of them. Association begets assimilation. Nothing has a greater power and energy to effect holiness than the communion of saints.

30

THE JUSTICE OF GOD

*He is the Rock . . . a God of truth and
without iniquity, just and right is he.*

DEUTERONOMY 32:4

All God's attributes are identical, and the same with His fundamental nature. He has several attributes whereby He is made known to us, but only one spirit. A cedar tree has several branches, yet they are one cedar. There are several attributes of God whereby we conceive of Him, but only one entire essence.

Concerning God's justice: "Touching the Almighty, we cannot find him out: he is excellent . . . in plenty of justice" (Job 37:23). God is said to dwell in justice: "Justice and judgment are the habitation of thy throne" (Psalm 89:14). In God, power and justice meet. Power holds the scepter, and justice holds the balance.

What is God's justice? Justice is to give every one his due. God's justice is the righteousness of His nature, whereby He is carried to do that which is righteous and equal. "Shall not he render to every man according to his works?" (Proverbs 24:12). God is an impartial judge. He judges the cause. Men often judge the person, but not the cause; which is not justice, but malice. "I will go down now, and see whether they have done altogether according to the cry of it, which is come up unto me" (Genesis 18:21). When the Lord is dealing with a disciplinary act, He weighs every piece of evidence and does not punish rashly; He does not move toward riot, but toward a wise decision against offenders.

God Loves Justice

Thou lovest righteousness.

Psalm 45:7

God's holiness, the cause of His justice, will not allow Him to do anything except what is righteous. He can not be unjust or unholy. God's will is the supreme rule of justice, the standard of equity, and is wise and good. God wills nothing except what is just; it is just because He wills it. God does justice voluntarily. Justice flows from His nature. God will not be bribed, because of His justice; He cannot be forced, because of His power. He does justice out of love to justice. Justice is the perfection of the divine nature. God is just, and He is all that is excellent: perfections meet in Him. He is just and justice itself.

God can do no wrong to His creatures. God's justice has been wronged. God does not function according to the rigor of the law; He abates something of His severity. Our mercies are more than we deserve, and our punishments, less.

God's justice is such that man or angel should not argue with Him or demand a reason for His actions. Authority and equity are on His side. It is beneath Him to give an account to us of His proceedings. Which of these two is more likely, God's justice or man's reason? The plumb line of our reason is too short to fathom the depth of God's justice. We are to adore God's justice, where we cannot see a reason of it.

1

GOD'S PATTERNS OF JUSTICE

God is not unrighteous to forget your work and labour
of love, which ye have shewed toward his name.

HEBREWS 6:10

God's justice runs through the distribution of rewards and punishments. In rewarding the virtuous: "Verily there is a reward for the righteous" (Psalm 58:11). The saints will not serve Him without reward. Though they may be losers for Him, they will not be losers by Him. He gives rewards not because we deserve it, but because He promised it.

God punishes offenders justly, by a law: "Where there is no law, there is no transgression" (Romans 4:15). God gave men the law, and they break it. Therefore He punishes them justly. God punishes the wicked justly, only with full proof and evidence. What greater evidence than for a man's own conscience to be witness against him! There is nothing God charges upon a sinner but conscience sets its seal to the truth of it.

God is just and righteous, the exemplar and pattern of justice. "Wherefore doth the way of the wicked prosper?" (Jeremiah 12:1). The wicked may be sometimes instruments to do God's work. Though they do not design His glory, they may promote it. There is justice, that they should have a temporal reward. God lets those prosper under whose wing His people are sheltered. God will not be in any man's debt.

2

GOD IS KNOWN BY HIS JUDGMENTS

Against thee, thee only, have I sinned . . .
That thou mightest be justified when thou speakest,
and be clear when thou judgest.

PSALM 51:4

God lets men go on in sin, and prosper, that He may leave them more inexcusable. "I gave her space to repent of her fornication; and she repented not" (Revelation 2:21). God adjourns the sessions and spins out His mercies toward sinners. If they repent not, His patience will be a witness against them, and His justice will be clearer in their condemnation.

God does not always let the wicked prosper in their sin. Some He punishes openly, that His justice may be taken notice of. "The LORD is known by the judgment which he executeth" (Psalm 9:16). That is, His justice is seen by striking men dead in the very act of sin.

If God lets men prosper awhile in their sin, His vial of wrath is all this while filling; His sword is all this time being sharpened. Though God may be tolerant with men for a while, long forbearance does not equate forgiveness. The longer God is in taking His blow, the heavier it will be at last. Justice may be like a sleeping lion, but the lion *will* wake and roar upon the sinner. As long as there is eternity, God has time enough to reckon with His enemies.

3

GOD IS ALWAYS JUST

I know, O LORD, that thy judgments are right,
and that thou in faithfulness hast afflicted me.

PSALM 119:75

God's people suffer great afflictions, are injured, and are persecuted. "All the day long have I been plagued, and chastened every morning" (Psalm 74:14).

God's ways of judgment are sometimes secret, but never unjust. The Lord never afflicts His people without a cause, so He cannot be unjust. There is some good in the godly, therefore the wicked afflict them. And there is some evil in the godly, therefore God afflicts them. God's own children have their blemishes. "Are there not with you, even with you, sins against the Lord?" (2 Chronicles 28:10). These spiritual diamonds, have they no flaws? Do we not read of the spots on God's children? Are not they guilty of much pride, highly critical passion, and worldliness? Though, by their profession, they seem to resemble the birds of paradise, to fly above and to feed upon the dew of heaven; yet, like the serpent, they lick the dust. And these sins of God's people provoke God more than others do. The sins of the lost pierce Christ's side; these from His people wound His heart. Therefore is not God just in all the evils that befall them?

The trials and sufferings of the godly are to refine and purify them. What more proclaims God's faithfulness than to take such a course with them as may make them better?

4

GOD CANNOT BE UNJUST

*Hath not the potter power over the clay, of the same lump
to make one vessel unto honour, and another to dishonour?*

ROMANS 9:21

What injustice is in God to inflict less punishment and prevent a greater? The best of God's children have that in them that is commendable of hell. God does no wrong if He uses only the rod when they deserve poison. If God deals so favorably with His children, He only puts wormwood in their cup, whereas He might put fire and brimstone. They should rather admire His mercy than complain that He is unjust.

How can it stand with God's justice, that all men being equally guilty by nature, He does pass by one and save another? Why does He not deal with all alike? "Is there unrighteousness with God? God forbid" (Romans 9:14). "Doth the Almighty pervert justice?" (Job 8:3).

God is not bound to give an account for His actions. God is Lord supreme with sovereign power; therefore He can do no injustice. God has liberty in His own breast to save one and not another; and His justice is not at all impeached or blemished. Though some are saved and others perish, there is no unrighteousness in God. Whoever perishes, his destruction is of himself. God is not bound to force his mercies upon men. If they willfully oppose the offer of grace, their sin is to be regarded as the cause of their perishing, and not God's justice.

5

IMITATE GOD IN JUSTICE

The balances of deceit are in his hand.

HOSEA 12:7

God is just; a great part of the world is unjust. In their courts they pervert justice: They "decree unrighteous decrees" (Isaiah 10:1). The Hebrew word for a judge's robe signifies deceit, misrepresentation, or injustice, which is more often true of the judge than of the robe. What is a good law without a good judge? Injustice lies in two things: either not to punish where there is a fault or to punish where there is no fault. Men are often unjust using false weights: they hold the Bible in one hand and false weights in the other. "Thy wine is mixed with water" (Isaiah 1:22) when bad grain is mixed with good and sold as pure grain. He cannot be godly who is not just. Though God does not propose that you be as omnipotent as He is, yet He bids you be as just.

Let Christ's golden maxim be observed: "Whatsoever ye would that men to do to you, do ye even so to them" (Matthew 7:12). You would not have them wrong you, neither do you wrong them. Rather suffer wrong than do wrong. "Why do ye not rather take wrong?" (1 Corinthians 6:7). Oh, be exemplary for justice! Let justice be your ornament. "I put on righteousness, and it clothed me; my judgment was as a robe and a diadem" (Job 29:14). A robe for its graceful beauty: I put it on, and I was clothed in righteousness.

"He hath covered me with the robe of righteousness, as a bridegroom decketh himself with ornaments" (Isaiah 61:10).

6

GOD'S JUSTICE WILL COME

[God] will judge the world in righteousness.

ACTS 17:31

A judge puts his robe on and removes it again at night, but Job did so put on justice that he did not put it off until death; forever clothed. We must not take our robe of justice off until we lay down our tabernacle. If God be in you, you will be like Him. By every unjust action, you deny Christ; you stain the glory of your profession. Heathens will rise up in judgment against you.

Because God is just, there will be a day of judgment. God will administer justice; He will crown the righteous and condemn the wicked. "He hath appointed a day" (Acts 17:31). God is just, and He will take vengeance. Men break the laws God gave: the day cometh for the execution of offenders. A law not executed is like a wooden dagger, for show. The wicked shall drink a sea of wrath, but not sip one drop of injustice. At that day God's justice shall be fully vindicated from all the objections and demands of unjust men. At the last day, God's sword will be drawn against offenders; His justice shall be revealed before the world: "Shall not the Judge of all the earth do right?" (Genesis 18:25).

If thy heart has been broken for and from sin, thou may plead not only God's mercy, but also His justice for the pardoning of thy sin. Show Him His hand and seal, and He cannot deny Himself.

7

THE MERCY OF GOD

He loveth righteousness and judgment:
the earth is full of the goodness of the Lord.

PSALM 33:5

Mercy is an attribute of God, both the result and effect of God's goodness. The most learned of the heathens thought they gave their god Jupiter two golden characters when they gave him a distinctive form, good and great. Both these meet in God, goodness and greatness, majesty and mercy.

God is essentially good in Himself and relatively good to us. They are both put together in "Thou art good, and doest good" (Psalm 119:68). This relative goodness is His mercy, which is an inherent propensity in God to pity and comfort those that suffer.

Scripture's great design is to represent God as merciful. This is a loadstone to draw sinners to Him. "The LORD God [is] merciful, gracious, long-suffering, abundant in goodness" (Exodus 34:6), and He "will by no means clear the guilty" (Psalm 57:10). God's "mercy is great above the heavens" (Psalm 108:4). God is represented as a king, with a rainbow about His throne. The rainbow was an emblem of mercy. The Scripture represents God in white robes of mercy more often than with garments rolled in blood; with His golden scepter more often than His iron rod.

God is more inclined to mercy than wrath. Mercy is His darling attribute, which He most delights in (Micah 7:18). Mercy is God's right hand, and His desire, that He is most used to in His dealing with His children.

8

SEEK GOD'S MERCY

The LORD is merciful and gracious, slow to
anger . . . and ready to forgive.

PSALM 103:8, 86:5

It is delightful to God to have the breasts of His mercy drawn. "Fury
is not in me," (Isaiah 27:4); that is, I do not delight in it. Acts of
severity are rather forced from God; He does not afflict willingly.
The bee naturally gives honey; it stings only when it is provoked. So
God does not punish until He can bear no longer. "The LORD
could bear no longer, because of the evil of your doings" (Jeremiah
44:22). Inflicting punishment is called God's strange work. He is
not used to it. When the Lord would shave off the pride of a nation,
He is said to hire a razor, as if He had none of His own. He shall
"shave with a razor that is hired" (Isaiah 7:20).

There is no condition that we cannot seek mercy in it. When the
church was in captivity, she cried out, "It is of the LORD's mercies
that we are not consumed" (Lamentations 3:22). In all afflictions
we see some sunshine of mercy.

Mercy sweetens all God's other attributes. God's holiness without mercy, and His justice without mercy, were terrible. How bitter
and dreadful were the other attributes of God, did not mercy
sweeten them! Mercy sets God's power on work to help us; it makes
His justice become our friend; it shall avenge our quarrels.

GOD'S MERCY, A PEARL IN HIS CROWN

The LORD is good to all.

PSALM 145:9

God's mercy makes His Godhead appear amiable and lovely. When Moses said to God, "I beseech thee, shew me thy glory," the Lord answered him, "I will make all my goodness pass before thee . . . and will shew mercy on whom I will shew mercy" (Exodus 33:18-19). God's mercy is His glory. His holiness makes Him illustrious; His mercy makes Him kindly.

Even the worst people taste God's mercy; even though they fight against it.

Sweet dewdrops are on the thistle as well as on the rose. The church where mercy visits is very large.

Mercy coming to us in a covenant is sweetest. It was mercy that God would give Israel rain, bread to fill them, peace, and victory over their enemies, but it was a greater mercy that God would be their God. To have health is a mercy, but to have Christ and salvation is a greater mercy: it is like the diamond in the ring, which casts a more sparkling luster.

One act of mercy engages God to another. Men argue thus: "I have shown you kindness already. Therefore trouble me no more." But because God has shown mercy, He is more ready still to show mercy. His mercy in election makes Him justify, adopt, glorify. One act of mercy engages God to more. A parent's love to his child makes him always giving.

GOD, THE FATHER OF MERCIES

Blessed be God . . . the Father of mercies . . .

2 CORINTHIANS 1:3

All the mercy in the creature is derived from God, and is only a drop in the ocean. The mercy and pity a mother has to her child is from God; He who puts the milk in her breast puts the compassion in her heart. The Father of mercies begets all the mercies in the world (2 Corinthians 1:3). If God has put any kindness into the creature, how much kindness is in Him who is the Father of mercy!

As God's mercy makes the saints happy, so it should make them humble. Mercy is not the fruit of our goodness, but the fruit of God's goodness. Mercy is a charity that God bestows. They have no cause to be proud who live upon the charity of God's mercy. "If I be righteous, yet will I not lift up my head" (Job 10:15): all my righteousness is the effect of God's mercy. Therefore I will be humble and will not lift up my head.

Mercy stays the speedy execution of God's justice. Sinners continually provoke God and make "the fury come up in his face" (Ezekiel 38:18). Whence does God not presently arrest and condemn them? It is not that God cannot do it, for He is armed with omnipotence, but it is from His mercy. Mercy provides a reprieve for the sinner and stops the speedy process of justice. God would, by His goodness, lead sinners to repentance.

GOD'S MERCY IS FREE

I will love them freely.

HOSEA 14:4

How dreadful to have mercy as a witness against us! It was sad for Haman when the queen herself accused him (Esther 7:6). So will it be when this queen of mercy shall stand up against a person and accuse him. It is only mercy that saves a sinner. How sad, then, to have mercy become an enemy! If mercy is an accuser, then who shall be our advocate? The sinner never escapes hell when mercy draws up the indictment.

There are several kinds of mercy: preventing mercy, sparing mercy, supplying mercy, guiding mercy, accepting mercy, healing mercy, quickening mercy, supporting mercy, forgiving mercy, correcting mercy, comforting mercy, delivering mercy, and crowning mercy.

To set up merit is to destroy mercy. Nothing can deserve mercy (because we are polluted in our blood) nor force it. We may force God to punish us, but not to love us. Every link in the chain of salvation is wrought and interwoven with free grace. Election is free. God "hath chosen us in [Christ], according to the good pleasure of his will" (Ephesians 1:4–5). Justification is free: "being justified freely by his grace" (Romans 3:24). Salvation is free: "According to his mercy he saved us" (Titus 3:5). Say not then, "I am unworthy," for mercy is free. If God should show mercy to such only as are worthy, He would show none at all.

12

MERCIES ARE NEW EVERY MORNING

For thou, LORD, are good, and ready to forgive;
and plenteous in mercy.

PSALM 86:5

God's mercy is overflowing; it is infinite. The vial of wrath drops, but the fountain of mercy runs. The sun is not as full of light as God is of mercy. God has morning and night mercies: His mercies are "new every morning" (Lamentations 3:23) and "In the night his song shall be with me" (Psalm 42:8). God has mercies under heaven, which we taste, and in heaven, which we hope for.

God's mercy is eternal: "The mercy of the LORD is from everlasting to everlasting" (Psalm 103:17). "His mercy endureth for ever" is repeated twenty-six times in Psalm 136. God's anger to His children lasts but a while, but "his mercy is everlasting" (Psalm 100:5). As long as He is God, He will be showing mercy. As His mercy is overflowing, so it is forever flowing.

We are to look upon God in prayer, not in His judgment robes, but clothed with a rainbow full of mercy and clemency. Add wings to prayer. When Jesus Christ ascended up to heaven, that which made Him go in that direction with joy was, "I go to my Father" (John 16:10). So that which should make our hearts ascend with joy in prayer is "We are going to the Father of mercy, who sits upon the throne of grace." Go with confidence in this mercy, as when one goes to a fire, not doubtingly, saying, "Perhaps it will warm me, perhaps not." God's mercy is plenteous.

13

BELIEVE IN HIS MERCY

I trust in the mercy of God for ever and ever.

PSALM 52:8

God's mercy is a fountain opened. We may drink of this fountain of salvation. What greater encouragement to believe than God's mercy? God counts it His glory to scatter pardons; He is desirous that sinners should touch the golden scepter of His mercy and live.

This willingness to show mercy appears by entreating sinners to come and take hold on His mercy. "Whosoever will let him take the water of life freely" (Revelation 22:17). Mercy woos sinners; it even kneels down to them. It was strange for a prince to entreat a condemned man to accept of pardon. God says, "Poor sinner, let Me love thee. Be willing to let Me save thee."

God's willingness to show mercy appears by His joyfulness when sinners take hold on His mercy. God's goodness is that He rejoices at the salvation of sinners and is glad when His mercy is accepted. God rejoices when a poor sinner comes in and takes hold of His mercy. What an encouragement to believe in God! He is a God of pardons. Mercy pleases Him. Nothing prejudices us but unbelief. Unbelief stops the current of God's mercy from running, shuts God's bowels, closes the cavity of Christ's wounds, so no healing virtue will come out. As far as the heavens are above the earth, so far is God's mercy above our sins. What will tempt us to believe, if not the mercy of God?

14

NOTHING SWEETER THAN GOD'S MERCY

The mercy of the Lord is . . . upon them that fear him.

PSALM 103:17

Take heed of abusing the mercy of God. Suck not poison out of the sweet flower of God's mercy. Think not that because God is merciful, you may go on in sin; this is to make mercy your enemy. None might touch the ark but the priests, who by their office were more holy. So none may touch the ark of God's mercy but such as are resolved to be holy. To sin because mercy abounds is the devil's logic. He who sins because of mercy is like one who wounds his head because he has a bandage. He who sins because of God's mercy shall have judgment without mercy. Mercy abused turns to fury. If "he bless himself, saying, I shall have peace, though I walk in the imagination of mine heart, to add drunkenness to thirst: the LORD will not spare him, but then the anger of the LORD, and his jealousy, shall smoke against that man" (Deuteronomy 29:19–20). Nothing is sweeter than mercy, when it is improved; nothing fiercer, when it is abused; as nothing is colder than lead when taken out of the mine, and nothing more scalding than boiling water. Nothing is blunter than iron, yet nothing is sharper when it is whetted. Mercy is not for them who sin and fear not, but for them who fear and sin not. God's mercy is a holy mercy; where it pardons, it heals.

TREASURES OF MERCY

In thee the fatherless findeth mercy.

HOSEA 14:3

What shall we do to be interested in God's mercy? Be sensible of your wants. See how much you stand in need of pardoning, saving mercy. See yourselves as orphans. God bestows the charity of mercy only on such as are destitute. Be emptied of all opinion of self-worthiness. God pours the golden oil of mercy into empty vessels.

Go to God for mercy: "Have mercy upon me, O God!" (Psalm 51:1). Put me not off with common mercy that reprobates may have. Give me not only acorns, but pearls. Give me not only mercy to feed and clothe me, but mercy to save me; Give me the cream of thy mercies. Lord! let me have mercy and lovingkindness, "who crowneth thee with lovingkindness and tender mercies" (Psalm 103:4). Give me such mercy as speaks Thy electing love to my soul.

Oh, pray for mercy! Prayer is the key that opens treasures of mercy, and all the mercy comes through Christ. "Samuel took a sucking lamb" (1 Samuel 7:9): carry the lamb Christ in your arms, go in His name, present His merits. Say, "Lord! Here is Christ's blood, which is the price of my pardon. Lord! Show me mercy, because Christ has purchased it." Though God may refuse us when we come for mercy in our own name, yet He will not when we come in Christ's name. Plead Christ's satisfaction, and this is an argument that God cannot deny.

16

MERCY SWEETLY FLOWS

Bless the LORD, O my soul:
and all that is within me, bless his holy name.

PSALM 103:1

Such as have found mercy are exhorted to be upon the mount of blessing and praising. They have not only heard the King of heaven is merciful, but they have found it so. The honeycomb of God's mercy has dropped upon them: when in wants, mercy supplied them; when they were near death, mercy raised them from the sick-bed; when they were covered with guilt, mercy pardoned them. The vessels of mercy run over with praise! "Who was before . . . a perse-cutor, and injurious; but I obtained mercy" (1 Timothy 1:13). I was blessed with mercy. As the sea overflows and breaks down the banks, so the mercy of God broke down the banks of my sin, and mercy sweetly flowed into my soul. You, who have been monuments of God's mercy, should be trumpets of praise; you, who have tasted the Lord is gracious, should tell others what experiences you have had of God's mercy, that you may encourage them to seek to Him for mercy. "I will declare what [God] has done for my soul" (Psalm 66:16). When I found my heart dead, God's Spirit came upon me mightily, and the blowing of that wind made the withering flowers of my grace revive. Oh, tell others of God's goodness, that you may set others to blessing Him, that God's praises live when you are dead.

17

MERCY, THE ATTRACTION OF LOVE

I will love thee, O LORD, my strength.

PSALM 18:1

The Hebrew word for *love* signifies love out of the inward bowels. God's justice may make us fear Him; His mercy makes us love Him. If mercy will not produce love, what will? We are to love God for giving us our food, much more for giving us grace; for sparing mercy, much more for saving mercy. Sure that heart is made of marble, which the mercy of God will not dissolve in love. "I would hate my own soul," says Augustine, "if I did not find it loving God."

We are to imitate God in showing mercy. As God is the Father of mercy, show yourselves to be His children by being like Him. Ambrose says, "The sum and definition of religion is, be rich in works of mercy, be helpful to the bodies and souls of others. Scatter your golden seeds; let the lamp of your profession be filled with the oil of charity. Be merciful in giving and forgiving. 'Be ye therefore merciful, as your Father also is merciful' (Luke 6:36)".

18

THE TRUTH OF GOD

For thy mercy is great unto the heavens,
and thy truth unto the clouds.

PSALM 57:10

Another attribute of God is His truth: "a God of truth and without iniquity; just and right is he" (Deuteronomy 32:4). God is the truth. He is true in a physical sense, true in His being: He has a real subsistence, and He gives a being to others. God is true in a moral sense: He is true and without errors, without deceit. God is the pattern and prototype of truth: there is nothing true but what is in God or comes from God. God's truth is taken from His veracity in making good His promises: "There hath not failed one word of all his good promise" (1 Kings 8:56). The promise is God's bond; God's truth is the seal set to His bond.

The power of God, whereby He is able to fulfill the promise to subdue our corruption. "He will subdue our iniquities" (Micah 7:19). "Oh," says a believer, "my corruption is so strong that I am sure I shall never get the mastery of it." Abraham looked at God's power and was "fully persuaded that, what [God] had promised, he was able also to perform" (Romans 4:21). There is nothing too hard for God. He who could bring water out of a rock is able to bring to pass His promises.

19

GOD'S TRUTH, GOD'S PROMISE

In hope of eternal life, which God,
that cannot lie promised before the world began.

TITUS 1:2

God's truth is the seal set to the promise. Eternal life is the sweetness promise: God cannot lie; there is the certainty of it. Mercy makes the promise; truth fulfills it. God's providences are uncertain, but His promises are the "sure mercies of David" (Acts 13:34). God "is not a man that he should repent" (1 Samuel 15:29). The word of a prince cannot always be taken, but God's promise is unbreakable. God's truth is one of the richest jewels of His crown, and He has pledged it in a promise: "Although my house be not so with God; yet he hath made with me an everlasting covenant, ordered in all things, and sure" (2 Samuel 23:5). That is, though I fail much of that exact purity the Lord requires, yet He has made with me an everlasting covenant, that He will pardon, adopt, and glorify me; and this covenant is ordered in all things and sure. This covenant abides firm and firm, being sealed with the truth of God. God has added to His word His oath, wherein He pledges His being, His life, and His righteousness to make good the promise. His truth is engaged in His promise, which cannot be altered. God cannot deceive the faith of His people. He is abundant in truth.

DELAYED, BUT NEVER BROKEN

The Lord shall give that which is good.

PSALM 85:12

The Lord may sometimes delay a promise, but He will not deny. God's promise may lie as good as seed under ground, but at last it will spring up into a crop. He promised to deliver Israel from the iron furnace, but this promise was above four hundred years in travail before it brought forth. Simeon had a promise that he should not depart "before he had seen the Lord's Christ" (Luke 2:26), but it was a short time before his death when he saw Christ. Though God delay the promise, He will not deny it.

God may change His promise, but He will not break it. Sometimes God changes a temporal promise into a spiritual; it may not be fulfilled in a temporal sense, but a spiritual. God may let a Christian be cut short in temporal things, but He makes it up in spirituals. If He does not increase the basket and the store, He gives increase of faith and inward peace. Here He changes His promise, but He does not break it: *He gives that which is better.* If a man promises to pay me the lowest value of a coin, and he pays me in a better coin, as in gold, he does not break his promise. Psalm 89:33 reminds us of God's promise to His own faithfulness: "[I will not] suffer my faithfulness to fail."

21

CHRIST DIED FOR ALL

Behold the Lamb of God,
which taketh away the sin of the world.

JOHN 1:29

In this verse, *the world* is taken either in a limited sense, for the world of the elect, or in a larger sense, for both elect and reprobates. "Christ takes away the sins of the world," that is, the world of the elect.

Christ died sufficiently for all, not effectually. Christ's blood has value enough to redeem the whole world, but its virtue is applied only to such who believe. Christ's blood is commendable for all, not effectual. All are not saved, because some turn away from salvation and malign Christ's blood, counting it an unholy thing.

The truth of God is a pillar for our faith. Were He not a God of truth, how could we believe in Him? *He is truth,* and not a word He has spoken shall fall to the ground. The object of trust, God's truth is an immovable rock on which we may venture our salvation. Truth on earth fails, but not truth in heaven. Nothing God has spoken will change. There is nothing else we can believe in but the truth of God. His truth is a pillar for faith to rest upon. A person of honor cannot be more affronted or provoked than when he is not believed. He who denies God's truth makes the promise no better than a forged deed; and can there be a greater affront offered to God?

JUNE

22

WORDS SMOOTHER THAN OIL

LORD, who shall abide in thy tabernacle? . . .
He that . . . speaketh the truth in his heart.

PSALM 15:2

God has threatened to "wound . . . the hairy scalp of such an one as goeth on still in his trespasses" (Psalm 68:21). He has threatened to judge adulterers and be avenged upon the malicious. "Thou beholdest mischief and spite, to requite it with thy hand" and to rain fire and brimstone upon the sinner (Psalm 11:6). God is as true to His aggression as to His promises. To show His truth, He has executed His aggression and let His thunderbolts of judgment fall upon sinners in this life. He has punished blasphemers. Let us fear the threatening that we may not feel it.

Let us be like God in truth. We must be true in our words. It is the note of a man who shall go to heaven. Truth in words is opposed to lying. A liar is most opposite to the God of truth. Some men tell lies for profit, as when a tradesman says his commodity cost him so much, when perhaps it did not cost him half so much. He who lies in business will lie in hell.

Some lie jokingly, in sport, to make others merry, and they laugh all the way to hell. He who tells a lie makes himself like the devil. The devil "is a liar, and the father of it" (John 8:44). Lying shuts men out of heaven. Falsehood in friendship is a lie. Counterfeiting friendship is worse than counterfeiting money. Our lips are to be the sounding voice of God's truth and not the enemies tool to deceive.

23

OH, TO BE LIKE GOD IN TRUTH

Put on the new man, which after God
is created in righteousness and true holiness.

EPHESIANS 4:24

We must be true in our profession of religion. Let the practice of being like God go along with profession. Hypocrisy in religion is a lie. The hypocrite is like a face in a glass, which is the show of a face, but no true face. He makes show of holiness, but it has no truth in it. Ephraim pretended to be that which he was not; and what says God of him? "Ephraim compasseth me about with lies" (Hosea 11:12). By a lie in our words, we deny the truth; by a lie in our profession, we disgrace it. Not to be to God what we profess is telling a lie, and the Scripture makes it little better than blasphemy. "I know the blasphemy of them which say they are Jews, and are not" (Revelation 2:9). Oh! I beseech you, labor to be like God. He is a God of truth. It would be as unthinkable that He can part with His Deity as He can with His Truth. Be like God: be true in your words and be true in your profession. God's children are "children that will not lie" (Isaiah 63:8). When God sees "truth in the inward parts" (Psalm 51:6) and "lips that . . . speak no guile," He sees His own image, which draws His heart toward us. Likeness produces love.

24

THE UNITY OF GOD

Hear, O Israel, the LORD our God is one LORD.

DEUTERONOMY 6:4

There is but one God only, the living and true God. That there is a God has been proved, and those who will not believe the reality of His essence shall feel the severity of His wrath. He is the only God: "Know therefore this day, and consider it in thine heart, that the LORD he is God in heaven above, and upon the earth beneath, there is none else" (Deuteronomy 4:39). "A just God and a Savior; there is none beside me" (Isaiah 45:21). There are many so-called gods. Kings represent God; their regal scepter is an emblem of his power and authority. Judges are called gods. "I have said, Ye are gods" (Psalm 82:6).

There is but one First Cause that has its Being of itself and on which all other beings depend. As in the heavens, the mobile moves all the other planets; so, God gives life and motion to everything that exists. There can be but one God, because there is but one First Cause.

There is but one infinite Being; therefore there is but one God. There cannot be two infinites. "Do not I fill heaven and earth? saith the LORD" (Jeremiah 23:24). If there be one Infinite, filling all places at once, how can there be any room for another infinite to subsist?

25

ONE OMNIPOTENT POWER

*I am the first, and I am the last;
and beside me there is no God.*

ISAIAH 44:6

If there be two Omnipotents, there will be a contest between them, and there would be confusion. The order and harmony in the world, or the constant and uniform government of all things, is a clear argument that there is but one Omnipotent, one God who rules all.

Those who contrive many gods are in error, not knowing the Scriptures. God has given them up to "strong delusions, that they should believe a lie: that they all might be damned who believed not the truth" (2 Thessalonians 2:11).

One God means one true religion in the world: "one Lord, one faith" (Ephesians 4:5). Many gods would mean many religions, and every god would be worshiped in his way. But if there be but one God, there is but one religion: one Lord, one faith. Some say, "We may be saved in any religion." But it is absurd to imagine that God, who is One in essence, should appoint several religions in which He will be worshipped. It is as dangerous to set up a false religion as to set up a false god. There are many ways to hell; men may go in the direction their fancy leads them. But there is only one direct road to heaven, that is, faith and holiness. There is no way to be saved but this. As there is but one God, so there is but one true religion.

26

PLEASE GOD BY DOING HIS WILL

*And this I pray, that your love may abound yet more and
more in knowledge and in all judgment; That ye may approve things
that are excellent; that ye may be sincere and without offence till
the day of Christ. Being filled with the fruits of righteousness,
which are by Jesus Christ, unto the glory and praise of God.*

PHILIPPIANS 1:9–11

We please God when we comply with His will. It was Christ's desire
to do His Father's will (John 4:34), and so He pleased Him. A
voice came from heaven, saying, "This is my beloved Son, in whom
I am well pleased" (Matthew 3:17). It is God's will that we be holy:
when we are adorned with holiness, our lives are walking Bibles
according to God's will, and it pleases Him.

We please God when we do the work He sets before us: "I have
finished the work which thou gavest me to do" (John 17:4). *Many finish
their lives, but do not finish their work.* God wants us to observe the first and
second tablets Moses brought down from Sinai. On the first is set
down our duty toward God; in the second, our duty toward man.
Such as make morality the chief and sole part of religion, set the
second table above the first; nay, they take away the first tablet. For if
prudence, justice, temperance be enough to save, then what needs
the first tablet? Our worship toward God will be quite left out. But
those two tablets that God has joined together, let no man put asunder. We please God when we dedicate our hearts to giving Him the
best of everything. We please God when we serve Him with love, fervency, and zeal. There is but one God. Therefore there is but One
whom we must please, namely, God.

27

GOD IS ABOVE ALL

There is none upon earth that I desire beside thee.

PSALM 73:25

There is one God, and we must pray to none but God. Some pray to saints and angels. The saints above know not our wants; if they did, we have no warrant to pray to them. "Abraham [is] ignorant of us" (Isaiah 63:16). Prayer is a part of divine worship, which must be given to God only. Angel worship is forbidden (Colossians 2:18–19). That we may not pray to angels is clear: "How then shall they call on him in whom they have not believed?" (Romans 10:14). We may not pray to any but whom we may believe in. We may believe in angels, but we may not pray to them.

There is one God, and it is sin to invoke any but Him. There is one God, who is "above all" (Ephesians 4:6), and He must be loved above all. We must love Him with a love of appreciation and set the highest estimate on Him, who is the only fountain of being and bliss. We must love Him with a love that desires to please. The lover's effort to please the beloved, this is love. Our love to other things must be more indifferent. Some drops of love may run beside to the creature, but the full stream must run toward God. He who is above all, must be loved above all.

28

No Other Gods Before Me

Their sorrows shall be multiplied,
that hasten after another god . . .

PSALM 16:4

God is a jealous God, not enduring His children to have other gods. Some make a god of pleasure: they are "lovers of pleasures more than lovers of God" (2 Timothy 3:4). Whatever we love more than God is our god. Whatever man trusts is his god; he makes the wedge of gold his hope; he makes money his creator, redeemer, and comforter. It is his creator: if he has money, he thinks he made. It is his redeemer: if he is in danger, he trusts in his money to redeem him: it is his comforter; if at any time he is sad, the golden harp drives away the evil spirit: so that money is his god. God made man from dust, and man makes his god from the dust. Some make their children gods, provoking God to take them away. If you lean too hard upon glass, it will break, and many break their children by leaning too hard upon them. Others make a god of their belly (Philippians 3:19). The wicked man's trinity is "the lust of the flesh, the lust of the eye, and the pride of life" (1 John 2:16). The lust of the flesh is pleasure; the lust of the eye, money; the pride of life, honor. Whatever you worship besides God will be a bramble, and fire will come out of it and devour you. The prickly bush is not one to rest upon.

29

THAT THEY ALL MAY BE ONE

Be kindly affectioned one to another with brotherly love . . .

ROMANS 12:10

There is but one God, and they that serve Him should be one. They should be one in affection; they should have one heart. Christ prayed for His disciples: "that they all may be one" (John 17:21). The apostle exhorts to be all of one mind. How sad to see Christians of many opinions going many different ways! Satan has sown division. He first divided men from God and then one man from another. "The multitude of them that believed were of one heart and of one soul" (Acts 4:32). As in music, though there be several stringed instruments, yet all make one sweet harmony. Though there are several Christians, yet there should be one sweet harmony of affection among them. "Behold, how good and how pleasant it is, for brethren to dwell together in unity!" (Psalm 133:1). If God be one, let all who profess Him be of one mind, and one heart, and thus fulfill Christ's prayer, "that they all may be one."

30

To Know Him and to Make Him Known

This God is our God: for ever and ever.

PSALM 48:14

What comfort to hear that there is a God, and that He is the only God, and that He is our God! What is Deity without property in Him? Let us labor to make clear the title! Beg the Holy Spirit. The Spirit works by faith. By faith we are one with Christ, and through Christ we come to have God for our God; all His glorious fullness is given to us by a deed of gift.

We are to be thankful for the knowledge of the only true God! Many are blind and worship the devil. Such as know not the true God will stumble into hell in the dark. Oh, let us be thankful that we are born in such a land where the light of the gospel has shone. To have the knowledge of the true God is more than if we had mines of gold, rocks of diamonds, islands of spices; especially since God has by His saving grace revealed Himself to us; since He has given us eyes to see the light; if we so know God as to be known of Him, to love Him, and believe in Him (Matthew 11:25). We can never be thankful enough to God, that He has hid the knowledge of Himself from the wise and prudent of the world, and has revealed it unto us.

1

THE TRINITY

There are three that bear record
in heaven, the Father, the Word, and
the Holy Ghost: and these three are one.

1 JOHN 5:7

God is but one, yet are there three distinct persons subsisting in the one Godhead. This is a sacred mystery, which the light within man could never have discovered. As the two natures in Christ, yet but one person, is a wonder, so three persons, yet but one Godhead. Here is the great depth: the Father God, the Son God, the Holy Ghost God; yet not three Gods, but only one God. The three persons in the blessed Trinity are distinguished, but not divided; three substances, but one essence. This is a divine riddle where one makes three, and three make one. Our narrow thoughts can no more comprehend the Trinity in unity than a nutshell will hold all the water in the sea.

Let me explain it better by the shared characteristics. In the body of the sun, there are the substance of the sun, the beams, and the heat. The beams are begotten of the sun, and the heat proceeds both from the sun and the beams. But these three, though different, are not divided; they all three make but one sun. So in the blessed Trinity, the Son is begotten of the Father, and the Holy Ghost proceeds from both. Yet though they are three distinct persons, they are but one God.

2

UNITY IN THE TRINITY

Thou, Father, art in me, and I in thee.

JOHN 17:21

There is unity in the persons in the Godhead, identity of essence, and oneness in essence, three persons, the same divine nature and substance, so that there are no degrees in the Godhead.

God the Father is called the first person, in respect of order, not dignity for God. The Father is not wiser, not holier, nor any more powerful than the other persons in the Trinity. There is a priority, not superiority.

The second person in the Trinity is Jesus Christ, who was begotten by the Father before time. He is Jehovah, our Jesus, the branch of David.

The third person in the Trinity is the Holy Ghost, who proceeds from the Father and the Son, whose work is to illuminate the mind and kindle sacred motions. The essence of the Spirit is in heaven and everywhere; but His influence is in the hearts of believers. Though Christ merits grace for us, it is the Holy Ghost who works it in us. Though Christ makes the purchase, it is the Holy Ghost who makes the assurance and seals us to the day of redemption. He who spoke with a voice from heaven was God the Father; He who was baptized in the Jordan was God the Son; He who descended in the likeness of a dove was God the Holy Ghost. Thus, the Unity of essence, and the Trinity of persons.

3

CHRIST IS GOD!

In [Jesus] dwelleth all the fullness of the Godhead bodily.

COLOSSIANS 2:9

Without distinction in the persons in the Trinity, man's redemption is overthrown: God the Father being offended with man for sin requires a mediator who is Christ, who makes our peace. Christ having died and shed His blood, how shall this blood be applied except by the Holy Ghost? Apart from three persons in the Godhead, man's salvation cannot be worked out. Without the second person in the Trinity, there is no Redeemer; if no third person, there is no Comforter; thus there is no way to get to heaven.

Jesus Christ is co-equal, co-eternal, and co-essential with God the Father. Not only was Christ with God before the beginning, but He was God: "God manifest in the flesh" (1 Timothy 3:16). The title of *Lord*, given to Christ in the New Testament, is the same as *Jehovah* in the Old Testament. Christ has a co-eternity and co-substantiality with His Father: "I and my Father are one" (John 10:30). The glorious attributes belonging to God the Father are ascribed to Christ. God the Father omnipotent is Jesus Christ. While Christ was on the earth in bodily presence, He was also in the bosom of the Father by divine presence. God the Father, the adequate object of faith, is to be believed in; so is His Son. Adoration belongs to God the Father and to God the Son.

4

THE ETERNAL GODHEAD

He shall guide you into all truth.

JOHN 16:13

The eternal Godhead subsists in the Holy Ghost. Christ speaks not of an attribute, but of a person. That the Godhead subsists *in the person* of the Holy Ghost appears in this: that the Spirit, who gives diversity of gifts, is said to be the same Lord and the same God. The black and unpardonable sin is said, in a special manner, to be committed against the Godhead subsisting in the Holy Ghost. The mighty power of God is made manifest by the Holy Ghost, for He changes the hearts of men. The devil would have Christ prove Himself to be God by turning stones into bread; but the Holy Ghost shows His Godhead by turning stones into flesh. The power and Godhead of the Holy Ghost appeared in effecting the glorious conception of our Lord Jesus Christ. The very shadow of the Holy Ghost made a virgin conceive. The Holy Ghost works miracles, which transcend the sphere of nature, miracles like raising the dead. To Him belongs divine worship; our souls and bodies are the temples of the Holy Ghost. We are baptized in the name of the Holy Ghost. Therefore we must believe His Godhead or renounce our baptism in His name. Those who would wittingly and willingly blot out the third person shall have their names blotted out of the Book of Life.

5

AN EXHORTATION

All men should honor the Son even as they honor the Father.

JOHN 5:23

Believe the doctrine of the Trinity in the unity of essence. The Trinity is an object of faith; the plumb line of reason is too short to fathom this mystery; but where reason cannot wade, there faith may swim. There are some truths in religion that may be demonstrated by reason; that there is a God. But the Trinity of persons in the unity of essence is wholly supernatural and must be believed by faith. This sacred doctrine is not against reason, but above it. Illuminated philosophers who could find out the causes of many things, the discourse of the magnitude and influence of the stars, the nature of minerals, could never, by their deepest search, learn the mystery of the Trinity. This is divine revelation and must be adored with humble believing. We cannot be good Christians without the firm belief of the Trinity. How can we pray to God the Father except in the name of Christ and through the help of the Spirit?

If there be one God subsisting in three persons, then let us give equal reverence to all the persons in the Trinity. The Father is not more God than the Son and Holy Ghost in the Trinity. There is an order in the Godhead, but no degrees; one person has not a majority or supereminence above another, therefore we must give equal worship to all the persons. Adore Unity in Trinity.

6

THE CREATION

In the beginning God created the heaven and the earth.

GENESIS 1:1

The decrees of God are His eternal purpose, according to the counsel of His will, whereby, for His own glory, He has foreordained whatsoever shall come to pass.

God is unchangeable in His essence, and He is unchangeable in His decrees: His counsel shall stand. He decrees the issue of all things, and He carries them on to their accomplishment by His providence.

The work of creation is God making all things from nothing by the word of His power. The creation is glorious to behold, and it is a pleasant and profitable study. The creation is the heathen man's Bible, the ploughman's primer, and the traveler's perspective glass, through which he receives a representation of the infinite excellencies which are in God. The creation is a large volume, in which God's works are bound up; and this volume has three great leaves in it: heaven, earth, and sea.

The world was created by God in time, and it could not be from eternity. "In the beginning God created." To imagine that the work of the creation was not framed by the Lord Jehovah is to conceive an unusual landscape to be drawn without the hand of an artist. "God that made the world and all things therein" (Acts 17:24).

7

MAKING AND ADORING CREATION

By the word of the LORD were the heavens made.

PSALM 33:6

We should consider the making and the adorning of creation. God made the world without pre-existent matter. This is the difference between generation and creation. In generation there is suitable material at hand, some matter to work upon; but in creation there is no pre-existent matter. Our beginning was of nothing.

God made the world with a word. The disciples wondered that Christ could speak a word and calm the sea; but it was a word that made the sea.

Creation came out of God's hands without any blot, written with God's own fingers. His work was perfect.

God made the world with neither shape nor order, and then He made it beautiful. He divided the sea and the earth, He decked the earth with flowers, the trees with fruit, and He made the light. We admire the heavens, the sun, the moon, and the stars. Man is the most exquisite piece in the creation. He is a microcosm or miniature copy. Man was made with deliberation and counsel: "Let us make man" (Genesis 1:26). Man was to be the masterpiece of this visible world; therefore God consulted about making so rare a piece. A solemn council of the sacred persons in the Trinity was called: "Let us make man, and let us make him in our own image." God stamped His image on man and made him partaker of many divine qualities.

WONDERFULLY MADE BY GOD

I am wonderfully made . . . I was . . .
curiously wrought in the lowest parts of the earth.

PSALM 139:14—15

God created man. The head, the most excellent architectural part, is the fountain of spirits and the seat of reason. In nature, the head is the best piece, but in grace, the heart excels. The eye is the beauty of the face; it shines and sparkles like a lesser sun in the body. The eye occasions much sin and therefore may well have tears in it. The ear is the conduit-pipe through which knowledge is conveyed. Better lose our seeing than our hearing, for "faith cometh by hearing" (Romans 10:17). The tongue is an instrument to set forth the glory of God. The soul at first was an instrument in tune to praise God, and the tongue made the music. God has given us two ears, but one tongue, to show that we should be swift to hear, but slow to speak. God has set a double fence before the tongue—the teeth and the lips—to teach us to be wary that we offend not with our tongue. The heart is a noble part and the seat of life.

The soul of man is the man of the man. The soul is a vessel of honor: God Himself is served in this vessel. How richly is the soul embroidered! Thus you see how glorious a work the creation is, and man especially, who is the epitome of the world.

9

A Demonstration of God's Glory

The elements shall melt with fervent heat,
the earth also and the works that are therein shall be burnt up.

2 Peter 3:10

God didn't make the world for Himself; He did not need it, being infinite. God did not make the world to be a mansion for us, since we are not to abide here forever. Heaven is the mansion house. The world is a passage room to eternity; the world is to us as the wilderness was to Israel, not to rest in, but to travel through to the glorious Canaan. The world is a dressing room to dress our souls, not a place to reside forever. The apostle tells us of the world's funeral (2 Peter 3:10).

God made the world to demonstrate His own glory as a looking glass, that we may see His power and goodness shine forth. "The heavens declare the glory of God" (Psalm 19:1). The world is like a beautiful piece of tapestry, in which we may see the skill and wisdom of Him who made it.

The world convinces us of the truth of His Godhead. To create is proper to a Deity. God proves He is the true God and distinguishes Himself from idols. Only God can create. Creation is enough to convince the lost that there is a God. Every star in the sky, every bird that flies in the air is a witness against the heathen. A creature could not make itself.

THORNS AND THISTLES

Our help is in the name of the LORD, who made heaven and earth.

PSALM 124:8

Did God make this world full of beauty and glory and everything good? Sin eclipsed the beauty, soured the sweetness, and marred the harmony of the world. One drop of sin's bitter gall can embitter a whole sea! Sin brought pride, displeasure, and a curse to the world. God cursed the ground for man's sake. Innocently, Adam tilled the ground without toiling, which was a delight. Eating in sorrow and the sweat of the brow came after sin. And after sin, the earth produced plenty of thorns, which are hurtful, choking the corn, which was not a hurtful quality before. Ever since the Fall, life's comforts have been laden with thorns and thistles.

One fruit of the curse was to drive man out of Paradise. God first brought Adam into Paradise as a king into his palace. Driving Adam out of Paradise signified God dethroning and banishing him that he might look after a heavenly and a better paradise.

Another fruit of the curse was death. Death was not natural to Adam, but it came in after sin. Death grew out from the root of sin. See how cursed sin is, that has brought so many curses upon the creation. If we will not hate sin for its deformity, let us hate it for the curse it brings.

11

SWEETNESS IN GOD

How sweet are Your words to my taste!
Yes, sweeter than honey to my mouth!
From Your precepts I get understanding;
Therefore I hate every false way.

PSALM 119:103–104 NASB

God creates a mighty support of faith with a word. He can create strength in weakness and provide for His children. He who made the world can do more than we can imagine, "Now unto him that is able to do exceeding abundantly above all that we ask or think" (Ephesians 3:20), so trust God for help, who made heaven and earth. Creation is a monument to God's power, so it is a deferment to faith. He can with a word create softness in a hard heart. He can create purity. There is no golden pillar for faith to abide in other than creating power.

Did God make the world and everything in it good? Was there in the creature so much beauty and sweetness? What sweetness is there in God! And how much more should we trust in God that made them! Is there beauty in a rose? What beauty then is there in Christ, the Rose of Sharon! Does oil make the face shine? How will the light of God's countenance make it shine! What is Christ, in who are hid all treasures? We should ascend from the creature to the Creator. If there be any comfort below, much more comfort is in God, who made all these things! We are to delight in Him who made the world. We are to set our hearts on Him, and long to be with Him, who has infinitely more sweetness in Him than any creature!

HIS, BY RIGHT OF CREATION

O LORD, how manifold are thy works!
in wisdom hast thou made them all.

PSALM 104:24

God gave us the Scriptures to read and the book of the creation. Look up, for the heavens show God's glory. The sun gilds the world with its bright beams. Behold the stars, their regular motion in their orbs, their magnitude, their light, and their influence. God's glory blazes in the sun and twinkles in the stars. Look into the sea and see the wonders of God in the deep. Look into the air and hear birds singing forth the praises of their Creator. Look to the earth and wonder at the nature of minerals, the power of the magnet, the virtue of herbs. See the earth decked as a bride with flowers. These are the glorious effects of God's power. God has fashioned the creation as with intriguing needlework, that we may observe His wisdom and goodness, giving praise due to Him.

We owe ourselves to God, so we should serve and obey God who gives us our life: "In him we live, and move" (Acts 17:28). God has made everything for man's service—the corn for nourishment, the beasts for usefulness, the birds for music—that man should be for God's service. The rivers come from the sea, and they run into the sea again. All we have is from God. Let us honor our Creator and live to Him who made us.

GRACE IS THE CHRISTIAN'S BEAUTY

I was . . . curiously wrought.

PSALM 139:15

God made our bodies out of the dust, and that dust out of nothing. Let this keep down pride! When God would humble Adam, He used this expression: "Out of the ground wast thou taken: for dust thou art" (Genesis 3:19). Why are you proud, O dust and ashes? You are made but of coarse metal. Since you are humble, why do you not walk humbly? You, being remarkably formed, may make you thankful; but being made of the dust may keep you humble. If you have beauty, it is but well-colored earth. Your body is but air and dust mingled together, and this dust will drop into the dust.

Did God create our souls after His image, but we lost it? Let us never rest until we are restored to God's image again. For now we have the devil's image revealed in us as pride, malice, and envy. Let us get God's image restored, which consists in knowledge and righteousness (Colossians 3:10). Grace is our best beauty; it makes us like God and angels. As the sun is to the world, so is holiness to the soul. Let us go to God to repair His image in us.

Lord! Thou hast once made me; make me anew. Sin has defaced Thy image in me. Oh, draw it again by the pencil of the Holy Ghost.

14

PROVIDENCE OF GOD

My Father worketh hitherto, and I work.

JOHN 5:17

God's works of providence are acts of His most holy, wise, and powerful government for His creatures and of their actions.

God has rested from the works of creation. He does not create any new species of things. "He rested . . . from all his works" (Genesis 2:2), and therefore it must be meant of His works of providence: "My Father worketh . . . and I work" (John 5:17). "His kingdom ruleth over all" (Psalm 103:19); that is, His providential kingdom.

There is providence, but no such thing as blind fate. There is a providence that guides and governs the world. "The lot is cast into the lap; but the whole disposing thereof is of the LORD" (Proverbs 16:33).

Providence is God's ordering all issues and events of things, after the counsel of His will, to His glory. God's decree ordains things that shall fall out; God's providence orders them after the counsel of God's will.

God orders all events after the counsel of His will, to His own glory, His glory being the ultimate end of all His directions and the heart where all the lines of providence meet. The providence of God is the eye that sees and the hand that turns all the wheels in the universe. God is not like an artificer who builds a house and then leaves it, but like a pilot who steers the ship of the whole creation.

15

GOD CARES FOR HIS CHILDREN

Am I a God at hand . . . and not a God afar off?

JEREMIAH 23:23

God's providence reaches to all places, persons, and occurrences. The church where Providence visits is very large, reaching heaven, earth, and sea. That the sea, which is higher than the earth, does not drown the earth, is a wonder of Providence. God takes care of every saint in particular, as if He had none else to care for. God, by His providential care, shields off dangers from His people and sets a lifeguard of angels about them. God's providence keeps the bones of the saints, bottles their tears, strengthens them in their weakness, supplies all their wants out of its alms basket, and wonderfully supplies the wants of the elect. The raven, that unnatural creature that will hardly feed its own young, providentially brought sustenance to the prophet Elijah (1 Kings 17:6). Mary, through bearing and bringing forth the Messiah, helped to make the world rich though she was poor; and being warned of the angel to go into Egypt, (Matthew 2:13), she had scarce enough to bear her charges thither; but see how God provided for her beforehand. God's providence sent wise men from the east, bringing costly gifts for the Christ-child, providing Mary enough to defray her charges into Egypt. God's children sometimes don't know how except that Providence feeds them. If God will give His people a kingdom when they die, He will not deny them daily bread while they live.

16

GOD'S PROVIDENCE USES THE LEAST THINGS

The hairs of your head are all numbered.

MATTHEW 10:30

God's providence reaches to all affairs and occurrences in the world. There is nothing that moves from God's providence that He does not have final say in. Is it the raising of a man to honor? He puts down one and raises up another. Success and victory in battle is the result of Providence. Saul had the victory, but God wrought the salvation (1 Samuel 11:13). That among all virgins brought before the king, Esther should find favor in the eyes of the king, was not without God's special providence; for, by this means, the Lord saved the Jews alive who were destined to destruction. Providence reaches to the least of things, to birds and ants. Providence feeds the young raven when the dam forsakes it and will give it no food (Psalm 147:9). Providence reaches to the very hairs of our head (Matthew 10:30), so how much more to our souls.

There are many disorderly and irregular things in the world, and we wonder if God's providence is in them. God makes use of even irregular things for His own glory. The silversmith makes use of every tool in his shop to master his craft, no matter how strange those tools might appear to a visitor. Thus it is with the providences of God: they seem to us to be very crooked and strange, yet they all carry on God's work.

GOD'S PROVIDENCES ARE FULL OF WISDOM

Thou hast ordained [the Chaldeans] for correction.

HABAKKUK 1:12

God's people are sometimes downcast, and it seems unrealistic that they who are best are in the lowest condition, yet there is much wisdom in this providence. Perhaps riches or success created pride: God comes with a humbling providence to afflict them and fleece them. *Better is the loss that makes them humble than the success that makes them proud.* If the godly don't suffer affliction in outward comforts, how could their graces, like faith and patience, be seen? If the sun always shines, we can't see stars; if we always prosper, faith can't be seen. God's providences are wise and regular, though they seem strange and crooked.

The wicked flourishing seems out of order, but God, in His providence, sees good in the worst of men exalted and working for Him, though it is against their will. God will be in no man's debt. He makes use of the wicked to protect and shield His church and to refine and purify it. God ordained the wicked to correct His children. As iron brightens a file, so the godly are obliged to the wicked, though it is against their will, to brighten and refine their graces. If the wicked do God's own work, though against their will, He will not let them be losers by it. He will raise them in the world and give a full cup of earthly comforts. God's providences are wise and regular, which to us seem strange and crooked.

God Has No Hand in Sin

[He] suffered all nations to walk in their own ways.

Acts 14:16

God has a hand in all things, so does He have a hand in the sins of men? No! He has no hand in any man's sin. God cannot go contrary to His own nature, He cannot commit unholy acts, any more than the sun can be darkened. As you must take heed of making God ignorant of men's sins, so you must take heed of making God to have a hand in men's sins. Is God not the author of sin, and the avenger of it? Would God make a law against sin and then have a hand in breaking His own law? God permits sin, which He never would if He could not bring good out of it. Had not sin been permitted, God's justice in punishing sin and His mercy in pardoning it had not been so well known.

God does not infuse evil into men. He withdraws the influence of His graces, and then the heart hardens itself. As the light is withdrawn, darkness presently follows, but it is absurd to say that the light darkens the air. God does not cause man's sin. God has a hand in the action where sin is, but no hand in the sin of the action. So here: the natural actions of men are from God, but the sinful actions are from men themselves, and God has no hand at all in them.

19

PROVIDENCE: A CHRISTIAN'S DIARY

Whoso is wise, and will observe these things,
Even they shall understand the lovingkindness of the LORD.

PSALM 107:43

Providences are predetermined by the Lord. The falling of a tile upon one's head, the breaking out of a fire is casual to us, but it is ordered by a providence of God. A clear instance of this is in 1 Kings 22:34: "A certain man drew a bow at a venture, and smote the king of Israel between the joints of the harness." This accident was casual to the man who drew the bow, but it was divinely ordered by the providence of God. God's providence directed the arrow to hit the mark. Things that seem to happen by chance are issues of God's decrees, interpretations of His will.

God's providence is to be observed, but we must not make it our rule to walk by. *Providence is a Christian's diary but not his Bible.* Sometimes a bad cause prevails and roots, but it is not to be liked because it prevails. We must not think good of sin even if it succeeds. This is no rule for our actions. There is no standing in the way of God's providence to hinder it.

20

PROMISES AND PROVIDENCES CROSSING

I will sing of mercy and judgment.

PSALM 101:1

Trust God when His providences seem to run contrary to His promises. God promised to give David the crown to making him king, but Providence ran contrary. David was pursued by Saul, his life in danger, but it was David's duty to trust God. The Lord, by crossing providences, often brings to pass His promise. God promised Paul the lives of those with him in the ship, but God's providence seemed to run contrary to His promise. The winds blew, and the ship split and broke in pieces. But God fulfilled His promise: upon the broken pieces of the ship, they all came safely to shore.

The providences of God are intermingled. In hell, there will be nothing but bitter; in heaven, nothing but sweet. But in this life the providences of God are mixed, something sweet and something of the bitter. Providences are like Israel's pillar of cloud that led them in their march, dark on one side and light on the other. When Joseph was in prison, there was the dark side of the cloud. But God was with Joseph: there was the light side of the cloud. Asher's shoes were of brass, but his feet were dipped in oil. So affliction is the shoe of brass that pinches; but there is mercy mingled with the affliction, for there is the foot dipped in oil.

SUBMITTING TO DIVINE PROVIDENCE

I was dumb, and opened not my mouth; because thou didst it.

PSALM 39:9

Do not murmur at things that are ordered by divine wisdom. We may no more find fault with the works of Providence than we may with the works of creation. It is a sin to quarrel with God's providence or to deny His providence. If men do not act as we would have them, they shall act as God would have them. His providence is His master-wheel that turns these lesser wheels, and God will bring His glory out of all at last. We may think we could order things better if we had the government of the world in our hands. But alas! Should we be left to our own choice, we should choose those things that are hurtful for us. David earnestly desired the life of his child, which was the fruit of his sin, but had the child lived, it would have been a perpetual monument of David's shame. Let us be content that God should rule the world. Learn to accept in His will and submit to His providence. Does any affliction befall you? Remember, God sees that which is fit for you, or it would not come. Your clothes cannot fit you as well as your crosses. God's providence may sometimes be secret, but it is always wise.

22

GOD'S PROVIDENCES ARE FOR OUR GOOD

And we know that all things work together for good . . .

ROMANS 8:28

The providences of God are sometimes dark, and our eyes so dim, we can hardly make them out. We cannot unbridle Providence, but we can believe that it will work together for the good of the elect. The clock's movements seem to work contrary to one another, but they forward the motion of the clock, making it strike. So the providences of God carry on the good of the elect. Pricking a vein is in itself evil and hurtful, but as it tends to the health of the patient, it is good. Affliction is not joyous, but grievous, yet the Lord turns it to the good of His saints. Poverty shall starve their sins, and afflictions shall prepare them for a kingdom. Christians, believe that God loves you and that He will cross providences to promote His glory and your good.

Nothing comes to pass except what is ordained by God's decree and ordered by His providence. We sometimes fear what the issue of things will be when men grow high in their professions, but let us not make things worse by our fear. Men are limited in their power and cannot go further than God's providence permits. When Israel was encompassed between Pharaoh and the Red Sea, some of their hearts began to tremble, and they were dead men. But Providence ordered that the sea was a safe passage to Israel—and a sepulcher to Pharaoh and his host.

23

THANKFUL FOR GOD'S PROVIDENCE

He shall cover thee with his feathers, and under his wings
shalt thou trust: his truth shall be thy shield and buckler.

PSALM 91:4

Let God's merciful providence cause thankfulness. We are kept alive by wonderful working Providence making our clothes warm us and our meat to nourish us. We are fed every day out of the charity basket of God's providence. Our health and our wealth are not our diligence, but God's providence. If we go a step higher, we see cause for thankfulness, that we were born and bred in a gospel land and that we live in such a place where the Sun of Righteousness shines, which incites providence. We might have been born in places where pagans prevail. That Christ should make Himself known to us, touching our hearts with His Spirit, when He passes by others—this is from the miraculous providence of God, the effect of His free grace.

God's providence reaches in a special manner to His church: He waters His vineyard with His blessings and watches over it by His providence. Dissenters of the church must work when it is neither day nor night, for the Lord keeps it by His providence night and day. God by His providence preserves His church in the midst of enemies, like a spark kept alive in the ocean or a flock of sheep among wolves. God saves His church by giving unexpected mercies to His church, when she looked for nothing but ruin.

WONDER AND MERCY EXIST IN GOD'S PROVIDENCE

*Both riches and honour come of thee, and thou reignest
over all; and in thine hand is power and might; and in
thine hand it is to make great, and to give strength unto all.*

1 CHRONICLES 29:12

God raised up Queen Esther to save the Jews when Haman had a bloody warrant signed for their execution! By saving in a way we think He will destroy, God works by contraries, raising His church by bringing it low. The blood of the martyrs has watered the church and made it more fruitful. The church is like a plant that lives by dying and grows when pruned. The church is the apple of God's eye, and the eyelid of His providence daily covers and defends it.

We long for the time when the great mystery of God's providence shall be unfolded. We often don't know what to make of God's providence, and we are ready to censure what we do not understand. In heaven we shall see how His providences contributed to our salvation. Here we only see dark pieces of God's providence, making it impossible to judge His works. But in heaven we will see full body and portrait of His providence drawn out into its lively colors, and it will be glorious to behold. Then we shall see how all God's providences helped to fulfill His promises.

THE FALL: THE COVENANT OF WORKS

Of the tree of the knowledge of good and evil, thou shalt not eat of it.

GENESIS 2:17

God created man and entered a covenant of life with him upon condition of perfect obedience, forbidding him to eat of the tree of knowledge [of good and evil] upon pain of death.

The covenant was made with Adam and all mankind (Adam represented the world) to show God's sovereignty. We were His creatures, and He was the King of heaven and earth, so He might impose upon us terms of a covenant.

God commanded Adam not to eat of the tree of knowledge, but gave him freedom to eat of all the other trees of the garden. God did not deny him happiness, but He would try Adam's obedience. Adam had knowledge and the garment of original righteousness, but his touching the tree of knowledge was aspiring for omniscience. Adam had power to keep the law written in his heart, but he didn't. This covenant of works had a promise: "Do this and live!" And a warning: "Thou shalt die the death," both a natural death and an eternal death.

God knew Adam would transgress, yet that was not a sufficient reason that no law should be given him. By the same reasoning, God should not have given His written Word to men because He knew that some would not believe. Shall laws not be made in the land because some will break them? God knew Adam would break the law, and He knew how to turn it to greater good by sending Christ.

PERSONAL AND PERPETUAL OBEDIENCE

And the law is not of faith: but,
The man who doeth them shall live in them.

GALATIANS 3:12

With the first covenant being broken, God knew how to establish a second, and a better.

The form of the first covenant in innocence was working: "Do this and live." Working was the ground condition of man's justification. Not that working is required in the covenant of grace, for we are bid to work out our salvation and be rich in good works. Works in the covenant of grace are not required as in the first covenant with Adam. Works are not required for justification, but as evidence of our love for God; not as the cause of our salvation, but as evidence of our adoption. Works are required in the covenant of grace, not so much in our own strength as in the strength of another. "It is God which worketh in you" (Philippians 2:13).

The covenant of works was very strict. God required perfect obedience: Adam must do all things written in the Book of the Law and not fail, either in the matter or manner. Adam was to live exactly by the whole moral law; one sinful thought would forfeit the covenant. God required personal obedience: Adam must not do his work by proxy or have any surety bound for him; he must do it himself. God required perpetual obedience: He must continue in all things written in the Scriptures. Thus it was very strict. There was no mercy in case of failure.

AN ANCHOR OF HOPE

Blessed are the undefiled in the way,
Who walk in the law of the LORD.

PSALM 119:1

The covenant of works leaves men full of fears and doubts. The covenant of works rested upon the strength of man's inherent righteousness; though in innocence perfect, yet was subject to change. Adam was created holy, but changeable: he had power to stand and power to fall. He had a stock of original righteousness to begin the world with, but he was not sure he would not break. He steered right in the time of innocence; but he was not so secure that he might not dart against the rock of temptation, and he and his posterity be shipwrecked. So the covenant of works must leave jealousies and doubt in Adam's heart; he had no security given him that he should not fall from that glorious state.

The covenant of works being broken by sin, man's condition was very deplorable and desperate. He was left helpless; there was no place for repentance. The justice of God being offended set all the other attributes against him. Adam lost his righteousness, his anchor of hope, and his crown. There was no way for relief unless God would find out such a way as neither man nor angel could devise.

God's glory made a covenant with dust and ashes; He bound Himself to us and gave life in case of obedience. For Him to enter into covenant with us was a sign of friendship and a royal act of favor.

To be a Perfect Pattern of Sanctity

Man being in honor abideth not:
He is like the beasts that perish.

PSALM 49:12

God entered into covenant with man, placing him in the garden of God, and because of the pleasure, it was called Paradise. Man had his choice of all the trees, except one; he had all kinds of precious stones, pure metals, rich cedars; he was a king upon the throne, and all the creation did respect him, as in Joseph's dream all his brothers' sheaves bowed to his sheaf. Man, in innocence, had all kinds of pleasure that might ravish his senses with delight and be as baits to lure him to serve and worship his Maker. He was full of holiness. Paradise was not more adorned with fruit than Adam's soul was with grace. He was the coin on which God had stamped His lively image. Light sparkled in his understanding, so that he was like an earthly angel; and his will and affections were full of order, tuning harmoniously to the will of God. Adam was a perfect pattern of sanctity. Adam had intimate communion with God and conversed with Him, as a favorite with his prince. Adam knew God's mind and had His heart. He not only enjoyed the light of the sun in Paradise, but the light of God's countenance. *Adam's teeth watered at the apple, and ever since it has made our eyes water.*

THE SURE COVENANT

*Now hath he obtained a more excellent ministry, by
how much also He is also the mediator of a better
covenant, which was established on better promises.*

HEBREWS 8:6

We can learn from Adam's fall how unable we are to stand in our own strength. If Adam, in the state of integrity, did not stand, how unable are we now, when the lock of our original righteousness is cut? If purified nature did not stand, how then shall corrupt nature? We need more strength to uphold us than our own.

See what a sad condition all unbelievers and unrepentant persons are in. As long as they continue in their sins, they continue under the curse, under the first covenant. Faith entitles us to the mercy of the second covenant; but while men are under the power of their sins, they are under the curse of the first covenant. If they die in that condition, they are damned to eternity.

The wonderful goodness of God, who was pleased when man had forfeited the first covenant, enters into a new covenant with him. Well it is called a covenant of grace, for it is as decorated with promises as heaven with stars. When the angels fell, God did not enter into a new covenant with them to be their God, but He let them lie broken. Yet He has entered into a second covenant with us, better than the first. It is better, because it is sure: it is made in Christ and cannot be reversed. Christ has engaged His strength to keep every believer.

The Covenant of Grace is Like a Court of Law

Believe on the Lord Jesus, and thou shalt be saved.

ACTS 16:31

Whosoever they are who look for righteousness and salvation by the power of their free will, or by the inherent goodness of their nature, or by virtue of their merit, they are all under the covenant of works. They do not submit to the righteousness of faith. Therefore they are bound to keep the whole law, and in case of failure, they are condemned. The covenant of grace is like a court of law to relieve the sinner and help him who is cast by the first covenant. Such will stand upon their own inherent righteousness, free will, and merit, but all under the first covenant of works, and they are in a perishing estate.

Let us labor by faith to get into the second covenant of grace, and then the curse of the first covenant will be taken away by Christ. If we once get to be heirs of the covenant of grace, we are in a better state than before. Adam stood on his own legs, and therefore he fell; we stand in the strength of Christ. Under the first covenant, the justice of God, as an avenger of blood, pursues us; but if we get into the second covenant, we are in the city of refuge. We are safe, and the justice of God is pacified toward us for all eternity.

31

SIN: AN ACCURSED THING

Sin is the transgression of the law.

1 JOHN 3:4

Sin is a violation of the law of God or a transgression of it. *To transgress* signifies "to go beyond one's bounds." The moral law keeps us within the bounds of duty. Sin takes us beyond our bounds.

The law of God is not the law of an inferior prince, but of Jehovah, who gives laws to angels and to men. It is a law that is just, and holy, and good. It is just: there is nothing in it unequal; holy, nothing in it impure; good, nothing in it prejudicial. There is no reason to break this law.

Sin is a heinous and deplorable thing: the complication of all evil, the spirits of mischief distilled. It is compared to the venom of serpents and the stench of burial places. The apostle uses this expression of sin: "exceeding sinful"(Romans 7:13) or, as it is in the Greek, "hyperbolically sinful." The devil would paint sin with the vermilion color of pleasure and profit that he may make it look good. But when the paint is pulled off, you may see its ugly face. We are apt to have slight thoughts of sin and say to it, as Lot of Zoar, "Is it not a little one?" (Genesis 19:20). But sin fetches its pedigree from hell; sin is of the devil. Satan was the first actor of sin and the first tempter to sin. Sin is the devil's firstborn.

1

SIN: STAMP OF THE DEVIL

Let us cleanse ourselves from all filthiness of the flesh and spirit.

2 CORINTHIANS 7:1

Sin is a defiling thing, not only a defection, but pollution. It is to the soul as rust is to gold, as a stain is to beauty. *Sin makes the soul red with guilt and black with filth.* Sin in Scripture is compared to a "menstruous cloth" (Isaiah 30:22) and to an epidemic disease. Joshua's filthy garments, in which he stood before the angel, were a type and symbol of sin. Sin has blotted God's image and stained the orient brightness of the soul. It makes God detest a sinner, and when a sinner sees his sin, he cannot bear himself. Sin drops poison on our holy things; it infects our prayers. The high priest was to make atonement for sin on the altar, to typify that our holiest services need Christ to make atonement for them. Duties of religion in themselves are good, but sin corrupts them, as the purest water is polluted by running through mud. If the leper, under the law, had touched the altar, the altar would not have cleansed him, but he would have defiled the altar. Sin stamps the devil's image on a man. Malice is the devil's eye; hypocrisy, his cloven foot. It turns a man into a devil. "Have not I chosen you twelve, and one of you is a devil?" (John 6:70). The persistence of sins harassing is the very thing Christians need to turn away from trusting God to cleanse our hearts to purity before Him.

2

SIN CAUSES GRIEF

Grieve not the holy Spirit of God.

EPHESIANS 4:30

How can the Spirit be grieved when He is God? He cannot be subject to any passion.

This is spoken metaphorically. Sin is said to grieve the Spirit because it is an injury offered to the Spirit. He takes it unkindly and, as it were, lays it to heart. And is it not much thus to grieve the Spirit? The Holy Ghost descended in the likeness of a dove, and sin makes this blessed dove mourn. Were it only an angel, we should not grieve him, much less the Spirit of God. Is it not sad to grieve our Comforter?

Sin is an act of defiance against God; it is walking opposite to heaven: "if ye will . . . walk contrary to me" (Leviticus 26:27). A sinner tramples upon God's law, crosses His will, and does all he can to affront, to spite God. The Hebrew word for sin, *pasha*, signifies rebellion: there is the heart of a rebel in every sin. "We will certainly do whatsoever thing goeth forth out of our own mouth, to burn incense unto the queen of heaven" (Jeremiah 44:17). Sin strikes at the Deity; sin is God's would-be murderer. Sin would dethrone God and un-God Him. If the sinner could help it, God would no longer be God. But through the Spirit in us, we are free from a sin-filled death. "For the wages of sin is death; but the gift of God is eternal life through Jesus Christ our Lord" (Romans 6:23).

3

SIN: A DISEASE REQUIRING THE GREAT PHYSICIAN

Is this thy kindness to thy friend?

2 SAMUEL 16:17

Sin is an act of disingenuousness and unkindness toward God. God feeds the sinner, holds evils from him, blesses him with mercy; but the sinner not only forgets God's mercies, but abuses them. He is the worse for mercy; like Absalom, who, as soon as David had kissed him and taken him into favor, plotted treason against him (2 Samuel 15:10). Like the mule, who kicks the cow after she has given it milk. God may upbraid the sinner by saying, "I have given thee thy health, strength, and estate; but thou requitest Me evil for good. Thou woundest Me with My own mercies. Is this thy kindness to thy friend? Did I give thee life to sin? Did I give thee wages to serve the devil?"

Sin is a disease: "the whole head is sick" (Isaiah 1:5). Some are sick of pride; others, of lust; others, of envy. Sin has distempered the intellectual part; it is leprosy in the head; it has poisoned the organs. The sinner's "conscience is defiled" (Titus 1:15). It is with a sinner as with a sick patient: his palate is distempered, and the sweetest things taste bitter to him. The Word, which is sweeter than the honeycomb (Psalm 19:10), tastes bitter to him; he makes "sweet for bitter" (Isaiah 5:20). This is a disease, and nothing can cure this disease but the blood of the Physician.

4

SERVING SIN

Oh, do not do this abominable thing that I hate.

JEREMIAH 44:4

Sin is an irrational thing that makes man act wickedly and foolishly. It is absurd and irrational to prefer the less before the greater; the pleasures of life before the rivers of pleasures at God's right hand for evermore. Is it not irrational to lose heaven for the satisfying or indulging of lust to gratify an enemy? In sin we do so. *When lust or anger burns in the soul, Satan warms himself at this fire.* Men's sins feed the devil.

Sin is a painful thing that costs men much labor. They "weary themselves to commit iniquity" (Jeremiah 9:5). It is more difficult for some to follow their sins than for others to worship God. While the sinner travails in sin, he brings forth sorrow; he is "serving divers lusts" (Titus 3:3). Not enjoying, but serving, because not only of the slavery in sin, but also the hard labor. Many men go to hell in the sweat of his brow.

Sin is the only thing God hates. If the sinner dies under God's hatred, he cannot be admitted into the celestial mansions. Will God let the man live with Him whom He hates? God will never lay a viper in His bosom. The feathers of the eagle will not mix with the feathers of other fowls. So God will not mix and incorporate with a sinner. Until sin is removed, there is no coming to where God is.

5

SIN'S EVIL EFFECTS

But God, who is rich in mercy . . . even when we were dead in sins,
hath quickened us together with Christ, (by grace ye are saved;).

EPHESIANS 2:4–5

See the evil of sin in the price paid for it. It cost the blood of God to expiate it. All the princes on earth, or angels in heaven, could not satisfy for sin; only Christ. Nay, Christ's active obedience was not enough to make atonement for sin, but He had to suffer upon the cross; for, without blood, there is no remission of sin. Oh, what an accursed thing is sin that Christ should die for it!

The evil of sin is not so much seen in that one thousand are damned for it, as that Christ died for it. Sin has degraded us of our honor. God made us in His own image, a little lower than the angels, but sin has debased us. Before Adam sinned, he was like a herald whom all reverence, because he carries the king's coat of arms. But pull it off and he is despised; no man regards him. Sin did this: it has plucked off our coat of innocence, and now it has debased us, turning our glory into shame.

Sin disquiets the peace of the soul. Whatever defiles, disturbs. As poison tortures the bowels and corrupts the blood, so sin does the soul. Sin breeds a trembling heart, creates fears, and "fear hath torment" (1 John 4:18). Sin makes sad convulsions in the conscience. And is not he to be ill cured who throws himself into hell for ease?

6

SIN: UNREPENTED, BRINGS FINAL DAMNATION

Hell . . . where their worm dieth not, and the fire is not quenched.

MARK 9:44

Sin produces all temporal evil. "Jerusalem hath grievously sinned, therefore she is removed" (Lamentations 1:8). It is the Trojan horse that has sword, famine, and pestilence in its belly. Sin's hot coal not only blackens, but burns. Sin creates all our troubles; it puts gravel into our bread, wormwood in our cup. Sin rots the name, consumes wealth, and destroys relationships. Sin shoots the flying roll of God's curses into a family and kingdom.

Cankers in the rose cause it to perish, and corruptions that breed in men's souls cause their damning. Sin, without repentance, brings the "second death," a death always dying (Revelation 20:14). Sin's pleasure will turn to sorrow at last, like the book the prophet did eat, sweet in the mouth, bitter in the belly. Sin brings the wrath of God, and nothing can quench that fire. Sin is deadly, yet many love it!

"How long will ye love vanity?" (Psalm 4:2). Sin is a dish men cannot refrain from even though it makes them sick. What pity when sweet affection and love should be poured upon so filthy a thing as sin! Sin brings a sting in the conscience, a curse into wealth, yet men love it. A sinner is a self-denier: in exchange for his sin, he will deny himself a part in heaven.

7

SIN: THE EMBODIMENT OF EVIL

For you have been my hope, O Sovereign LORD.

PSALM 75:1

There is more evil in the least sin than in the greatest bodily evils that can befall us.

There is more evil in a drop of sin than in a sea of affliction. Affliction is like a tear in a coat; sin, a prick at the heart. In affliction there is some good: in this lion there is some honey to be found. "It is good for me that I have been afflicted" (Psalm 119:71). There is no good in sin; it is the spirit and embodiment of evil. Sin is worse than hell; for the pains of hell are a burden to the creature only, but sin is a burden to God.

Sin is a great evil, so we should be thankful to God that He takes away our sins: "I have caused thine iniquity to pass from thee" (Zechariah 3:4). If you had a diseased body, how thankful would you be to have the illness taken away? Much more to have God take away the guilt of sin by pardoning grace and the power of sin by mortifying grace. Thank God that this sickness is "not unto death"; that God has changed your nature and, by grafting you into Christ, made you partake of the sweetness of that olive; and that sin, though it live, does not reign. Sin, the elder, serves grace, the younger.

8

ADAM'S SIN

She took of the fruit thereof, and did eat,
and gave also unto her husband.

GENESIS 3:6

Adam and Eve's first sin, where they fell, was in eating the forbidden fruit: they fell from their glorious innocence. Adam was perfectly holy; he had righteousness of mind and liberty of will to good. But he invented his own—and our—death; His fall was voluntary. He had a power not to fall. Free will was sufficient to repel temptation. The devil could not have forced him unless he had given his consent. *Satan was only a suitor to woo, not a king to compel;* but Adam gave away his own power and was lured into sin. Adam was lord of the world. "Have dominion over the fish of the sea, and over the fowl of the air, and over every living thing that moveth upon the earth" (Genesis 1:28). But he lost all as soon as he sinned and forfeited Paradise. Adam's fall was sudden; he did not long continue in his royal majesty.

Satan "was a murderer from the beginning" (John 8:44). As soon as Satan fell, he began to tempt mankind to sin; his was a murderous temptation. It appears Adam did not stay long in Paradise. Soon after his creation, the devil set upon him and murdered him by his temptation. The enemy is alive and actively seeking those whom he may destroy and kill.

9

GOD: OUR REFUGE

The eternal God is thy refuge,
and underneath are the everlasting arms . . .

DEUTERONOMY 33:27

The Tree of Life was placed in the midst of Paradise; it was one of the choicest in the garden. It is likely Adam would have eaten of this Tree of Life had not the serpent beguiled him with the Tree of Knowledge. I think Adam fell the day of his creation: he had not tasted the Tree of Life, that tree that was visible and had delicious fruit growing upon it.

"Man being in honor abideth not: he is like the beasts that perish" (Psalm 49:12). In the Hebrew, *abideth* signifies "to stay or lodge all night." Adam did not take up one night's lodging in Paradise, from which we learn the weakness of human nature.

Adam, in a state of integrity, quickly defected and lost the robe of innocence and the glory of Paradise. If our nature was weak when it was at the best, what is it now when it is at the worst? *If Adam did not stand when he was perfectly righteous, can we stand when sin cuts our original righteousness?* In hours, Adam sinned himself out of Paradise. How quickly would we sin ourselves into hell if we were not saved by a greater power than our own! But God puts underneath us His everlasting arms (Deuteronomy 33:27).

SATAN: A LIAR AND A MURDERER

My strength is made perfect in weakness.

2 CORINTHIANS 12:9

Adam, being left to himself, fell. How soon will we fall if God should leave us to ourselves! *A man without God's grace, left to himself, is like a ship in a storm, without pilot or anchor, and is ready to crash upon every rock.* Make this prayer to God: *Lord, do not leave me to myself. If Adam fell so soon who had strength, how soon shall I fall who have no strength?* "My strength is made perfect in weakness."

The devil crept into the serpent and spoke through the serpent. His trickery is worse than his darts. He dealt as an impostor, ushering in his temptation by lies: "Ye shall not surely die" (Genesis 3:4) and that God did envy our first parents their happiness. "God doth know, that in the day ye eat thereof, then your eyes shall be opened" (v. 5).

It is God's envying your happiness that He forbids you this tree. They should be made like unto God: "Ye shall be as gods" (v. 5). Here was his tack in tempting: the devil was first a liar; then a murderer.

Our first parents were not confirmed in their obedience and not fixed in their sphere of holiness. Though they had a possibility of standing, they had not an impossibility of falling; they were holy, but changeable. Satan's subtleness is seen in tempting our first parents before they were confirmed in their obedience.

11

GOD SPEAKS TRUTH

Ye shall not surely die.

GENESIS 3:4

Satan's strategy in tempting our first parents was that he put upon Eve first because he thought she was less able to resist. Satan broke over the hedge where it was weakest; he knew he could easily worm his way in and wind himself into her by temptation. Satan observes where there is a breach, or how he may enter with more skill, as he did to Eve. He tempted Eve first, because he knew, if once he could prevail with her, she would easily draw her husband. Thus the devil handed over a temptation to Job by his wife. "Curse God, and die" (Job 2:9). Satan knew a temptation coming to Adam from his wife would be more effective and would be less suspected. Sometimes relations prove temptations. A wife may be a snare when she dissuades her husband from doing his duty or entices him to evil. Ahab sold himself "to work wickedness in the sight of the Lord, whom Jezebel his wife stirred up" (I Kings 21:25). She blew the coals and made his sin flame even more. Satan's clever strategy was in tempting Adam through his wife; Satan thought she would draw him to sin.

Satan's subtleness in tempting was in assaulting Eve's faith. He would persuade her that God had not spoken truth: This was Satan's masterpiece, to weaken her faith. When he had shaken that, and had brought her once to distrust, then she yielded and put forth her hand to evil.

12

TO DIE, CONTINUE TO DIE, AND EVENTUALLY DIE

*But of the tree of the knowledge of good
and evil, thou shalt not eat of it:for in the day
that thou eatest thereof thou shalt surely die.*

GENESIS 2:17

When Adam was invested in all his glory, the devil cruelly, on the day of Adam's coronation, dethroned him, bringing him and all his posterity under a curse. Satan has an implacable antagonism against us, and that hostility can never be reconciled. So much for the occasion of Adam's sin, or his being tempted by the serpent.

The sin itself — "eating the forbidden fruit" —was heinous, and that appears three ways: in respect of the person who committed it, the aggravation of the sin, and the dreadfulness of the effect. Adam had excellent and noble endowments; he was illumined with knowledge, embellished with holiness. He knew his duty, and it was as easy to him to obey God's command as to know it. He might have chosen whether he would sin or not, yet he willfully did eat of the forbidden tree when he was tempted.

The aggravation of Adam's sin was but the seizing of an apple. Was it such a great matter to pluck an apple? It was against an infinite God. It was a voluminous sin, so there were many sins in this one sin of Adam. It was a big-bellied sin, a chain with many links that was against God Almighty. Oh, the weight of sin!

13

UNBELIEF!

The woman saw that the tree was good for food . . .
she took of the fruit thereof, and did eat.

GENESIS 3:6

Adam and Eve did not believe God that they would die the death in the day they ate of that tree. They did not believe they should die; they were not persuaded such fair fruit had death at its door. Their unbelief made God a liar; they believed the devil rather than God.

Un-thankfulness is the epitome of all sin. Adam's sin was committed in the midst of Paradise. God had enriched him with mercies, had stamped His own image upon him, making him lord of the world, and had given him every tree of the garden to eat, with one exception, not to take of that tree! This was ingratitude; it was like the dye to the wool that makes it crimson. When Adam's eyes were opened and he saw what he had done, he was ashamed and hid himself. How could he look God in the face without blushing!

In Adam's sin was discontent. Had he not been discontent, he would never have sought to have altered his condition. Adam, one would think, had enough: he differed but little from the angels, he had the robe of innocence to clothe him, and he had the glory of Paradise to crown him. Yet he was not content: he would have more; he would be above the ordinary rank of creatures. How wide was Adam's heart, that a whole world could not fill it!

14

PRIDE, DISOBEDIENCE, CURIOSITY, AND WANTONNESS

*But of the tree of the knowledge of good
and evil, thou shalt not eat of it.*

GENESIS 2:17

Pride, in that he would be like God, was in Adam's sin. This worm, that was but newly crept out of the dust, now aspired after Deity. "Ye shall be as gods," said Satan, and Adam hoped to have been so indeed. He supposed that the tree of knowledge would have anointed his eyes and made him omniscient. But, by climbing too high, he fell to the bottom.

Adam would eat of the tree even though it cost him his life. Such disobedience is a sin against equity. It is right we should serve Him from whom we have our subsistence. God gave Adam his allowance, therefore it was but right he should give God his allegiance. How could God endure to see His laws trampled on before His face? This made him place a flaming sword at the end of the garden.

Adam meddled with that which was out of his sphere and did not belong to him. Adam would be prying into God's secrets and tasting what was forbidden.

Though Adam had a choice of all the other trees, yet his palate grew wanton, and he must have this tree. Like Israel, God sent them manna, angels' food, but they had a hankering after quails. It was not enough that God supplied their wants unless He should satisfy their lusts. Adam had not only for necessity, but for delight, yet his wanton palate lusted after forbidden fruit.

15

Sacrilege, Murder, and Presumption

*The voice of thy brother's blood crieth
unto me from the ground.*

Genesis 4:10

The tree of knowledge was not Adam's, but he ate of it sacrilegiously, robbing God of His due. It was a crime for Adam to steal fruit from that tree that God had peculiarly enclosed for Himself.

Adam was a public person: his posterity was involved and wrapped up in him. By sinning he destroyed all his posterity if free grace had not stepped in. If Abel's blood cried so loud in God's ears, how loud did the blood of all Adam's posterity cry against him for vengeance!

Adam presumed on God's mercy: he blessed himself, saying he should have peace; though he did transgress, saying he should not die; that God would sooner reverse His decree than punish him. This was great presumption. What a heinous sin was Adam's breach of covenant!

We are apt to have slight thoughts of sin and say it is but a little one. How many sins were in Adam's sin! Oh, take heed of any sin! As many works are bound in one volume, so there may be many sins in one sin. The dreadfulness of the effect has corrupted man's nature. One drop could poison a whole sea! And how deadly is that sin of Adam, that could poison all mankind, and bring a curse upon them, till it is taken away by Him who was made a curse for us.

16

ORIGINAL SIN

By one man sin entered into the world, and death by sin.

ROMANS 5:12

The covenant was made with Adam, for himself and for his posterity. All mankind descending from him, by ordinary generation, sinned in him and fell with him in his first transgression.

Adam was a representative person: while he stood, we stood; when he fell, we fell. We sinned in Adam: "Wherefore, as by one man sin entered into the world, and death by sin; and so death passed upon all men, for that all have sinned" (Romans 5:12). Adam was the head of mankind, and being guilty, we are guilty, as the children of a traitor have their blood stained.

When Adam fell, all mankind fell with him. Why, when one angel fell, did not all fall? Angels, called the morning stars, had no relation to one another; they have no dependence one upon another. We were in Adam's loins, a part of him as a child is a branch of the parent. Therefore when he sinned, we sinned.

Adam's sin is ours by propagation. The guilt of Adam's sin is imputed to us, and the depravity and corruption of his nature are transmitted to us. This is that which we call original sin: "In sin did my mother conceive me" (Psalm 51:5). Adam's leprosy cleaves to us. It is said to be the "old man" (Ephesians 4:22); not that it is weak, as old men are, but for its long standing and for its deformity. In old age the fair blossoms of beauty fall. So original sin is the old man, because it has withered our beauty and made us deformed in God's eye.

AN APPETITE FOR THE FORBIDDEN

How much more abominable and filthy is man,
which drinketh iniquity like water?

JOB 15:16

Original lust is called the law of sin, and it has the power of a law that binds the subject to allegiance. Men have needs to do what sin will have them, when they have both the love of sin to draw them and the law of sin to force them.

We lack righteousness that should be ours: We have lost that excellent quintessential frame of soul that we once had. Sin has cut the lock of original purity, where our strength lay. Original sin has contaminated and defiled our virgin nature.

That sin has poisoned the spring of our nature; it turned beauty into leprosy and the azure brightness of our souls into midnight darkness.

Original sin has become co-natural to us. A man, by nature, sins. Though there were no devil to tempt, no bad examples to imitate, there is such an innate principle in him that he cannot forbear sinning. In original sin there is an aversion from good. Man has a desire to be happy, yet he opposes that which promotes his happiness, a disgust of holiness, and he hates to be reformed. Since we fell from God, we have no mind to return to Him. The natural bias of the soul is bad. God has set flaming swords to stop men in their sin, yet they go on in it, showing what a strong appetite they have for the forbidden fruit.

18

THE NATURE OF ORIGINAL SIN

The whole head is sick, and the whole heart is faint.

ISAIAH 1:5

The universality of original sin is poison diffusing itself into all the parts and powers of the soul. Like a sick patient whose feet are infected with gangrene, his lungs are perished; infected Christians have gangrened souls until Christ, who made medicine of His blood, cures us.

Original sin depraved our intellectual part. Just as in the creation "darkness was upon the face of the deep" (Genesis 1:2), so it is with the understanding: darkness is upon the face of this deep. There is salt in every drop of the sea, bitterness in every branch of wormwood, so there is sin in our senses. The mind is darkened; we know little of God. Ever since Adam ate of the Tree of Knowledge and his eyes were opened, we lost our eyesight. Besides ignorance in the mind, there is error and mistake; we do not judge things rightly; we put bitter for sweet, and sweet for bitter. There is much pride, arrogance, and prejudice, and much fleshly logical thinking: "How long shall thy vain thoughts lodge within thee?" (Jeremiah 4:14).

Original sin defiled the heart and made it deadly wicked. It is a lesser hell. In the heart are legions of lusts, stubbornness, infidelity, and hypocrisy boiling as the sea with passion and revenge. "Madness is in their heart while they live" (Ecclesiastes 9:3). The heart is the devil's workhouse, where all mischief is framed.

19

MAN'S FREE WILL

Now then it is no more I that do it,
but sin that dwelleth in me.

ROMANS 7:17

Defiance of authority is the seat of rebellion. The sinner crosses God's will to fulfill his own. In the will there is a rooted enmity against holiness; it is like an iron tendon refusing to bend to God. Where is the freedom of the will, when it is so full not only of unwillingness, but opposition to what is spiritual?

The affections, as the strings of a viol, are out of tune. They are the lesser wheels, which are strongly carried by the will, the master wheel. Our affections are set on wrong objects. Our love is set on sin; our joy, on the creature. Our affections are naturally as a sick man's appetite, who desires things that are toxic and hurtful to him; he calls for wine in a fever. So we have impure desires instead of holy longings.

The adhesion of original sin cleaves to us so that we cannot get rid of it. Paul shook the viper from his hand (Acts 28:3–5), but we cannot shake off this inbred corruption. It may be compared to a wild fig tree growing on a wall, the roots of which are pulled up, and yet there are some fibers of it in the joints of the stonework, which will not be eradicated, but will sprout forth until the wall is pulled apart. Original desire comes not as a lodger for a night, but as an indweller.

20

SIN HINDERS WORSHIP

The good that I would I do not.

ROMANS 7:19

All the dullness and deadness in religion is the fruit of original sin. This it is what rocks us asleep in duty. Sin is compared to a weight. A man with weights tied to his legs cannot run fast.

Original sin, though dormant in the soul and a spring that runs underground, often breaks forth unexpectedly. Christian, you cannot believe that evil which is in your heart, and which will break forth suddenly if God should leave you. "Is thy servant a dog, that he should do this great thing?" (2 Kings 8:13). Is His servant a dog? Yes, and worse than a dog when that original corruption within is stirred up. If one had come to Peter and said, "Peter, within a few hours thou will deny Christ," he would have said, "Is thy servant a dog?" Peter did not know his own heart, nor how far that corruption within would prevail upon him. The sea may be calm and look clear, but when the wind blows, it rages and foams! Though your heart seems good, when temptation blows, how may original sin discover itself, making you foam with lust and passion! Who would have thought to have found adultery in David, and drunkenness in Noah, and cursing in Job? If God leave a man to himself, how suddenly and scandalously may original sin break forth in the holiest men on the earth!

21

SIN, LIKE A PULSE EVER BEATING

What I hate, that do I.

ROMANS 7:15

Original sin mixes and incorporates itself with our duties. As the hand that is paralytic cannot move without shaking, as wanting some inward strength, so we cannot do any holy action without sinning, as wanting a principle of original righteousness. As whatever the leper touched became unclean, such leprosy is original sin; it defiles our prayers and tears. Though I do not say that the holy duties and good works of the regenerate are sins, for that were to reproach the Spirit of Christ, by which they are wrought; yet the best works of the godly have sin cleaving to them. Christ's blood alone makes atonement for our holy things.

There is some unbelief mixed with faith, lukewarmness with zeal, pride with humility. As weak lungs cause asthma or shortness of breath, so original corruption has infected our hearts, and graces breathe faintly.

Original sin is a vigorous, active principle within us. It does not lie still, but is ever stirring us up to evil; it is an inmate out of control. How came Paul to do that which he hated? Original sin irritated and stirred him up to it. Original sin is like quicksilver, always in motion. When we are asleep, sin is awake in dreams. Original sin makes the mind plot evil and the hands to do the work. It has in it a principle of restlessness, not of tranquility; it is like the pulse, ever beating.

22

ORIGINAL SIN: THE CAUSE OF ALL ACTUAL SIN

*Hew the tree down, and destroy it; yet leave
the stump of the roots thereof in the earth.*

DANIEL 4:23

Original sin is the kindling wood of sin and the womb in which all actual sins are conceived, and so comes murders, adulteries, and plunderings. Actual sins may be more scandalous, but original sin is more heinous; the cause is more than the effect and not perfectly cured in this life.

Though grace does subdue sin, it does not wholly remove it. We are like Christ, having the first fruits of the Spirit, yet we are unlike Him, having the remainders of the flesh. Original sin is like a tree: though the branches and the trunk are cut down, the stumps and root of the tree are left. Though the Spirit is still breaking and cutting down sin in the godly, the stump of original sin is left, like a sea that will not, in this life, be dried up.

God shows the power of His grace in the weakest believer. Grace shall prevail against a torrent of corruption. Corruption is ours, but the grace is God's.

God leaves original corruption to make us long for heaven, where there shall be no sin to defile and no devil to tempt. When Elijah was taken up to heaven, his mantle dropped off (2 Kings 2:13); when the angels shall carry us up to heaven, the mantle of sin shall drop off. We shall never more complain of an aching head or an unbelieving heart.

23

GRACE PURIFIES BUT DOES NOT PERFECT

There is not a just man upon earth,
that doeth good, and sinneth not.

ECCLESIASTES 7:20

Original sin is propagated to us and is inherent in us while we live here. It proves wrong those who say they are without sin and hold to perfection, showing pride and ignorance. The seeds of original sin remain in the best. Though grace purifies human nature, it does not perfect it.

The apostles say of believers that their "old man is crucified" (Romans 6:6) and they are "dead indeed unto sin" (Romans 6:11). They are dead spiritually, dead as to the guilt of it and the power of it; the love of sin is crucified.

They are dead to sin spiritually. A man sentenced to death is dead in law, so they are legally dead to sin. A sentence of death has gone out against sin. It shall die and drop into the grave; at present, sin has its life lengthened. Only the death of the body can free us from the body of this death.

Let us take to heart original sin, being deeply humbled by it. Sin is an active principle in us, stirring us up to evil. Original sin is worse than all actual sin: the fountain is more than the stream, the nature poisoned. A river may have clear streams, but vermin at the bottom. You carry a hell inside; you do nothing, but you defile it. Your heart defiles the purest water that runs through it. Though regenerate, there is much of the old man in the new man. Oh, how original sin should humble us!

24

GRACE REPELS SIN

*And God saw that the wickedness of man was
great in the earth, and that every imagination of
the thoughts of his heart was only evil continually.*

GENESIS 6:5

God left original sin in us, because He would have it as a thorn in
our side to humble us. God leaves original sin to pull down the
plumes of pride. Under our silver wings of grace are black feet.

Let the sense of this make us daily look up to heaven for help.
Beg Christ's blood to wash away the guilt of sin and His Spirit to
mortify the power of it; beg further degrees of grace. Though grace
cannot make sin nonexistent, it makes it not to reign; though grace
cannot expel sin, it can repel it. And for our comfort, where grace
makes a combat with sin, death shall make a conquest.

Let original sin make us walk with continual jealousy and
watchfulness over our hearts. The sin of our nature is like a sleeping lion, the least thing that awakens it makes it rage. Though the
sin of our nature seems quiet, and lies as fire hid under the embers,
yet if it be a little stirred and blown up by a temptation, how quickly
may it flame forth into scandalous evils! Therefore, we need always
to walk watchfully: "I say to you all, Watch" (Mark 13:37). A wandering heart needs a watchful eye.

MAN'S MISERY BY THE FALL

They that hated them ruled over them.

PSALM 106:41

Mankind by the Fall lost communion with God; we are under His wrath and curse, and so made liable to the miseries in life, to death itself, and to the pains of hell forever.

We "were by nature the children of wrath" (Ephesians 2:3). Adam left an unhappy portion to his posterity, sin. There is misery ensuing from original sin: Sin put Adam and us all out of favor with God. When we lost God's image, we lost His acquaintance. God's banishing Adam out of Paradise showed how sin has banished us out of God's love and favor.

By nature we are under the power of Satan, who is called "the prince of the power of the air" (Ephesians 2:2). Before the Fall, man was a free citizen, now a slave; before, a king on the throne, now in chains. Man is enslaved to the one who hates him. By sin we are enslaved to Satan, who is a hater of mankind and who writes all his laws in blood. A sinner before conversion is under Satan's command, so he does all the devil's drudgery. No sooner Satan tempts, but he obeys. As the ship is at the command of the pilot, who steers it which way he will, so is the sinner at the command of Satan—and he steers the ship into hell's mouth. The devil rules all the powers and faculties of a sinner.

26

Sin is Founded upon Ignorance

The lusts of your father ye will do.

John 8:44

Satan rules man's understanding. He blinds men with ignorance and then rules them. Satan can do what he will with an ignorant man; because man does not see the error of his way, the devil can lead him into any sin.

Satan rules the will: he cannot force the will, but he can, by temptation, draw it. He woos hearts, and we obey him. When the devil spurs a sinner by temptation, he will hedge and break all God's laws, that he may obey Satan. Where then is free will if Satan has such power over the will? No member of the body is not at the devil's service. Satan is the worst tyrant. Some tyrants rule the body; Satan, rules the conscience. Others have some pity on their slaves, but Satan is a merciless tyrant, allowing no rest. What pains did Judas take? The devil would let him have no rest till he had betrayed Christ, and afterwards stained his hands in his own blood.

Satan is said to work effectually in the children of disobedience. If the devil bids a man lie or steal, he does not refuse; what is worse, he willingly obeys this tyrant. Sinners are willing to be slaves: they will not take their freedom; they kiss their chains.

Fight to get out of this deplorable condition, to get out from under the power of Satan.

27

REPENT AND BE FREE!

*To open their eyes, and to turn [men] from darkness
to light, and from the power of Satan unto God.*

ACTS 26:18

If any of your children were slaves, you would give great sums of money to purchase their freedom. When your souls are enslaved, will you not labor for their freedom? The gospel proclaims a jubilee to captives. Sin binds men; the gospel looses them. The gospel star leads you to Christ. If you get Christ, then you are made free, though not from the being of sin, yet from Satan's tyranny. "If the Son therefore shall make you free, ye shall be free indeed" (John 8:36)! You hope to be kings to reign in heaven. Will you let Satan reign in you now? Never think to be kings when you die and slaves while you live. *The crown of glory is for conquerors, not for captives.* Get out of Satan's jurisdiction; get your chains of sin filed off by repentance.

By "children of wrath," the apostle means "heirs of wrath," exposed to God's displeasure. Sin broke the knot of friendship with God; we are now bound over to the governing body and have become children of wrath. "The king's wrath is as the roaring of a lion" (Proverbs 19:12). God's wrath is infinite; all other is but as a spark to a flame. Wrath in God is not a passion, as in us; but it is an act of God's holy will. He abhors sin and decrees to punish it.

28

HEIRS TO GOD'S BLESSINGS AND CURSES

And were by nature the children of wrath . . .

EPHESIANS 2:3

The wrath of God embitters afflictions in this life, for when sickness comes attended with God's wrath, it puts conscience into agony. The mingling of the fire with the hail made it most terrible (Exodus 9:24). So mingling God's wrath with affliction makes it torturing; it is the nail in the yoke. God's wrath, when a warning (as a shower hanging in the cloud), made Eli's ears tingle. What is it then when this wrath is executed?

While we are children of wrath, we have nothing to do with any of the promises. They are as the Tree of Life, bearing different fruit, but we have no right to pluck one leaf. We are strangers to the covenant of promise (Ephesians 2:12); the promises are as a fountain sealed. While we are in the state of nature, we see nothing but the flaming sword. While children of wrath, we are heirs to all God's curses (Galatians 3:10). How can the sinner eat and drink in that condition? The sword of God's wrath and curse hangs every moment over a sinner's head. There is a curse on the sinner's name, on his soul, on his estate and posterity, and on the ordinances. Thus it is before conversion: as the love of God makes every bitter thing sweet, so the curse of God makes every sweet thing bitter.

29

HEIRS OF WRATH

Jesus, which delivered us from the wrath to come.

1 THESSALONIANS 1:10

Is this current estate to be rested in? If a man be fallen under the King's displeasure, will he not labor to win himself into His favor? Oh, let us flee from the wrath of God and fly to Jesus Christ! There is none else to shield off the wrath of God from us.

All the troubles in man's life are bitter fruits of original sin. The sin of Adam has made the creature "subject to vanity" (Romans 8:20). Is it not a part of the creature's vanity that all the comforts below will not fill the heart, any more than the mariner's breath can fill the sails of a ship? "In the fullness of his sufficiency he shall be in straits" (Job 20:22). There is still something wanting, and a man would have more. The heart is always thirsty and not satisfied.

Solomon put all the creatures into a crucible; and when he came to extract the spirit and quintessence, there was nothing but froth: "all was vanity" (Ecclesiastes 2:11). It is vexing vanity; not only emptiness, but bitterness. Our life is labor and sorrow: we come into the world with a cry and go out with a groan. Some have said that they would not live the life they have lived over again, because their life has had more water of tears than wine of joy. "Man is born unto trouble" (Job 5:7). Every one is not born heir to land, but he is born heir to trouble. We do not finish our troubles in this life, but by God's grace we change them.

30

Sin Dissolves Harmony

Sin entered into the world, and death by sin.

Romans 5:12

Where we look for comfort, there is a cross. Where we expect honey, there we taste wormwood. The apostle speaks of some who entertained angels in their houses (Hebrews 13:2); but how often, instead of entertaining angels in their houses, do some entertain devils! All this is but the apple's sour core of which Adam and Eve ate, the fruit of original sin. The deformities and diseases of the body are from sin: famine and a new crop of fevers oppressed the lands. There would never have been a stone in the kidneys if there had not been first a stone in the heart. The death of the body is the fruit and result of original sin. Adam was made immortal conditionally: if he had not sinned. Sin dug Adam's grave. Death is terrible to nature. But the apostle says, "That as sin hath reigned unto death, even so might grace reign through righteousness unto eternal life by Jesus Christ our Lord" (Romans 5:21). If Adam had not eaten of the Tree of Knowledge, he had not died: "In the day that thou eatest thereof thou shalt surely die" (Genesis 2:17): implying, if Adam had not eaten, he should not have died. Oh, then, see the misery ensuing upon original sin! Sin dissolves the harmony and good temperature of the body, and pulls its frame in pieces.

31

THE SECOND DEATH

In whom we have redemption through his blood.

EPHESIANS 1:7

Original sin without repentance exposes us to hell and damnation. This is the second death. Two things are in it. Punishment of loss: the soul is banished from the presence of God where there is fullness of joy. Punishment of sense: the sinner feels scalding vials of God's wrath, penetrating, abiding, and reserved. How terrible when a little of God's anger is kindled and a spark flies into a man's conscience in this life! What will it be when God stirs up all His anger? Hell is the accent and emphasis of misery; judgment without mercy. What flames of wrath, seas of vengeance, and rivers of brimstone are poured out upon the damned! One glimpse of hell fire is enough to make notorious sinners turn Christian. These hell torments are forever: "They shall seek death, and shall not find it" (Revelation 9:6). The breath of the Lord kindles that fire: "And the smoke of their torment ascendeth up for ever and ever, and they have no rest day nor night" (Revelation 14:11). Thank original sin for this fire!

How are all believers bound to Jesus Christ, who has freed them from that misery to which sin has exposed them! Sin brought trouble and a curse into the world: Christ sanctified the trouble and removed the curse. He not only freed believers from misery, but He purchased for them a crown of glory and immortality.

1

COVENANT OF GRACE

I will make an everlasting covenant with you.

ISAIAH 55:3

God entered into a covenant of grace to deliver the elect out of sin and misery, to bring them into a state of grace by a Redeemer. Man, by his fall, plunged into a labyrinth of misery, and having no way to recover himself, God was pleased to enter into a new covenant with him and restore him to life.

There is a new covenant ratified between God and the elect. It is a solemn agreement made between God and fallen man, where the Lord is our God and He makes us His people.

It is called the covenant of peace (Ezekiel 37:26) because it seals up reconciliation between God and humble sinners. Before this covenant, there was nothing but hostility. God did not love us, for a creature that offends cannot be loved by a holy God; and we did not love Him, since a God that condemns cannot be loved by a guilty creature. So there was war on both sides. God found a way in the new covenant to reconcile differing parties, so it is fitly called the covenant of peace.

It is called a covenant of grace, for it was of grace that, when we had forfeited the first covenant, God entered into a new one, after we had cast away ourselves. Oh, the free grace of God that He should confer with sinners, and set His wisdom and mercy to work to bring rebels into the bond of the covenant!

2

A ROYAL CHARTER

I will establish an everlasting covenant with you.

EZEKIEL 16:60 NASB

It is called a covenant of grace, because it is a royal charter made up of terms of grace. That He will give us a will to accept the mercy of the covenant and strength to perform the conditions of the covenant—all is pure grace.

God makes a covenant with us out of indulgence, favor, and regard to us. A tyrant will not enter into a covenant with slaves: he will not show them such respect. God's entering into a covenant with us, to be our God, is a dignity He grants us: a covenant of honors, a note of distinction between God's people and heathens.

God makes a covenant with us, to tie us firmly to Him; as it is called in Ezekiel, the "bond of the covenant" (20:37). God knows we have slippery hearts; therefore He will have a covenant to bind us. It is horrid transgression to go away from God after covenant. It is perjury to depart from God after solemn covenant.

How does the covenant of grace differ from the first covenant? The terms of the first covenant were more strict and severe. The least failing would have made the covenant with Adam null and void, but many failings do not annul the covenant of grace. The least sin trespasses against the covenant, but does not void it. How sad, if, as often as we break covenant with God He should break covenant with us; but God will not take advantage of every failing, but in "anger remember mercy."

3

Faith: A Humble Grace

Jesus the mediator of the new covenant.

HEBREWS 12:24

The first covenant, broken, allowed sinners no remedy or hope, but the new covenant allows a remedy: it leaves room for repentance, and it provides a mediator.

The first covenant was all about working; the second is about believing (Romans 4:3–5). Works are required in the covenant of grace: "This is a faithful saying . . . that they which have believed in God might be careful to maintain good works" (Titus 3:8). But the covenant of grace does not require works in the same manner as the covenant of works did. In the first covenant, works were required as the condition of life; in the second, they are required only as the signs of life. In the first, works were required as grounds of salvation; in the new covenant, they are required as evidences of our love to God. In the first, they were required for the justification of us; in the new, as the manifestation of our grace.

The main condition of the covenant of grace is faith, and faith is more the condition of the new covenant than any other grace in order to exclude glorying in the creature. If works were the condition of the covenant, man could say, "It is *my* righteousness that saved me." But if it is of faith, where is boasting? Faith takes all from Christ and gives all the glory to Christ; it is a most humble grace. Hence it is that God has singled out this grace to be the condition of the covenant.

4

In Covenant with God

God resisteth the proud . . .

1 Peter 5:5

If faith is a condition of the covenant of grace, it excludes desperate sinners from the covenant. There is a covenant of grace, but did you ever know a bond without a condition? The condition of the covenant is faith, and if thou have no faith, thou have no more to do with the covenant than a foreigner or a country farmer with the city charter.

God's amazing goodness caused Him to enter into covenant with us. He never entered into covenant with angels when they fell. It was much condescension in God to enter into covenant with us in a state of innocence, but more so when we were in a state of antagonism. In this covenant of grace, we may see the cream of God's love and the working of His bowels to sinners. This is a marriage covenant: "I am married unto you, saith the LORD" (Jeremiah 3:14). In the new covenant, God makes Himself over to us, and what more can He give? He makes over His promises to us, and what better bonds can we have?

God's covenant-people are a humble people: "Be clothed with humility" (1 Peter 5:5a). God's people esteem others better than themselves; they shrink into nothing in their own thoughts. When God's people shine most in grace, they are covered with the veil of humility. Pride excludes from the covenant, for "God resisteth the proud" and sure such are not in covenant with God whom he resists.

5

GOD'S COVENANT PEOPLE

Thy people shall be willing in the day of thy power.

PSALM 110:3

A people in covenant with God are a willing people; though they cannot serve God perfectly, they serve Him willingly. They do not grudge God a little time spent in His worship nor hesitate or murmur at sufferings; they will go through a sea and a wilderness if God calls. This spontaneity and willingness are from the power of God's Spirit which does not force, but sweetly draws the will; this willingness in Christianity makes all our services accepted. God does sometimes accept willingness without the work, but never the work without willingness.

God's covenant people are a consecrated people; they have holiness to the Lord written upon them. "Thou art holy people unto the LORD thy God" (Deuteronomy 7:6). God's covenant people are separated from the world and sanctified by the Spirit. God's people are not only washed from gross sins, but adorned with holiness of heart: they bear not only God's name, but His image. Holiness is God's stamp; if He does not see this stamp upon us, He will not own us for His covenant people.

Christ is a mediator only for such as are in covenant. Till you are in covenant with God, there is no mercy. The mercy seat was placed upon the ark, and the mercy seat was no larger than the ark to show that the mercy of God reaches no further than the covenant.

The Covenant of Grace is Sure

He hath made with me an everlasting
covenant, ordered in all things, and sure.

2 Samuel 23:5

The excellencies of the covenant of grace make it a better covenant than the covenant made with Adam, because it is more friendly and promising. Those services that would have been rejected in the first covenant are accepted in the second. God accepts the will for the deed. Here sincerity is crowned in the covenant of grace: where we are weak, God will give strength; and where we are without funds, God will accept a guarantee.

It is a better covenant, because it is surer. The first covenant was not sure, and it stood upon a tottering foundation of works. Adam had no sooner a stock of righteousness to trade with, but he broke; but the covenant of grace is sure. It is confirmed with God's decree, and it rests upon two mighty pillars: the oath of God and the blood of God.

The covenant of grace has better privileges: it brings advancement. Our nature now is more elevated: we are raised to higher glory than in innocence, and we are advanced to sit upon Christ's throne (Revelation 3:21). We are, by virtue of the covenant of grace, nearer to Christ than the angels: they are His friends; we, His spouse. God is willing to be in covenant with you. Why does God woo and beseech you by His ambassadors to be reconciled if He were not willing to be in covenant?

7

HE IS OUR GOD, WE ARE HIS PEOPLE

They shall call on my name, and I will hear them: I will say,
It is my people: and they shall say, The LORD is my God.

ZECHARIAH 13:9

Some say, "I would eagerly be in covenant with God, but I have been a great sinner, and I fear God will not admit me into covenant." If you see your sins and dislike yourself for them, God will take you into covenant. As the sea covers great rocks, so God's covenant mercy covers great sins. Some of the Jews who crucified Christ had their sins washed away in His blood.

"But I am not worthy that God should admit me into covenant." It never came into God's thoughts to make a new covenant upon terms of worthiness. If God should show mercy to none but such as are worthy, then must He show mercy to none. But it is God's design in the new covenant to advance the riches of grace, to love us freely, and, when we have no worthiness of our own, to accept us through Christ's worthiness. Therefore let not unworthiness discourage you; it is not unworthiness that excludes any from the covenant, but unwillingness.

To be in covenant with God, we need to seek God in prayer and demand compassion from the Lord. The Lord has made an express promise that, upon our prayer to Him, the covenant should be ratified, He will be our God, and we shall be His people.

8

BLOOD ATONEMENT

Ye . . . are made nigh by the blood of Christ.

EPHESIANS 2:13

When in covenant with God, break off the covenant with sin. Will any king enter into covenant with that man who is in league with his enemies?

If you would enter into the bond of the covenant, get faith in the blood of the covenant. Christ's blood is the blood of atonement; believe in this blood and you are safe in God's mercy.

When in covenant with God, all your sins are pardoned: pardon is the crowning mercy. "Who forgiveth all thine iniquities . . . who crowneth thee with lovingkindness and tender mercies" (Psalm 103:3). "[I] will be their God . . . I will forgive their iniquity" (Jeremiah 31:33–34). Sin being pardoned, all wrath ceases. How terrible is it when a spark of God's wrath flies into a man's conscience, but sin forgiven, there is no more wrath. God does not appear now in the fire or earthquake, but covered with a rainbow full of mercy.

All temporal mercies are fruits of the covenant. Wicked men have mercies by Providence, not by virtue of a covenant; with God's permission, not with His love. But those in covenant have their mercies sweetened with God's love, and they swim to them in the blood of Christ. "Take two talents" (2 Kings 5:23). So says God to such as are in covenant: "Take two talents: take health, and take Christ with it; take riches, and take my love with them; take the venison, and take the blessing with it. Take two talents."

9

PLEAD THE COVENANT

As thou, Father, art in me, and I in thee,
that they also may be one in us.

JOHN 17:21

"Lord, thou hast promised to bruise Satan under my feet. Wilt thou suffer thy child to be worried?" Take off the roaring lion. If in need, plead the covenant: "Lord, wilt thou save me from hell and not from want, or give me a kingdom and deny me daily bread?"

If in covenant with God, all things work for your good. Every wind of Providence shall blow you nearer heaven. Affliction shall humble and purify. Afflictions add glory to the saints. The more the diamond is cut, the more it sparkles; the heavier the saints' crosses are, the heavier their crown.

When in covenant, you are forever in covenant. Those in covenant are elected, and God's electing love is unchangeable: "I will make an everlasting covenant with them, that I will not turn away from them . . . but I will put my fear in their hearts, that they shall not depart from me" (Jeremiah 32:40). God loves the saints, and He will not forsake them; the saints shall so fear God that they shall not forsake Him. It is a covenant of eternity made with believers: Christ is the head; they are the body. This is union, much like that union between God the Father and Christ. The union between Christ and the saints is inseparable, it can never be dissolved, or the covenant made void; so that you may die with comfort.

10

COVENANT COMMUNION

*For I am in a strait betwixt two, having a desire to depart,
and to be with Christ; which is far better*

PHILIPPIANS 1:23

Death breaks the union between the body and the soul, but perfects the union between Christ and the soul. This has made the saints desire death as the bride the wedding day.

To show you how you should walk who have tasted of covenant mercy, live as a people in covenant with God. You must love this God. His love to you calls for love. God's love is a free love. Why should God pass by others and take you into a league of friendship with Himself? In the law, God passed by the lion and eagle, and chose the dove; so He passes by the noble and mighty.

God's love is a full love. When God takes you into covenant, you are His, and His delight is in you. He gives you the key of all His treasure, He settles heaven and earth upon you, He gives you a bunch of grapes by the way, and He says, "Son, all I have is thine." And does not all this call for love?

The covenant has made you a royal nation; therefore be a holy people. Shine as lights in the world; live as earthly angels. God has taken you into covenant, that you and He may have communion together.

11

THE NEW COVENANT: THE BIBLE WITHIN THE BIBLE

Jesus the mediator of the New Covenant . . .

HEBREWS 12:24

Jesus Christ is the sum and embodiment of the gospel; the wonder of angels; the joy and triumph of saints. The name of Christ is sweet: it is music in the ear, honey in the mouth, and a cordial at the heart. Having spoken of the covenant of grace, I shall speak now of the Mediator of the covenant and the Restorer of lapsed sinners.

There are several names and titles in Scripture given to Christ, as the great restorer of mankind. Sometimes He is called a Savior: "Thou shalt call his name JESUS," (Matthew 1:21). The Hebrew word for *Jesus* signifies a Savior, and whom He saves from hell, He saves from sin. Where Christ is a Savior, He is a sanctifier: "He shall save his people from their sins" (Matthew 1:21). There is no other savior: "Neither is there salvation in any other" (Acts 4:12). There was one ark to save the world from drowning; so there is one Jesus to save sinners from hell. Christ alone is the wellspring of life. The ordinance is the channel that conveys salvation, but Christ is the spring that feeds it. "Neither is there salvation in any other."

12

CHRIST THE REDEEMER

The Redeemer Shall Come to Zion

ISAIAH 59:20

Christ is called a Redeemer, the Redeemer of the elect. "My redeemer liveth" (Job 19:25). The Hebrew word for *Redeemer* signifies "one who is related and has the right to redeem a mortgage." So Christ is like a relative to us, being our elder brother, and therefore has the best right to redeem us.

Christ is called a Mediator. The Greek word for *Mediator* signifies "a middle person, one making up the breach between two disagreeing parties." God and we were at variance by sin; now Christ is our Mediator. He reconciles us to God through His blood, so He is called the Mediator of the new covenant.

There is no communion between God and man but in and through a Mediator. Christ takes away the hostility in us, and the wrath of God, and makes peace. Nor is Christ a Mediator of reconciliation only, but an intercessor: "Christ is not entered into the holy places made with hands . . . but into heaven itself, now to appear in the presence of God for us" (Hebrews 9:24). His person is amiable; He is made up of all love and beauty. He is the image of His Father.

John 1:14 says, "The Word was made flesh." It is spoken of Christ the promised Messiah. Christ took our flesh, that the same nature which sinned might suffer; and "the Word was made flesh," that through the glass of His human nature we might look upon God.

13

JACOB'S LADDER

He knoweth our frame.

PSALM 103:14

As a word is the interpreter of the mind, revealing what is in a man's breast; so Jesus Christ reveals His Father's mind to us concerning the great matters of our salvation. Were it not for Christ's manhood, the sight of the Godhead would be formidable to us; but through Christ's flesh, we may look upon God without terror. Christ took our flesh, that He might know how to pity us; He knows what it is to be weak, sorrowful, tempted. He took our flesh that He might elevate our human nature with honor. Christ, having married our flesh, has exalted it above the angelic nature.

Christ may be fitly compared to Jacob's ladder, which reached to heaven: His human nature was the foot of the ladder, which stood upon earth; His divine nature, the top which reached to heaven. This is a grand article of our faith, and the Scripture is clear: Jesus is the mighty God, and He is of the same nature and essence with the Father. God the Father is called Almighty, and so is Christ: "the Almighty" (Revelation 1:8). God the Father is the heart-searcher, and so is Christ: "He knew what was in man" (John 2:25). God the Father is omnipresent, and so is Christ: "the Son of man which is in heaven" (John 3:13).

14

DIVINE WORSHIP

Let all the angels of God worship him.

HEBREWS 1:6

Divine worship belongs to the first person in the Trinity; so it does to Christ. Creation is proper to the Deity: a flower of Christ's crown. "By him were all things created" (Colossians 1:16). Invocation is proper to the Deity: this is given to Christ. "Lord Jesus, receive my spirit" (Acts 7:59). Is lying and trust peculiar to God the Father? This is given to Christ. "Ye believe in God, believe also in me" (John 14:1). Christ must be God, not only that the divine nature support the human from sinking under God's wrath, but giving value and weight to His sufferings.

Christ being God, His death and passion are praiseworthy. Christ's blood is called the blood of God, in Acts 20:28, because the person who was offered in sacrifice was God as well as man. This is an invincible support to believers; it was God who was offended, and it was God who satisfied. Thus Christ's person is in two natures.

Christ's two natures are in one person, God-man. "God was manifest in the flesh" (1 Timothy 3:16). Christ had a twofold substance, divine and human, yet not a twofold subsistence; both natures make but one Christ. So Christ's manhood is united to the Godhead in an ineffable manner; though there are two natures, yet but one person. But both the natures of Christ remain distinct, and yet make not two distinct persons, but one person; the human nature not God, yet one with God.

15

THE GRACE OF OUR MEDIATOR

The Word was made flesh . . . full of grace and truth.

JOHN 1:14

Christ is our Mediator. His graces are the sweet savor of His ointments. Christ, our blessed Mediator, had the anointing of the Spirit without measure (John 3:34). Grace in Christ is after a more eminent and glorious manner than it is in any of the saints.

Jesus Christ, our Mediator, has perfection in every grace (Colossians 1:19). He is a covering, magazine, and storehouse of all heavenly treasure, all fullness. This no saint on earth has: he may excel in one grace, but not in all. Abraham was eminent for faith, Moses for meekness; but Christ excels in every grace.

There is a never-failing fullness of grace in Christ. Grace in the saints is ebbing and flowing; it is not always in the same degree and proportion. At one time David's faith was strong; at another time, so faint and weak that you could hardly feel any pulse: "I said in my haste, I am cut off from before thine eyes" (Psalm 31:22). But grace in Christ is a never-failing fullness; it never becomes less. He never lost a drop of His holiness. What was said of Joseph in Genesis 49:23 may more truly be applied to Christ: "The archers shot at him, but his bow abode in strength." Men and devils shot at Him, but His grace remained in its full vigor and strength. "His bow abode in strength."

16

CHRIST, A TREASURY OF GRACE

Of his fullness have all we received, and grace for grace.

JOHN 1:16

God's grace is for us; the holy oil of the Spirit was poured on the head of this blessed Aaron that it might run down upon us. The saints have not grace to bestow on others. When the foolish virgins would have bought oil from their neighbor virgins, saying, "Give us of your oil; for our lamps are gone out," the wise virgins answered, "Not so; lest there be not enough for us and you" (Matthew 25:8–10). The saints have no grace to spare for others; but Christ diffuses His grace to others. Grace in the saints is as water in the vessel; grace in Christ is as water in the spring. Set a glass under a still, and it receives water from it, drop by drop. So the saints have the drops and influences of Christ's grace distilling upon them.

Christ, the Mediator, is a treasury of grace: "All my springs are in thee" (Psalm 87:7). I am guilty, and Thou hast blood to pardon me; polluted, Thou hast grace to cleanse me; sick unto death, Thou hast the balm of Gilead to heal me. Joseph opened all the storehouses of corn: Christ is our Joseph who opens the treasuries and storehouses of grace and communicates to us. He is sweet as the honeycomb. In Christ our Mediator there is a fullness of all grace; and Christ desires that we should come to Him for grace.

17

GODHEAD AND MAN UNITED

That I may win Christ, and be found in him,
not having mine own righteousness.

PHILIPPIANS 3:8–9

Admire the glory of this Mediator: He is God-man and co-essentially glorious with the Father. The Jews who saw Christ in the flesh did not see His Godhead; they saw the man, not the Messiah. The temple of Solomon within was embellished with gold. As travelers passed by, they saw the outside of the temple, but only the priests saw the glory within the temple. So believers only, made priests unto God, see Christ's glorious inside, the Godhead shining through the manhood.

If Christ be God-man in one person, then look unto Jesus Christ alone for salvation. If we could arrive at the highest degree of sanctification in this life, all that would not save us without looking to the merits of Him who is God. Our perfect holiness in heaven is not the cause of our salvation, but the righteousness of Jesus Christ. We may look to our graces as evidences of salvation, but to Christ's blood only as the cause.

All that Christ in either of His natures can do for believers, He will do. In His human nature He prays for them; in His divine nature He merits for them.

Admire the love of Christ our Mediator; that He should humble Himself, and take our flesh, that He might redeem us. Believers should put Christ in their bosom, as the spouse did, and they should have Jesus written in their heart.

18

CHRIST AS PROPHET

The LORD thy God will raise up unto thee a Prophet.

DEUTERONOMY 18:15

Christ's offices are Prophetic, Priestly, and Regal.

There are several names given to Christ as a Prophet. He is called "the Counselor" in Isaiah 9:6; "the messenger of the covenant" in Malachi 3:1; "a Lamp" in 2 Samuel 22:29; the "morning star" in Revelation 22:16. Jesus Christ is the great Prophet of His church. He is the best teacher; He makes all other teaching effectual. "Then opened he their understanding" (Luke 24:45). He not only opened the Scriptures, but opened their understanding. He teaches to profit. "I am the LORD thy God, which teacheth thee to profit" (Isaiah 48:17).

Christ teaches externally, by His Word. "Thy word is a lamp unto my feet" (Psalm 119:105). Such as pretend to have a light or revelation above the Word, or contrary to it, never had their teaching from Christ.

Christ teaches these sacred mysteries, inwardly, by the Spirit. "The natural man receiveth not the things of the Spirit of God . . . neither can he know them" (1 Corinthians 2:14). He knows not what it is to be transformed by the renewing of the mind (Romans 12:2), or what the inward workings of the Spirit mean. He does not see the deep things of God. He who is taught of Christ sees the secrets of the kingdom of heaven.

19

THE DISCERNMENT OF THINGS UNSEEN

We look not at the things which are seen,
but at the things which are not seen.

2 CORINTHIANS 4:18

Christ teaches us to see into our own hearts. Take lively wits, the greatest politicians who understand the mysteries of state, who know not the mysteries of their own hearts: they cannot believe the evil that is in them. The heart is a great deep, not easily comprehended. But when Christ teaches, He removes the veil of ignorance and lights a man into his own heart. Now that he sees swarms of vain thoughts, he blushes at how sin mingles with his duties, how stars are mixed with clouds; he prays that God would deliver him from himself.

A natural man sets up his happiness here and worships golden images; but he whom Christ has anointed has a spirit of discerning. He looks upon the creature and sees it to be empty and unsatisfying, not commensurate to a heaven-born soul. Solomon had put all the creatures into a still, and when he came to extract the spirit, all was vanity (Ecclesiastes 2:11). The apostle calls the vanity of vanity a show or vision, having no intrinsic goodness (1 Corinthians 7:31).

Christ gives the soul a sight of glory, a prospect of eternity. Moses saw him who is "invisible" (Hebrews 11:27). And the patriarchs saw a better country that was heavenly, where there were delights of angels, rivers of pleasure, the flower of joy, fully ripe and blown (Hebrews 11:16).

20

God's Grace is Irresistible

A certain woman named Lydia . . .
whose heart the Lord opened.

ACTS 16:14

Christ teaches the heart; others may teach the ear. All the dispensers of the Word can do is to work knowledge, but Christ works grace. They can give the light of the truth; Christ gives love of the truth. They can only teach what to believe; Christ teaches how to believe.

Christ gives us a taste of the Word. Ministers may set the food of the Word before you, but it is only Christ who can cause you to taste it. "Taste and see that the LORD is good" (Psalm 34:8). It is one thing to hear a truth preached, another to taste it; one thing to read a promise, another thing to taste it. David had a taste of the Word: "Thou hast taught me. How sweet are thy words unto my taste! yea, sweeter than honey to my mouth" (Psalm 119:102–103). The light of knowledge is one thing; to savor, another. Christ makes us taste a savouriness in the Word.

When Christ teaches, He makes us obey. Others may instruct, but cannot command obedience. The prophet had denounced judgments against the people of Judah, but they would not hear: "We will certainly do whatsoever thing goeth forth out of our own mouth, to burn incense unto the queen of heaven" (Jeremiah 44:17). When Christ comes to teach, He removes obstinacy; He not only informs the judgment, but He inclines the will. He comes with the light of His Word and the rod of His strength, making the stubborn sinner yield to Him. His grace is irresistible.

21

CHRIST THE TEACHER

Precept must be upon precept . . . and line upon line.
ISAIAH 28:10

Christ teaches easily; others teach with difficulty—difficulty in finding a truth and in impressing it. Some teach all their lives, but the Word makes no impression. They complain, "I have laboured in vain, I have spent my strength for nought" (Isaiah 49:4); but Christ the great Prophet teaches with ease. He can, with the least touch of His Spirit, convert: He can say, "Let there be light"; with a word he can convey grace.

When Christ teaches, He makes men willing to learn. Men may teach others, but they have no mind to learn. "Fools despise . . . wisdom and instruction" (Proverbs 1:7). They rage at the Word, as if a patient should rage at the physician; backward are men to their own salvation. Christ makes His people a "willing" people (Psalm 110:3). They prize knowledge. Those whom Christ teaches, say, as Isaiah 2:3, "Come ye, and let us go up to the mountain of the LORD . . . and he will teach us of his ways, and we will walk in his paths."

When Christ teaches, He not only illuminates but animates. His lessons quicken: "I am the light of the world: he that followeth me . . . shall have the light of life" (John 8:12). By nature we are dead, therefore unfit for teaching. Christ teaches them who are dead! He gives the light of life. Where Christ comes with His light, there is the heat of spiritual life going along with it.

22

CHRIST'S DIVINITY

*Looking for that blessed hope, and the glorious appearing
of the great God and our Saviour Jesus Christ; who
gave himself for us, that he might redeem us from all iniquity,
and purify unto himself a peculiar people, zealous of good works.*

TITUS 2:13–14

Had Christ not been God, He could never have known the mind of God or revealed to us the secrets of heaven. Only God can enlighten the conscience and make the stony heart bleed.

The wisdom in Christ, who is the great doctor of His church, gives saving knowledge to all the elect. Christ is the great luminary: in Him are hid all treasures of knowledge.

See the misery of man in the state of nature. Men in the dark cannot discern colors; so, in the state of nature, they cannot discern between moralities and grace: they mistake the cloud for the goddess herself. In the dark the greatest beauty is hid. Though there be transcendent beauty in Christ as amazes the angels, man in the state of nature sees none of this beauty. A man in the dark is in danger, every step he takes, of falling into hell. The darkness in which a sinner is, an unregenerate state, is worse than natural darkness, for natural darkness affrights. But the spiritual darkness is not accompanied with horror; men tremble not at their condition. Men love darkness (John 3:19) until Jesus Christ comes to teach and turn them from darkness to light, from Satan's power to God.

September

23

THE NEED FOR CHRIST'S TEACHINGS

All thy children shall be taught of the LORD.

ISAIAH 54:13

See the happy condition of the children of God: Christ is their prophet. One man cannot see by another's eyes, but believers see with Christ's eyes. Christ gives them the light of grace and the light of glory.

So labor to have Christ for your prophet. He teaches, saving believers from danger: He is an interpreter of thousands, and He can untie those knots that puzzle angels. Until Christ teaches, we never learn; until Christ is made to us wisdom, we shall never be wise to salvation.

See your need of Christ's teaching. Some speak much of the light of reason improved: the plumbline of reason is too short to fathom the deep things of God. The light of reason will no more help a man to believe than the light of a candle will help him to understand.

Go to Christ to teach you: "Lead me in thy truth, and teach me" (Psalm 25:5).

Do Thou light my lamp, O Thou great Prophet of Thy church! Give me a spirit of wisdom and revelation, that I may see things in another manner than I ever saw them before; teach me in the Word to hear Thy voice, and in the sacrament to discern Thy body. "Lighten mine eyes" (Psalm 13:3). His pulpit in heaven is where Christ converts souls. Oh, that we would go to our great Prophet.

24

GO TO CHRIST FOR TEACHING

*Jesus went about all Galilee, teaching in their synagogues and
preaching the gospel of the kingdom, and healing all manner
of sickness and all manner of disease among the people.*

MATTHEW 4:23

Jesus Christ is willing to teach us. Why else did He enter into the
calling of the ministry, but to teach the mysteries of heaven? Why
did He take the prophetic office upon Him? Why was Christ so
angry with those who had "taken away the key of knowledge" (Luke
11:52)? Why was Christ anointed with the Spirit without measure
except that He might anoint us with knowledge? Knowledge is in
Christ. Those blind in the gospel who came to Christ had their
sight restored; none in the gospel came to Christ for sight, but He
restored their eyesight. Christ is more willing to work a cure upon
a blind soul than ever He was to do so upon a blind body.

There are none so dull and ignorant that Christ cannot teach.
Every one is not fit to make a scholar, but there is none so dull that
Christ cannot make him a good scholar. Christ delights in teaching
the ignorant in such a manner that they know more than the wise
men of the world. "The eyes of the blind shall be opened, and the
ears of the deaf shall be unstopped" (Isaiah 35:5). Who would go to
teach a blind or a deaf man? Yet such dull scholars Christ teaches.
Such as are blinded with ignorance shall see the mysteries of the
gospel, and the deaf ears shall be unstopped.

25

MYSTERIES OF HEAVEN REVEALED

If any man will do his will, he shall know of the doctrine,
whether it be of God, or whether I speak of myself.

JOHN 7:17

Wait upon the grace that Christ has appointed. Christ teaches by His Spirit, yet He teaches in the use of ordinances. Wait at the gates of wisdom's door. Ministers are teachers under Christ. We read of pitchers and of lamps within the pitchers. Ministers are earthen vessels, but these pitchers have lamps within them to light souls to heaven. Christ speaks to us from heaven by His ministers. Those weaned from the breast of ordinances seldom thrive, growing light in their head or lame in their feet. The Word preached is Christ's voice in the minister's mouth; those refusing to hear Christ speaking in the ministry, Christ will refuse to hear speaking on their deathbed.

If you have the teachings of Christ, walk according to that knowledge. Use knowledge well, and Christ will teach you more. A master seeing his servant improve a little stock well gives him more to trade with.

It is your honor to have God for your teacher, and that He should teach you is a matter of admiration and congratulation. Oh, how many knowing men are ignorant! They have Christ's Word to enlighten them, but not His Spirit to sanctify them. But you have the inward as well as the outward teaching, that Christ should anoint you with the heavenly unction (consecration) of His Spirit, so you can say, as John did, "Whereas I was blind, now I see!" (9:25).

26

CHRIST'S PRIESTLY OFFICE

*Now once in the end of the world hath he appeared
to put away sin by the sacrifice of himself.*

HEBREWS 9:26

Christ executes the office of a Priest in the offering up of Himself a sacrifice to satisfy divine justice and reconcile us to God, and in making continual intercession for us.

His satisfaction consists of His active obedience. Christ did everything that the law required. His Holy life was a perfect commentary on the law of God; He obeyed the law for us.

His satisfaction consists of His passive obedience. Our guilt being transferred and imputed to Him, He suffered the penalty that was due to us. He appeared to put away sin by the sacrificing of Himself. The Passover lamb, slain, was a type of Christ who was offered up in sacrifice for us. Sin could not be removed otherwise: "Without shedding of blood is no remission" (Hebrews 9:22). Christ was a Lamb without spot, a Lamb slain.

A priest was needed to mediate between a guilty creature and holy God. But if only Christ's humanity suffered, how could this suffering satisfy for sin? The human nature being united to the divine, the human nature suffered, and the divine satisfied. Christ's Godhead supported the human nature, that it did not faint and that it gave virtue to His sufferings. The altar sanctifies the thing offered on it (Matthew 23:19). The altar of Christ's divine nature sanctified the sacrifice of His death and made it of infinite value.

27

CHRIST'S SUFFERINGS, BODY AND SOUL

He saved others; himself he cannot save.

MATTHEW 27:42

The greatness of Christ's sufferings appears in the sufferings of His body. He suffered truly, not in appearance only. The apostle calls it "the death of the cross" (Philippians 2:8). The thoughts of this made Christ sweat great drops of blood in the garden (Luke 22:44). It was a disgraceful, painful, and cursed death. Christ suffered in every sense. His eyes beheld two sad objects: His enemies insulting and His mother weeping. His ears were filled with the verbal abuse of the people; His smell was offended when their spit fell upon His face; His taste, when they gave Him gall and vinegar to drink; His feelings, when His head suffered with thorns; His hands and feet, with the nails; His whole body, one great wound. Now was this white lily dyed with purple color.

In the sufferings of His soul, Jesus was pressed in the winepress of His Father's wrath, causing that vociferation and outcry on the cross, "My God, my God" (Mark 16:34). Christ suffered a double eclipse upon the cross, an eclipse of the sun and an eclipse of the light of God's countenance). How bitter was this agony! The evangelists use several statements to express it: "He began to be sore amazed" (Mark 14:33); He began to be "exceeding sorrowful" (Matthew 26:38). Christ felt the pains of hell in His soul, and all for us!

28

CHRIST'S SACRIFICIAL SUFFERING

Thus it behooved Christ to suffer.

LUKE 24:46

Christ did not suffer for any desert of His own. "The Messiah [shall] be cut off, but not for himself"; it was for *us* (Daniel 9:26; Isaiah 53:6). Jesus suffered, that He might satisfy God's justice for us. We sinners had infinitely wronged God. If we had shed rivers of tears and offered up millions of burnt offerings, we could never have pacified an angry Deity. Christ must die, that God's justice may be satisfied.

Could God have forgiven sin freely without a sacrifice? When He resolved to have the law satisfied, and to have man saved in a way of justice as well as mercy, it was necessary that Christ should lay down His life as a sacrifice.

This sacrifice fulfilled the predictions of Scripture and brought us into favor with God. It is one thing for a traitor to be pardoned, and another thing to be made a favorite. Christ's blood is not only called a sacrifice, whereby God is appeased, but a propitiation, whereby God becomes gracious and friendly to us. Christ is our mercy seat, from which God gives answers of peace to us.

There were many legacies that Christ bequeathed to believers, legacies that had been all null and void had He not died. A testament is in force after men are dead; the mission of the Spirit, the promises, those legacies, were not in force till Christ's death. Christ by His blood has sealed them, and believers may lay claim to them.

29

God's Goodness in Providing a Sacrifice

Behold therefore the goodness and severity of God.

ROMANS 11:22

Jesus died that He might purchase for us glorious mansions; therefore heaven is called a promised and a "purchased possession" (Ephesians 1:14). Christ died for our advancement; He suffered that we might reign; He hung upon the cross that we might sit upon the throne. Heaven was shut: the cross of Christ is the ladder by which we ascend to heaven. His crucifixion is our coronation.

In the bloody sacrifice of Christ, see the horrid nature of sin. Sin is repulsive, but that which makes it appear horrid is that it made Christ veil His glory and lose His blood. Look upon sin with indignation, pursue it with holy malice, and shed the blood of those sins that shed Christ's blood. The sight of Christ's bleeding body should incense us against sin. Do not negotiate with it; let not that be our joy, which made Christ a man of sorrow.

Is Christ our priest sacrificed? See God's mercy and justice displayed: "Behold the goodness and severity of God." Had not Christ suffered upon the cross, we would be in hell forever, satisfying God's justice.

Though it were His own Son, the Son of His love, and our sins were imputed to Him, yet God did not spare Him, but His wrath flamed against Him (Romans 8:32). God was severe to His own Son. How dreadful will He be to His enemies! Those in willful impenitence must feel the same wrath as Christ did; and because they cannot bear it at once, therefore they must endure it forever.

30

CHRIST SACRIFICED FOR US

He shall see of the travail of his soul, and shall be satisfied.

ISAIAH 53:11

Christ is our priest, who was sacrificed for us. Now we see the endeared affection of Christ to us sinners. That Christ should die was more than if all the angels had been turned to dust; and especially that Christ should die as a criminal, having the weight of all men's sins laid upon Him, and that He should die for His enemies. The balm tree weeps out its precious balm, to heal those that cut and mangle it; so Christ shed His blood, to heal those who crucified Him. He died freely. It is called the offering of Jesus' body (Hebrews 10:10). His sufferings were so great that they made Him sigh, weep, and bleed; but they could not make Him repent. Christ labored upon the cross, yet He does not repent of it, but thinks His sweat and blood well bestowed, because He sees redemption brought forth to the world.

Oh, infinite, amazing love of Christ, a love that passes knowledge, that neither man nor angel can parallel! How should we be affected with this love! If Saul was so affected with David's kindness in sparing his life, how should we be affected with Christ's kindness in parting with His life for us! At Christ's death and passion, the very stones break apart; "the rocks rent" (Matthew 27:51). Not to be affected with Christ's love in dying is to have hearts harder than rocks.

1

CHRIST, THE PERFECT SACRIFICE

By one offering he hath perfected
for ever them that are sanctified.

HEBREWS 10:14

See the excellence of Christ's sacrifice. It was perfect.

Christ's sacrifice is praiseworthy. He not only died for our example, but to merit salvation. The person who suffered being God as well as man put virtue into His sufferings; our sins were atoned for, and God was appeased. No sooner did Christ die, but God's anger was pacified.

This sacrifice is beneficial. It procures justification of our persons, acceptance of our service, access to God with boldness, and entrance into the holy place of heaven. Through the red sea of Christ's blood, we enter into the heavenly Canaan.

Let us apply this blood of Christ. All the virtue of a medicine is in the application; though the medicine is made of the blood of God, it will not heal unless applied by faith. As fire is to the chemist, so is faith to the Christian: the chemist can do nothing without fire, so there is nothing done without faith. Faith makes Christ's sacrifice ours: "Christ Jesus my Lord" (Philippians 3:8). It is not gold in the mine that enriches, but gold in the hand. Faith is the hand that receives Christ's golden merits. It is not a cordial in the glass that refreshes the spirit, but a cordial drunk down. By faith, we drink the blood of Christ. Faith opens the cavity of Christ's wounds and drinks the precious cordial of His blood. Without faith, Christ Himself will not avail us.

2

OUR BLEEDING SAVIOR

Lo, I come . . . to do thy will, O God.

HEBREWS 10:7

Let us love our bleeding Savior, let us show our love to Christ, by being ready to suffer for Him. Many rejoice at Christ's suffering for them, but dream not of their suffering for Him. Was Christ a sacrifice? Did He bear God's wrath for us? We should bear man's wrath for Him. Christ's death was voluntary: "I have a baptism to be baptized with; and how am I straitened till it be accomplished!" (Luke 12:50). He was to be baptized in His own blood, and how did He thirst for that time: "How am I straitened!" Oh, then, let us be willing to suffer for Christ! Christ has taken away the venom and sting of the saints' sufferings: there is no wrath in their cup. Our sufferings Christ can make sweet. As there was oil mixed in the peace offering, so God can mix the oil of gladness with our sufferings. Life must end shortly. What is it to part with it a little sooner, as a sacrifice to Christ, as a seal of sincerity, and a pledge of thankfulness!

This sacrifice of Christ's blood may infinitely comfort us. This is the blood of atonement. Christ's cross is the hinge of our deliverance. His blood comforts in case of guilt! Christ's blood was shed for the remission of sin. Let us see our sins laid on Christ, and then they are no more ours but His.

3

THE HEALING, CLEANSING BLOOD OF JESUS

For it is the blood that maketh an atonement for the soul.

LEVITICUS 17:11

Christ's blood is a healing and cleansing blood. It is healing: "With his stripes we are healed" (Isaiah 53:5). It is the best salve; it heals at a distance. Though Christ is in heaven, we may feel the virtue of His blood healing our bloody issue. And it is cleansing: "The blood of Jesus Christ his Son cleanseth us from all our sin" (1 John 1:7). It is therefore compared to fountain water. The Word is a glass to show us our spots, and Christ's blood is a fountain to wash them away; it turns leprosy into purity.

There is one black spot that Christ's blood does not wash away, and that is sin against the Holy Ghost. There is enough virtue in Christ's blood to wash it away; but he who has sinned that sin will not be washed. He shows contempt toward Christ's blood and tramples it under foot.

How strong Christ's blood is! It is the anchor of our faith, our spring of joy, the crown of our desires, and the only support, both in life and death. In our fears, let us comfort ourselves with the propitiatory sacrifice of Christ's blood. Christ died both as a purchaser and as a conqueror: as a purchaser in regard to God, His blood obtained our salvation; and as a conqueror in regard to Satan, the cross was His triumphant chariot, wherein He has held hell and death captive.

4

THOU ART WORTHY, LORD

Bless the LORD, O my soul.

PSALM 103:1

Bless God for the precious sacrifice of Christ's death as a sin offering for us!

If a man redeems another out of debt, will he not be grateful? How deeply do we stand obliged to Christ, who has redeemed us from hell and damnation! "And they sung a new song, saying," Thou art worthy to take the book, and to open the seals thereof; for thou wast slain, and hast redeemed us to God by thy blood" (Revelation 5:9). Let our hearts and tongues join in concert to bless God; let us show thankfulness to Christ by fruitfulness; let us bring forth the fruits of humility, zeal, and good works. This is to live unto Him who died for us (2 Corinthians 5:15). Let us present Christ with the fruits of righteousness, which are unto the glory and praise of God.

And that God "also maketh intercession for us" (Romans 8:34). When Aaron entered into the holy place, his bells gave a sound. So Christ, having entered into heaven, His intercession makes a melodious sound in the ears of God.

Though Christ is exalted to glory, He has not laid aside His compassion, "Who also maketh intercession for us": To intercede is to make request on behalf of another. Christ is the great Master of requests in heaven.

5

OUR FAITHFUL HIGH PRIEST

For such an high priest became us, who is holy . . .
undefiled, separate from sinners.

HEBREWS 7:26

Christ "knew no sin" (2 Corinthians 5:21). He knew sin in its weight, but not in the act. He, who was to do away the sins of others, should Himself be without sin. Holiness is one of the precious stones that shine on the breastplate of our High Priest.

He is faithful: "It behoved him to be like unto his brethren, that he might be a merciful and faithful high priest" (Hebrews 2:17). Moses was a faithful servant; Christ, a faithful Son. He does not forget the cause He pleads, nor does He use deceit in pleading. Christ is true to the cause He pleads. We may trust our concerns to Him and trust our lives and souls to His hand.

He never dies. While the office of the priests under the law lived, they themselves died. "They were not suffered to continue by reason of death" (Hebrews 7:23). But Christ "ever liveth to make intercession" (Hebrews 7:25).

The efficacy of Christ's prayer reaches no further than the efficacy of His blood: His blood was shed only for the elect; therefore His prayers reach them only. Christ goes into heaven with the names of the elect only upon His breast; He intercedes for the weakest believers and for all the sins of believers. David's sin was a bloody color, yet it did not exclude Him from Christ's intercession.

6

CHRIST INTERCEDES FOR HIS ELECT

Who shall lay anything to the charge of God's elect?
It is Christ that maketh intercession for us.

ROMANS 8:33–34

Christ' work of intercession includes Him presenting the merit of His blood to His Father; in the virtue of that price paid, He pleads for mercy. The high priest was a lively type of Christ. Aaron was to do four things: kill the beasts; enter with the blood into the Holy of Holies; sprinkle the mercy seat with the blood; and kindle the incense, and make a smoke cloud to rise over the mercy seat; and thus atonement was made (Leviticus 16:11–16).

Christ our high priest answered this type. He was offered up in sacrifice, which answers to the priest's killing the young bull. He is gone up to heaven, answering the priest's going into the Holy of Holies. Jesus spreads His blood before His Father, which responds to the priest's sprinkling the blood upon the mercy seat. Fourth, He prays to His Father, for His blood's sake, that He would have favor with sinners, which corresponds to the cloud of incense. Then, through His intercessions, God is pacified, which responds to the priest's making atonement.

Christ, by His intercession, answers all indictments brought against the elect. Christ answers all these accusations: when Satan accuses the saints, or when the justice of God lays anything to their charge, Christ shows His own wounds. By virtue of His bloody sufferings, He answers all the demands and challenges of the law, and He counters Satan's accusations.

7

EFFECTUAL INTERCESSION

*If any man sin, we have an advocate with
the Father, Jesus Christ the righteous.*

1 JOHN 1:2

Christ's intercession calls for our acquittal: He asks as an advocate that the sinner be absolved from guilt. He requires that the sinner be set free in the court. An orator uses rhetoric to persuade and entreat the judge to show mercy to another; but an advocate tells the judge the law. Christ in heaven represents what is law. When God's justice opens the debt book, Christ opens the law book. He argues thus: "God is a just God and wilt not be pacified without blood. Through the shed blood, in justice there is a discharge for the distressed creatures. The law satisfied, the sinner should be acquitted." Upon Christ's plea, God sets His hand to the sinner's pardon.

Christ pleads our cause in heaven, for *free!* Christ laid down His life freely, so He intercedes freely.

Christ intercedes with feeling. "We have not an high priest which cannot be touched with the feeling of our infirmities" (Hebrews 4:15). Jesus is full of sympathy and tenderness, and He is a merciful High Priest. Though He has left His passion at the cross, He has not left His compassion. Christ intercedes feelingly; and that which makes Him intercede with affection is His own cause, that He pleads. He has shed His blood to purchase life and salvation for the elect; and if they should not be saved, He would lose His purchase.

Christ intercedes efficaciously: Christ never lost any cause He pleaded. Christ's intercession must be effectual if we consider the excellency of His person.

8

THE EXCELLENCY OF CHRIST

I knew that thou hearest me always.

JOHN 11:42

The prayer of a saint is prevalent with God, as Moses' prayer bound God's hand, "Let me alone" (Exodus 32:10); and Jacob, a prince, prevailed with God; and Elijah by prayer opened and shut heaven, then what is Christ's prayer! He is the Son of God, the Son in whom He is well pleased. What will not a father grant a son! *If God could forget that Christ were a Priest, He could not forget that He is a Son.*

Christ prays for nothing except what His Father has a mind to grant. There is but one will between Christ and His Father. Christ prays, "Sanctify them through thy truth" (John 17:17) and "This is the will of God, even your sanctification" (1 Thessalonians 4:3). So then, if Christ prays for nothing except what God the Father has a mind to grant, then He is likely to succeed.

Christ prays for nothing except what He has power to give. He prays, as He is man, what He has power to give as He is God. "Father, I will" (John 17:24). *Father,* is prayed as man; *I will,* He gives as God. It is a great comfort to a believer, when his prayer is weak and he can hardly pray for himself, that Christ's prayer in heaven is mighty and powerful. Though God may refuse prayer as it comes from us, yet He will not as it comes from Christ.

9

CHRIST THE INTERCESSOR

The LORD our righteousness.

JEREMIAH 33:16

Christ's intercession is always ready at hand. The people of God have sins of daily occurrence. Besides these, they sometimes lapse into great sins, and God is provoked, and His justice is ready to break forth upon them. But Christ's intercession is ready at hand: He daily makes up the breaches between God and them. He presents the merits of His blood to His Father to pacify Him. When the wrath of God began to break out upon Israel, Aaron stepped in and offered incense, and so the plague was stopped. No sooner does a child of God offend, and God begins to be angry, but immediately Christ steps in and intercedes. "Father," He says, "it is My child who has offended. He has forgotten his duty. Oh, pity him, and let Thy anger be turned away from him." Christ's intercession is ready: upon the least failings of the godly, He stands up and makes request for them in heaven.

Justification is a fruit of intercession. Guilt is remitted and righteousness is imputed. We are reputed not only righteous, as the angels, but as Christ, having His robes put upon us. But whence is it that we are justified? It is from Christ's intercession. "And may be found in Him, not having a righteousness of my own derived from the law, but that which is through faith in Christ, the righteousness which comes from God on the basis of faith:" (Philippians 3:9).

10

THE ANOINTING OF THE SPIRIT

Ye have an unction from the Holy One.

1 JOHN 2:20

Unction, or anointing, is the work of sanctification in the heart, whereby the Spirit makes us partakers of the divine nature. The Spirit of God puts the soul into a divine nature; it makes it to be holy and to resemble God. The sanctifying work of the Spirit is the fruit of Christ's intercession. Christ glorified, and in heaven, prays to the Father, and the Father sends the Spirit, who pours out the holy anointing upon the elect.

Christ's work in heaven is not only to present His own prayers to His Father, but He prays our prayers over again. "Another angel came . . . having a golden censer; and there was given unto him much incense, that he should offer it with the prayers of all saints upon the golden altar" (Revelation 8:3). This angel was Christ; He takes the golden container of His merits, puts our prayers in it, and, with the incense of His intercession, makes our prayers go up as a sweet perfume in heaven.

Our best service is mixed with corruption. Christ purifies and sweetens these services, mixing the sweet odors of His intercession with them; and God accepts and crowns them. What would become of our duties without a high priest? Christ's intercession is to our prayers as the fan to the chaff.

OCTOBER

11

ACCESS TO THE THRONE OF GRACE

*Keep through thine own name
those whom thou hast given me.*

JOHN 17:11

We have a friend at court speaking a good word for us, who is following our cause in heaven to animate and encourage us in prayer. Do we think it too bold for sinners like us to come for pardon, and that we shall be denied? Surely this is a sinful modesty. Coming in our own name in prayer is presumption, but Christ intercedes for us in the force and value of His blood. "Let us come boldly to the throne of grace" (Hebrews 4:16). Being fearful to come to God in prayer dishonors Christ's intercession.

Christ promised, "I will pray the Father, and he shall give you another Comforter" (John 14:16). The comfort of the Spirit is distinct from the anointing. Here is sweet comfort, sweeter than the honey drops from the comb. It is the "earnest of the Spirit" (2 Corinthians 1:22). The Spirit gives us an earnest of heaven in our hand: "I will pray the Father, and he shall give the Comforter."

Our prayer keeps us, but it is God's care and maintenance that holds us. "I have prayed for thee, that thy faith fail not" (Luke 22:32) is the copy of His prayer now in heaven. Peter's faith failed in some degree when he denied Christ; but Christ prayed that it might not totally fail. The saints persevere in believing, because Christ perseveres in praying.

12

THE BOW OF CHRIST'S INTERCESSION

[God] hath committed all judgment unto the Son.

JOHN 5:22

Christ shall judge the world. Those for whom He prayed, He will absolve when He sits upon the bench of judge. Believers are His spouse: will He condemn His own spouse? See the constancy of His love to the elect: He not only died for the elect, but intercedes for them in heaven. When Christ was done dying, He was not done loving. He is now at work in heaven for the saints; He carries their names on His breast, and He will never stop praying until that prayer is granted.

See whence it is that the prayers of the saints are so powerful with God. It is Christ's prayer in heaven that makes the saints' prayers so effective. Christ's divine nature is the altar on which He offers up our prayers, and so they prevail. Prayer, as it comes from the saints, is but weak and lethargic, but when the arrow of a saint's prayer is put into the bow of Christ's intercession, it pierces the throne of grace, showing that a Christian, when he prays, must fix his eye on Christ's intercession. We are to look up to the mercy seat and hope for mercy through Christ's intercession.

13

CHRIST, OUR ADVOCATE

We have an advocate with the Father.

1 JOHN 2:1

An unbeliever has none in heaven to speak for him. "I pray not for the world, but for them which thou hast given me" (John 17:9). If we are shut out of Christ's prayer, we are shut out of heaven. Christ pleads for the saints, as Queen Esther did for the Jews, when they would have been destroyed: "Let my people be given me at my petition" (Esther 7:3). *When the devil shows the blackness of sins, Christ shows the redness of His wounds.* How sad is the condition of that man for whom Christ will not pray, or against whom He will pray! Then Queen Esther petitioned against Haman, and then his face was covered, and he was led away to execution (Esther 7:8). It is sad when the law shall be against the sinner—and conscience, and judge, and no friend to speak for him. There is no option but the jailer must take the prisoner.

If Christ makes intercession, then we have nothing to do with other intercessors. Christ only can intercede for us, for God has consecrated Him as High Priest. "Thou art a priest for ever" (Hebrews 5:6). Christ intercedes by virtue of His merit, in the virtue of His blood; He pleads His merits to His Father. The angels have no merits to bring to God and cannot intercede for us. Our advocate must be our propitiation to satisfy God. "We have an advocate with the Father . . . and he is the propitiation for our sins" (1 John 2:1–2). The angels cannot be our propitiation, and not therefore our advocates.

14

PRAYING WITH MOANING AND GROANING

*God hath sent forth the Spirit of his Son into
your hearts, crying, Abba, Father.*

GALATIANS 4:6

If Christ is praying for us, His Spirit is praying in us. The Spirit helps us with
sighs and moans and groans (Romans 8:26). We see the beauty of
the sun on earth, so we need not climb there to know if it be there.
So we need not go up into heaven to see if Christ is interceding for
us. But let us look into our hearts, to see if they are quickened and
inflamed in prayer, and we can cry, "Abba, Father." His children
know Christ is interceding above for us by the Spirit within us.

If we are given to Christ, then He intercedes for us. "I pray . . .
for them which thou hast given me" (John 17:9). It is one thing for
Christ to be given to us; another thing, for us to be given to Christ.
If you are a believer, then you are given to Christ, and He prays for
you.

Faith is an act of resting. We rest on Christ as the stones in the
building rest upon the cornerstone. Faith throws itself into Christ's
arms and says, "Christ is my priest; His blood, my sacrifice; His
divine nature, my altar—and here I rest." This faith is seen by its
effects, by a refining work and a resigning work. The refining work
purifies the heart, it gives up its use, its love to Him. There is also the
resigning work of faith: they who believe are given to Christ and have
a part in His prayer. "Neither pray I for these alone, but for them
also which shall believe on me through their word" (John 17:20).

15

CHRIST'S INTEREST

Now also Christ shall be magnified in my body,
whether it be by life, or by death.

PHILIPPIANS 1:20

If Christ appears for us in heaven, then we must appear for Him upon earth. Christ is not ashamed to carry our names on His breast, so shall we be ashamed of His truth? He plead our cause, so shall not we stand up in His cause? What a claim to stand for the honor of Christ in times of apostasy! Christ presents our names in heaven, so shall not we profess His name on earth?

Christ lays out His interest for us at the throne of grace, so we must lay out all our interest for Him. Trade your talents for Christ's glory. Every man has talent to trade: one, learning; another, wealth. Trade for Christ's glory: spend and be spent for Him. Let your heart study for Christ, your hands work for Him, and your tongue speak for Him. Christ is our advocate for us in heaven, so we are agents for Him on earth. Every one of us in our sphere must act vigorously for Him.

Believe in the glorious intercession of Christ: that He now intercedes for us and that for His sake God will accept us. Not believing dishonors Christ's intercession. Shall we not have our High Priest make intercession for us? Is not Christ our Aaron, who presents His blood and incense before the mercy seat? Oh, look up by faith to Christ's intercession! Christ did not only pray for His disciples and apostles, but for the weakest believer.

16

CHRIST'S KINDNESS INVITES OUR LOVE

If any man love not the Lord Jesus Christ, let him be anathema.

1 CORINTHIANS 16:22

If a friend, when you were questioned in court for delinquency or debt, pleaded with the judge for you, and your crime was dismissed, would you not love that friend? How often does Satan put in his bills against us in the court! Now Christ is at the judge's hand; He sits at His Father's right hand, ever to plead for us and to make our peace with God. Our hearts should be fired with love to Christ! Love Him with a sincere superlative love, more than your possessions and your family. Our fire of love should be an altar fire, never going out.

Christ is at work for you in heaven; He makes intercession for you. "But I am afraid Christ does not intercede for me. I am a sinner; and for whom does Christ intercede?" He "made intercession for the transgressors" (Isaiah 53:12).

But, Christian, do you mourn for unbelief? Be not discouraged: you may have a part in Christ's prayer. "The congregation . . . murmured . . . against Aaron;" but though they had sinned against their high priest, Aaron ran in with his incense, and "stood between the dead and the living" (Numbers 16:41, 48). If so much depth be in Aaron, who was but a type of Christ, how much more depths are in Christ, who will pray for them who have sinned against their High Priest! Did He not pray for them that crucified Him, "Father, forgive them" (Luke 23:34)?

17

CHRIST'S KINGLY OFFICE

"King of kings, and Lord of lords."

REVELATION 19:16

Christ executed the office of a king by subduing us to Himself, in ruling and defending us, and in restraining and conquering His and our enemies.

Jesus Christ is of mighty renown. He is a King with a kingly title: "the high and lofty One" (Isaiah 57:15). He has His insignia regalia, His ensigns of royalty. He has His crown (Revelation 6:2); His sword, "Gird thy sword upon thy thigh" (Psalm 45:3); and His scepter, "A scepter of righteousness is the scepter of thy kingdom" (Hebrews 1:8). He has His coat of arms; He inserts the lion in His coat of arms: "the Lion of the tribe of Judah" (Revelation 5:5). He has a pre-eminence over all other kings and is called "The prince of the kings of the earth" (Revelation 1:5). He must be so, for by him kings reign (Proverbs 8:15). Christ infinitely is above all other princes, having the highest throne, the largest dominions, and the longest possession: "Thy throne, O God, is for ever and ever" (Hebrews 1:8). He has many heirs, but no successors. The power of other kings is limited, but Christ's power is unlimited. Christ's power is as large as His will.

God the Father has decreed Him to be king: "Yet have I set my king upon my holy hill of Zion: I will declare the decree" (Psalm 2:6–7). God has anointed and sealed Him to His regal office. God has set the crown upon His head.

18

A Spiritual Kingdom

Thy people shall be willing in the day of thy power.

PSALM 110:3

Christ is king to govern His people. It was prophesied of Christ before He was born, "And thou Bethlehem . . . art not the least among the princes of Juda: for out of thee shall come a Governor, that shall rule my people Israel" (Matthew 2:6).

Christ's kingdom is spiritual. He rules in the hearts of men. He sets up His throne where no other king does; He rules the will and affections, His power binds the conscience; He subdues men's lusts. "He will subdue our iniquities" (Micah 7:19).

Christ rules by law and by love. It is one of the flowers of the crown to enact laws. Christ as a king makes laws, and by His laws He rules; as the law of faith, "Believe on the Lord Jesus Christ" (Acts 16:31), and the law of sanctity, "Be ye holy in all manner of conversation" (1 Peter 1:15). Many would admit Christ to be their advocate to plead for them, but not their king to rule over them.

He rules by love and is a king full of mercy and clemency; as He has a scepter in His hand, so an olive branch of peace in His mouth. Though He is the Lion of the tribe of Judah for majesty, yet He is the Lamb of God for meekness. His regal rod has honey at the end of it. He sheds abroad His love into the hearts of His subjects; He rules them with promises as well as precepts. This makes all His subjects become volunteers; they are willing to pay their allegiance to Him.

19

CHRIST, DEFENDER OF HIS PEOPLE

Thou, O LORD, art a shield for me.

PSALM 3:3

Christ has a scepter to rule and a shield to defend His elect. Christ preserves His church as a flock of sheep among wolves. That the sea should be higher than the earth, and yet not drown it, is a wonder; that the wicked should be so much higher than the church in power, and not devour it, is because Christ has this inscription on His clothing and His thigh: KING OF KINGS. "If it had not been the LORD who was on our side . . . they had swallowed us up quick" (Psalm 124:2–3). Christ never slumbers or sleeps, but watches over His church to defend it. "Sing ye unto her, A vineyard of red wine. I the LORD do keep it . . . lest any hurt it, I will keep it night and day" (Isaiah 27:2–3). Christ keeps the church day and night and is said to carry His church upon His wings. The arrow must first hit the mother eagle's wings before it can hurt the young; the enemies must first strike through Christ before they can destroy His church. Let the wind and storms be up, and the church almost covered with waves, Christ is in the ship of the church, and there is no danger of shipwreck. Christ will defend His church as He is King, and He will deliver it. Sometimes Christ is said to command deliverance, and deliverance shall come in His time.

20

THE KING'S REWARDS

Godliness is profitable unto all things,
having promise of the life that now is,
and of that which is to come.

1 TIMOTHY 4:8

Christ will deliver His people when the hearts of His people are humble, their prayers are most fervent, their faith is strongest, their forces are weakest, and their enemies are highest. Then is the usual time that Christ puts forth His kingly power for their deliverance.

Christ is a King to reward His people. There is nothing lost by serving this King. He rewards His subjects in this life. He gives them inward peace and joy; a bunch of grapes by the way; and often riches and honor. But the great reward is to come: an "eternal weight of glory" (2 Corinthians 4:17). Christ makes all His subjects kings: "I will give thee a crown of life" (Revelation 2:10). This crown will be full of jewels, and it will never fade (1 Peter 5:4).

Christ is a King in reference to His enemies, in subduing and conquering them. He pulls down their pride, corrects their policy, and restrains their malice. Christ will make His enemies His footstool. He can destroy them with ease: "LORD, it is nothing with thee to help" (2 Chronicles 14:11). He can do it with weak means and without means. He can make the enemies destroy themselves. Thus Christ is King in vanquishing the enemies of His church. The church has more with her than against her: she has Emmanuel on her side, even that great *King* to whom all knees must bend.

21

PREPARED FOR BATTLE

The LORD is a man of war.

EXODUS 15:3

Revelation describes Christ with seven eyes and seven horns: seven eyes to discern the conspiracies of His enemies, and the seven horns to push and perplex His enemies.

Christ is described with a crown and a bow. "Behold a white horse: and he that sat on him had a bow; and a crown was given unto him: and he went forth conquering, and to conquer" (Revelation 6:2). The crown is a standard ensign of His kingly office; the bow, to shoot His enemies to death.

Christ is described with clothes dipped in blood (Revelation 19:13). He has a golden scepter to rule His people, but an iron rod to break His enemies. "The ten horns which thou sawest are ten kings . . . . These shall make war with the Lamb, but the Lamb shall overcome them: for he is Lord of lords, and King of kings" (Revelation 17:12, 14). The enemies may set up their standard, but Christ will set up His trophies at last. "And the angel . . . gathered the vine of the earth, and cast it into the great winepress of the wrath of God. And the winepress was trodden . . . and blood came out of the winepress" (Revelation 14:19–20). Christ's enemies will be as many clusters of ripe grapes, cast into the great winepress of the wrath of God, trodden by Christ until their blood come out. Christ will be the victor, and all His enemies shall be put under His feet.

SERVING OUR JUDGE AND KING

The Father . . . hath committed all judgment unto the Son.

JOHN 5:22

It is no disparagement to serve Christ—He is a King—or to be employed in a King's service. Some reproach the saints for their piety; but they serve the Lord Christ, He who has KING OF KINGS inscribed on His clothing. Christ's servants are vessels of honor and a royal nation. It's an honor to serve Christ more than to have kings serve us.

Since Christ is King, it informs us that all matters must one day be brought before Him. Christ has the power of life and death in His hand. He who hung upon the cross shall sit upon the bench of judge. Kings must come before Him to be judged, who once sat upon the throne must appear at the bar. God has committed all judgment to the Son: Christ's is the highest court of authority: if this King condemns men, there is no appeal to any other court.

When foiled by corruption, we must go to Christ, for He is King. Desire Him by His kingly power to subdue our corruptions, to bind these kings with chains. Though our lusts are too strong for us, they are not for Christ to conquer, for by His Spirit He can break the power of sin. When Joshua had conquered five kings, he caused his servants to set their feet on the necks of those kings; Christ can and will set His feet on the necks of our lusts.

23

CHRIST, THE KEY OF GOVERNMENT

Ye shall walk after the LORD your God, and fear him,
and keep his commandments, and obey his voice,
and ye shall serve him, and cleave unto him.

DEUTERONOMY 13:4

Is Christ King of kings? Christ is a great King, so submit to Him willingly. The devils in hell submit to Christ; but it is against their will; they are His slaves, not His subjects. Submit cheerfully to Christ's person and His laws. Many would have Christ their savior, but not their prince; such as will not have Christ to be their King to rule over them, shall never have His blood to save them. Christ commands love, humility, and good works: we are to be drawn to His service.

Let those admire God's free grace that were once under the tyranny of Satan, and now Christ has made them to become the subjects of His kingdom. Christ did not need subjects: He has legions of angels ministering to Him. In His love He has honored you to make you His subjects. How long was it that Christ could prevail with you to come under His banner! How much opposition did He meet with ere you would wear this prince's colors! Omnipotent grace overcame you. When Peter was sleeping between two soldiers, an angel came and removed his chains (Acts 12:7). So when you were sleeping in the devil's arms, Christ by His Spirit smote your heart and caused the chains of sin to fall off. He made you a subject of His kingdom. Admire free grace, you who art a subject of Christ and are sure to reign with Him forever!

24

CHRIST'S HUMILIATION IN HIS INCARNATION

Great is the mystery of godliness: God was manifest in the flesh.

1 TIMOTHY 3:16

Christ's humiliation consisted of His being born, in a low condition, made under the law, undergoing the miseries of this life, the wrath of God, and the cursed death of the cross.

Christ's humiliation consisted of His incarnation, His taking flesh, and being born. It was real flesh that Christ took; not the image of a body, but a true body. Therefore He is said to be "made of a woman" (Galatians 4:4). As bread is made of wheat and wine is made of grapes, so Christ is made of a woman: His body was part of the flesh and substance of the virgin. This is a glorious mystery, "God manifest in the flesh." In the creation, man was made in God's image; in the incarnation, God was made in man's image.

Christ was made in the flesh by His Father's special designation: "God sent forth his Son, made of a woman" (Galatians 4:4). God the Father in a special manner appointed Christ to be incarnate, which shows how needful a call is to any business of weight and importance; *to act without a call is to act without a blessing.* Christ would not be incarnate, and take upon Him the work of a mediator, until He had a call. "God sent forth his Son, made of a woman."

25

GOD MADE FLESH AND BORN OF A VIRGIN

I will put enmity between thee and the woman,
and between thy seed and her seed; it shall
bruise they head, and thou shalt bruise his heel.

GENESIS 3:15

Was there no other way to restore fallen man but that God should take flesh? We must not ask a reason of God's will; we are not to dispute but adore. God saw it to be the best way for our redemption, that Christ should be incarnate. It was not fit for any to satisfy God's justice but man; none could do it but God; therefore Christ, being both God and man, is the fittest to undertake this work of redemption.

Christ was born of a woman that God might fulfill that promise in Genesis 3:15, that He might roll away that reproach from the woman, which she had contracted by being seduced by the serpent. Christ, in taking His flesh from the woman, has honored her gender; that at the first, the woman had made man a sinner, so now, to make Him amends, she should bring Him a savior.

Christ was born of a virgin for decency: It became not God to have any mother but a maid, and it became not a maid to have any other son but a God.

Christ was born of a virgin for necessity: Christ was to be a high priest, most pure and holy. Had He been born after the ordinary course of nature, He had been defiled, since all who spring out of Adam's loins have a tincture of sin, but, that "Christ's substance might remain pure and immaculate," he was born of a virgin.

26

BORN WITHOUT SIN

The Holy Ghost shall come upon thee, and the
power of the Highest shall overshadow thee:
therefore also that holy thing which shall be
born of thee shall be called the Son of God.

LUKE 1:35

Christ was without mother as He was God, without father as He was man. How could Christ be made of flesh and blood of a virgin, and yet be without sin? The purest virgin is stained with original sin. "The Holy Ghost shall come upon thee": that is, the Holy Ghost consecrated and purified that part of the virgin's flesh where Christ was made. Though the Virgin Mary herself had sin, yet that part of her flesh whereof Christ was made was without sin; otherwise it must have been an impure conception.

The Holy Ghost framed Christ in the virgin's womb in a wonderful manner, uniting Christ's human nature to His divine, making one person. This is a mystery: God incarnate.

"When the fulness of the time was come, God sent forth his Son, made of a woman" (Galatians 4:4). By "the fullness of time" we must understand the determinate time God set when all the prophecies of the coming of the Messiah were accomplished, all legal shadows and figures, where he was typified, were nullified. The comfort is, though at present we do not see that peace and purity in the church which we could desire, yet in the fullness of time, when God's time is come, then shall deliverance spring up, and God will come riding upon the chariots of salvation.

27

A Monument of Free Grace

Draw nigh to God, and he will draw nigh to you.

JAMES 4:8

The cause of Jesus being made flesh was free grace. It was God's love that sent Christ, and love in Christ that He came to be incarnate. Love was the motive. Christ is God-man, because He is a lover of man. Christ came out of pity and indulgence to us. Christ's taking flesh was free grace and a pure design of love. God Himself, the Almighty, was overcome with love. Christ incarnate is nothing but love covered with flesh. Christ's assuming our human nature was a masterpiece of wisdom and a monument of free grace.

Christ took our flesh that He might take our sins upon Him, and so appease God's wrath. The weight of the whole world's sins was upon Him.

Christ took our flesh that He might make the human nature appear lovely to God, and the divine nature appear lovely to man. When we fell from God, our nature became repulsive to Him; no vermin is as detestable to us as human nature was to God. It was so vile to God that He could not endure to look upon us. Christ, taking our flesh, makes this human nature appear lovely to God. As when the sun shines on the glass it casts a bright luster, so Christ, being clad with our flesh, makes the human nature shine and appear amiable in God's eyes. And Christ, being God incarnate, makes the sight of the Deity not formidable, but delightful to us.

28

CHRIST THE PEACEMAKER

*Behold, I bring you good tidings of great joy . . .
for unto you is born this day in the city of
David a Saviour, which is Christ the Lord.*

LUKE 2:10–11

Christ took our flesh, mediates for us, and brings us into favor with God. When God the Father was angry with us, Christ married Himself to our nature and now mediates for us with His Father, making us friends again, and God looks upon us with favor. Jesus Christ may well be called a peacemaker, having taken our flesh upon Him, making peace between us and His Father.

God, in the riches of His grace, sent forth His Son, made of a woman, to redeem us. Behold the infinite love of Christ, that He was willing to condescend to take our flesh. Surely the angels would have disdained to have taken our flesh; it would have been a disparagement to them. What king would be willing to wear sackcloth over his cloth of gold? But Christ did not despise taking our flesh. Had not Christ been made flesh, we had been made a curse; had He not been incarnate, we had been incarcerated forever.

Christ came from the richest place in heaven, His Father's bosom, that hive of sweetness. He came to sinful man who had defaced His image and abused His love. Christ leaves angels, those noble spirits, the gold and the pearl, and comes to poor sinful man, and draws Him into His embraces.

29

CHRIST'S HUMILITY

[Jesus] was made in the likeness of men.

PHILIPPIANS 2:7

Christ's taking our flesh was one of the lowest steps of humility. He humbled Himself more in lying in the virgin's womb than in hanging upon the cross. It was not so much for man to die, but for God to become man was the wonder of humility. Christ's wearing our flesh veiled His glory. For Him to be made flesh who was equal with God—oh, what humility! He stood upon even ground with God, He was co-essential and con-substantial with His Father, yet He stripped Himself of the robes of His glory and covered Himself with the rags of our humanity.

Christ not only took our flesh, but took it when it was at the worst, under disgrace, and he took all the infirmities of our flesh. There are two sorts of infirmities, such as are sinful without pain, and such as are painful without sin.

A further degree of Christ's humility was that He not only was made flesh, but in the likeness of sinful flesh. "[God] hath made [Jesus] to be sin for us, who knew no sin" (2 Corinthians 5:21). He was like a sinner; all sin laid upon Him, but no sin lived in Him. That Christ, who would not endure sin in the angels, should Himself endure to have sin imputed to Him is the most amazing humility that ever was. Oh, look on Christ, this rare pattern, and be humbled!

30

CHRIST, BORN IN YOUR HEART

Until Christ be formed in you.

GALATIANS 4:19

Let us pray that Christ may be spiritually born in our hearts. What will it profit us for Christ to have been born into the world, unless He is born in our hearts and united to our persons? Christ must be born in your hearts. But before Christ is born in the heart, there are spiritual pangs: "They were pricked in their heart" (Acts 2:37). Christ being born in our hearts is never without pangs. Those without any trouble of spirit thank God, but it is a sign Christ is not yet formed in them.

When Christ was born into the world, He was made flesh; so, if He is born in thy heart, He makes it a heart of flesh. It was a rocky heart that would not yield to God; now it is fleshy and tender like melted wax, to take any stamp of the Spirit. It is a sign Christ is born in our hearts, when they are hearts of flesh, when they shed tears and love. What is it the better that Christ was made flesh, unless He has given thee a heart of flesh?

If Christ be born in you, your heart is a virgin-heart, in respect of sincerity and sanctity. Art you purified from the love of sin? If Christ is born in your heart, it is a holy of holies. If your heart is polluted with the predominant love of sin, never think Christ is born there. Christ will never again lie in a stable. If He is born in the heart, it is consecrated by the Holy Ghost.

31

LET US BE LIKE CHRIST

The life which I now live in the flesh
I live by the faith of the Son of God.

GALATIANS 2:20

There is life when Christ is in our heart. Faith is the vital organ of the soul. There is appetite: "As newborn babes, desire the sincere milk of the word" (1 Peter 2:2). The Word is like breast milk, pure, sweet, nourishing; and the soul in which Christ is formed desires this milk. After Christ is born in the heart, there is a striving to enter in at the strait gate (Matthew 11:12). This is the only comfort, that as Christ was born into the world, so He is born in our hearts; as He was united to our flesh, so He is united to our person.

As Christ was made in our image, let us labor to be made in His image. He was of a most sweet disposition, the delight of human kind. He invites sinners to come to Him. He offers everything we need. He would not break our heart but with mercy. Let us be like Him in sweetness of disposition; be not of a pessimistic spirit. Let us be like Christ in mildness and sweetness. Let us pray for our enemies and conquer them by love. A frozen heart will be thawed with the fire of love.

Let us be like Christ in His grace and in humility. "He humbled himself" (Philippians 2:8). He left the bright robes of His glory to be clothed with the rags of our humanity: a wonder to humility! We are never as comely in God's eyes as when we are black in our own. In this, let us be like Christ. True religion is to imitate Christ.

1

LIKE HIM IN HOLINESS OF LIFE

Who made me a judge?

LUKE 12:14

Christ was not ambitious of titles or of honor. He declined worldly dignity and greatness as much as others seek it. When they would have made Him a king, He chose to ride upon a donkey rather than be drawn in a chariot; he hung upon a wooden cross rather than wear a golden crown. He scorned the pomp and glory of the world. He waived secular affairs. He came into the world to be a Redeemer. He minded nothing but heaven. Let us not be ambitious of the honors and high positions of the world. Let us not purchase the world with the loss of a good conscience. What wise man would curse self to grow rich or pull down his soul to build wealth? Be like Christ in a holy contempt of the world.

Let us be made like Him in holiness of life. No temptation could hold Him. Temptation to Christ was like a spark of fire upon a marble pillar, which glides off. Let us be like him in this: "Be ye holy in all manner of conversation" (1 Peter 1:15). A Christian should both draw others to Christ and cast a sparkling luster of holiness in his life. Let us be so just in our dealings, so true in our promises, so devout in our worship, so unblameable in our lives, that we may be the walking pictures of Christ. Thus as Christ was made in our likeness, let us labor to be made in His likeness.

NOVEMBER

2

CHRIST'S EXALTATION

*God also hath highly exalted him, and given
him a name which is above every name.*

PHILIPPIANS 2:9

The Sun of Righteousness shines in full glory upon rising from the dead, ascending into heaven, and sitting at the right hand of God the Father. Therein is Christ's exaltation.

In what sense has god exalted Christ? Not in respect of His Godhead, for that cannot be exalted higher than it is. But Christ is exalted as Mediator; His human nature is exalted. God has exalted Christ in His titles, in His office, in His ascension, in His session at God's right hand, and in assigning Him judge of the world.

Jesus is Lord in respect of His sovereignty; He is Lord over angels and men: "All power is given unto [Him] in heaven and in earth" (Matthew 28:18). Christ has the key to the grave, to open them at the resurrection; the key of heaven, to open the kingdom of heaven to whom He will; and the key of hell, to lock up the damned in that fiery prison.

To this Lord, all knees must bow: "at the name of Jesus every knee should bow" (Philippians 2:10). All must be subdued to Him as sons or captives, submit to Him as to the Lord or Judge. We must not only cast ourselves into Christ's arms to be saved by Him, but we must cast ourselves at His feet to serve Him.

Christ is exalted to be a great prince: "the prince of the kings of the earth" (Revelation 1:5. They hold their crowns by immediate tenure from Him; His throne is above the stars, He has angels and archangels for His attendants. Thus He is exalted in His titles of honor.

3

CHRIST AT GOD'S RIGHT HAND

He that descended is the same also that
ascended up far above all heavens . . .

EPHESIANS 4:10

For Christ to sit at the right hand of God is to be in the next place to God the Father in dignity and honor. The human nature of Christ, being united to the divine, is now set down on a royal throne in heaven and adored even by angels.

By virtue of the personal union of Christ's human nature with the divine, there is a communication of all that glory from the Deity of Christ of which His human nature is capable. Not that the manhood of Christ is advanced to an equality with the Godhead, but the divine nature being joined with the human, the human nature is wonderfully glorified, though not deified. Christ as Mediator is filled with all majesty and honor, beyond the comprehension of the highest order of angels. In His humiliation, He descended so low that it was not fit to go lower; and in His exaltation, He ascended so high that it is not possible to go higher. In His resurrection, He was exalted above the grave; in His ascension, He was exalted above the starry heavens; in sitting at God's right hand, He was exalted far above the highest heavens.

When He was on earth, He lay in a manger; now He sits on a throne. He is in the brightness of His Father's glory: Him hath God highly exalted (Philippians 2:9).

4

CHRIST IN HIS GLORIFIED STATE

He that humbleth himself shall be exalted.

LUKE 14:11

The world looks upon humility as that which will make contemptible, but it is the way to honor: the way to rise is to fall; the way to ascend is to descend. Humility exalts us in the esteem of men, and it exalts us to a higher throne in heaven. "Whosoever therefore shall humble himself as this little child, the same is the greatest in the kingdom of heaven" (Matthew 18:4).

Christ suffered and then was exalted: sufferings go before glory. Many desire to be glorified with Christ, but they are not content to suffer for Him: "If we suffer, we shall also reign with him" (2 Timothy 2:12). The wicked first reign and then suffer; the godly first suffer and then reign. There is no way to heaven but through sufferings; no way to the crown but by the cross. Jerusalem above is a pleasant city with streets of gold, gates of pearl; but we must travel through a dirty road to it, through many reproaches and sufferings. We must enter into glory as Christ did: He first suffered shame and death, and then He was exalted to sit at God's right hand.

Christ, being exalted, has ennobled our nature, crowned it with glory, and lifted it above angels and archangels. Christ is exalted to glory; which is an evident token that He has done and suffered all that was required of Him, for working out our redemption.

5

A HEAVENLY HOME AWAITS

*Father, I will that they also, whom thou
hast given me, be with me where I am.*

JOHN 17:24

Christ being exalted at God's right hand is for the comfort of believers, so they may be exalted to that place of glory where He is. Christ's exaltation is our exaltation. He is preparing a place for believers (John 14:2). Christ is called the head; the church is the body. The head being exalted to honor, the body shall be exalted too. As Christ is exalted far above all heavens, He will instate believers in that glory with which His human nature is adorned. As He here puts His grace upon the saints, He will put His glory upon them. What comfort for the poorest Christian who has no home, yet may look up to heaven and say, "There is my home and my country. I have already taken possession of heaven in my head Christ. It will not be long before I shall sit with Him. He is upon the throne of glory, and I have His word that I will sit upon the throne with Him" (Revelation 3:21).

Let us exalt Christ in our hearts: believe, adore, and love Him. We cannot lift Him up higher in heaven, but we may in our hearts. Let us exalt Him in our praises and by living holy lives. All the doxologies and prayers in the world do not exalt Christ like a holy life does. It makes Christ renowned, and lifts Him up indeed, when His children walk worthy of Him.

6

CHRIST'S PURCHASING REDEMPTION

*By his own blood he entered in once into the holy
place, having obtained eternal redemption for us.*

HEBREWS 9:12

The Spirit applies to us the redemption purchased by Christ by working faith in us and thereby uniting us to Christ in our effectual calling.

Jesus Christ is the glorious purchaser of our redemption. The doctrine of redemption by Jesus Christ is a glorious doctrine; it is the marrow and essence of the gospel, in which a Christian's comfort lies. Great was the work of creation, but greater the work of redemption. *It cost more to redeem us than to make us.* In one there was the speaking of a word; in the other, the shedding of blood. The creation was but the work of God's fingers. Redemption is the work of His arm. Christ's purchasing redemption for us implies that our sins mortgaged and sold us. Had there not been some kind of mortgaging, there had been no need of redemption. When we were thus mortgaged and sold by sin, Christ purchased our redemption. He had the best right to redeem us, for He is our kinsman. Christ being near akin to us, flesh of our flesh, is the fittest to redeem us.

Christ redeems us by His own precious blood: "in whom we have redemption through his blood" (Ephesians 1:7). He paid a price by His blood, and this blood, of that person who was God as well as man, is a price sufficient for the ransom of millions.

7

REDEEMED FROM SIN

*Now once in the end of the world hath he appeared
to put away sin by the sacrifice of himself.*

HEBREWS 9:26

Being redeemed from slavery is mercy, but it is infinitely more to be redeemed from sin. Only sin can hurt the soul. It is not affliction that hurts the soul; affliction often makes it better, as the furnace makes gold the purer. But it is sin that causes the damage.

Sin cannot stand with perfect redemption. Here it is begun only, but sin may stand with imperfect redemption. While our redemption is but begun, there may be sin; but not when perfect in glory.

Guilt binds a person over to punishment. Christ has redeemed justified persons from the guilt of sin, discharging their debts. Christ says to God's justice, as Paul to Philemon, "If he hath wronged thee, or oweth thee ought, put that on mine account" (Philemon 1:18).

A justified person is redeemed from the power and regency of sin, though not from its presence. Sin may rage in a child of God, but not reign. "Sin shall not have dominion over you" (Romans 6:14). Sin lives in a child of God, but is deposed from the throne. It lives not as a king, but a captive.

"Christ hath redeemed us from the curse of the law, being made a curse for us" (Galatians 3:13). Christ said to His Father, as Rebecca to Jacob, "Upon me be thy curse" (Genesis 27:13). Christ has redeemed the believer and set him away from the power of hell and damnation.

8

Redeemed from the World

Without shedding of blood [there] is no remission.

Hebrews 9:22

Christ came to purchase our redemption and redeem us from the guilt and curse due to sin (Galatians 3:13), then let us try whether we are the persons whom Christ has redeemed from the guilt and curse due to sin. This is a needful trial, for there is but a certain number whom Christ has redeemed. Christ came not to redeem all, for that would overthrow the decrees of God. Redemption is not as large as creation. There is a sufficiency of merit in Christ's blood to save all, but there is a difference between sufficiency and efficiency. Christ's blood is a sufficient price for all, but it is effectual only to them who believe. A plaster may have a sovereign virtue in it to heal any wound, but it does not heal unless applied to the wound. Since all do not have the benefit of Christ's redemption, but some only, it is a necessary question to ask our own souls, "Are we in the number of those who are redeemed by Christ or not?"

Those redeemed are reconciled to God, and enmity is taken away. Those redeemed by Christ are redeemed from the world: He "gave himself for our sins, that he might deliver us from this present evil world" (Galatians 1:4). Those redeemed by Christ are risen with Christ: You were once bound in the chains of sin, but God has begun to beat off your chains and has freed you from the power of sin and the curse due to it. Be content to wait for this full and glorious redemption when you shall have that which "the eye hath not seen, nor ear heard . . . the things which God hath prepared for them that love him" (1 Corinthians 2:9).

9

APPLICATION OF REDEMPTION

The life which I now live in the flesh
I live by the faith of the Son of God.

GALATIANS 2:20

The Spirit applies the redemption purchased by Christ by working faith in us. Christ is the glory—and faith in Christ, the comfort—of the gospel.

What are the kinds of faith? There is an historical or dogmatic faith, which is believing the truths revealed in the Word, because of divine authority. There is a temporary faith, which lasts for a time, and then vanishes (Matthew 13:21). A miraculous faith was granted to the apostles, to work miracles for the confirmation of the gospel. This Judas had: he cast out devils, yet was cast out to the devil. And true, justifying faith, called "a faith of the operation of God," is a jewel hung only upon the elect (Colossians 2:12).

Justifying faith is not a mere acknowledgment that Christ is a Savior. There must be an acknowledgment, but that is not sufficient to justify. The devils acknowledged Christ's Godhead: "Jesus, thou Son of God" (Matthew 8:29). There may be an assent to divine truth, and yet no work of grace on the heart. Many assent in their judgments, that sin is an evil thing, but they go on in sin, whose corruptions are stronger than their convictions; and that Christ is excellent. They cheapen the pearl, but do not buy.

10

FAITH JUSTIFIES

Not having mine own righteousness, but
that which is through the faith of Christ,
the righteousness which is of God by faith.

PHILIPPIANS 3:9

Faith is going out of one's self, being taken off from our own merits, and seeing we have no righteousness of our own. Repentance and faith are both humbling graces: by repentance a man abhors himself; by faith he extends himself. Israel in their wilderness march, behind them saw Pharaoh and his chariots pursuing; before them. The Red Sea ready to devour. So the sinner behind sees God's justice pursuing him for sin; before him, hell ready to devour him; and in this forlorn condition, he sees nothing in himself to help, but he must perish unless he can find help in another.

The soul casts itself upon Jesus Christ; faith rests on Christ's person. Faith believes the promise; but that which faith rests upon in the promise is the person of Christ. Faith is described as "[believing] on the name of the Son of God" (1 John 3:23); that is, on His person. The promise is but the cabinet: Christ is the jewel in it which faith embraces. The promise is but the dish: Christ is the food in it that faith feeds on. Faith rests on Christ's person as He was crucified. It glories in the cross of Christ. To consider Christ crowned with all manner of excellencies stirs up admiration and wonder; but Christ looked upon as bleeding and dying is the proper object of our faith. It is called therefore "faith in his blood" (Romans 3:25).

11

THE SPIRIT OF GOD

[May you know] the exceeding greatness
of God's power to us . . . who believe.

EPHESIANS 1:19

Faith is fashioned by the blessed Spirit. He is called the Spirit of grace, because He is the spring of all grace. Faith is the chief work that the Spirit of God works in a man's heart. In making the world, God did but speak a word, but in working faith He puts forth His arm. What a power was put forth in raising Christ from the grave when such a tombstone lay upon Him as "the sins of the world"! Yet He was raised up by the Spirit. The same power is put forth by the Spirit of God in working faith. The Spirit exposes the mind and subdues the will. The will is like a fort that holds out against God. The Spirit, with sweet violence, conquers, or rather changes it: the Spirit makes the sinner willing to have Christ upon any terms; to be ruled by Him as well as saved by Him.

In its being the chief gospel-grace, the head of the graces, as gold among the metals, so is faith among the graces. In heaven, love will be the chief grace; but while we are here, love must give place to faith. Love takes possession of glory, but faith gives a title to it. Love is the crowning grace in heaven, but faith is the conquering grace upon earth. "This is the victory that overcometh the world, even our faith" (1 John 5:4).

12

FAITH, THE MASTER WHEEL

For in Christ Jesus neither circumcision availeth anything
nor uncircumcision; but faith which worketh by love.

GALATIANS 5:6

Faith sets love to work: believing the mercy and merit of Christ causes a flame of love to ascend. Faith sets patience to work: Be "followers of them who through faith and patience inherit the promises" (Hebrews 6:12). Faith believes the glorious rewards given to suffering, making the soul patient in suffering. Faith is the master-wheel: it sets all the other graces running.

Faith is precious in its being the grace that God honors to justify and save. It is "precious faith," as the apostle calls it in 2 Peter 1:1. The other graces help to sanctify, but it is faith that justifies. Repentance or love cannot justify, but faith does.

Faith does not justify as it is a work, that would make a Christ of our faith; but faith justifies as it lays hold of the object, of Christ's merits. Faith saves and justifies, but it is not any inherent virtue in faith, but as it lays hold on Christ it justifies.

Faith invigorates the graces, puts strength and liveliness into them, but it does not justify under this notion. Faith works by love, but it does not justify as it works by love, but as it applies Christ's merits.

Faith saves and justifies more than any other grace because of God's purpose. He has appointed this grace to be justifying; and He does it because faith is a grace that keeps man from being prideful, and that gives all honor to Christ and free grace: "Strong in faith, giving glory to God" (Romans 4:20).

13

FAITH AND THE COVENANT OF GRACE

Above all, [take up] the shield of faith.

EPHESIANS 6:16

Faith justifies because faith makes us one with Christ. It is the espousing, incorporating grace; it gives us coalition and union with Christ's person. Other graces make us like Christ; faith makes us members of Christ.

Faith will be of more use to us than any grace. It is not knowledge, though angelic, not repentance, though we could shed rivers of tears, could justify us; only faith, whereby we look on Christ. "Without faith it is impossible to please [God]" (Hebrews 11:6). If we do not please Him by believing, He will not please us in saving. Faith is the condition of the covenant of grace; without faith, without covenant; and without covenant, without hope (Ephesians 2:12).

Faith is distinguished by the fruits. Let us be serious in the trial of our faith. Much depends upon our faith; for if our faith be not good, nothing good comes from us, even our duties and graces are adulterated.

Faith puts a high value upon Christ: "unto you therefore which believe he is precious" (1 Peter 2:7). Paul best knew Christ: "Have I not seen Jesus Christ our Lord?" (1 Corinthians 9:1). He saw Christ with his bodily eyes in a vision, when he was caught up into the third heaven; and with the eye of his faith in the Holy Supper; therefore he best knew Christ. And see how he shapes all things in comparison of Him: "I count [all things] but dung, that I may win Christ" (Philippians 3:8).

14

FAITH REFINES, OBEYS, AND GROWS

[Hold] the mystery of faith in a pure conscience.

1 TIMOTHY 3:9

Faith is a refining grace. Faith is in the soul as fire among metals: it refines and purifies. Morality may wash the outside; faith washes the inside: "purifying their hearts by faith" (Acts 15:9). Faith is a virgin-grace: though it does not take away the life of sin, yet it takes away the love of sin.

Faith is an obedient grace: "the obedience of faith" (Romans 16:26). Faith melts our will into God's. If God commands duty, faith obeys: "by faith Abraham obeyed" (Hebrews 11:8). Faith is not an idle grace; as it has an eye to see Christ, so it has a hand to work for Him. It not only believes God's promise, but obeys His command. It is not having knowledge that will evidence you to be believers; the devil has knowledge, but wants obedience, and that makes him a devil. The true obedience of faith is a cheerful obedience.

True faith grows: "from faith to faith" (Romans 1:17). Growth of faith is judged by strength. We can do that now, which we could not do before. Growth of faith is seen by doing duties in a more spiritual manner, with more fervency; from a principle of love to God. When an apple has completely grown in size, it grows in sweetness; so we perform duties in love and are sweeter, and come off with a better relish.

15

ARE YOU WEAK IN FAITH?

Him that is weak in the faith receive ye,
but not to doubtful disputations.

ROMANS 14:1

We must distinguish between weakness of faith and no faith. A weak faith is true and may receive a strong Christ. A weak hand can tie the knot in marriage as well as a strong one; and a weak eye might have seen the brazen serpent. The woman in the gospel did but touch Christ's garment and received virtue from Him. It was the touch of faith.

The promise is not made to strong faith, but to true faith. The promise says not whosoever has a giant faith, that can remove mountains, that can stop the mouths of lions, shall be saved; but whosoever believes, be his faith ever so small. Though Christ sometimes chides a weak faith, yet that it may not be discouraged, He makes it a promise: "Blessed are the poor in spirit: for theirs is the kingdom of heaven" (Matthew 5:3).

Weakest things multiply most; the vine is a weak plant, but it is fruitful. Weak Christians may have strong affections. How strong is the first love, which is after the first planting of faith!

Weak faith may be growing. Seeds spring up by degrees; first the blade, then the ear, then the full corn in the ear. Therefore, be not discouraged. God who would have us receive them who are weak in faith will not Himself refuse them. A weak believer is a member of Christ; and though Christ will cut off rotten members from His body, He will not cut off weak members.

16

EFFECTUAL CALLING

Whom he did predestinate, them he also called.

ROMANS 8:30

Effectual calling is a gracious work of the Spirit, where He causes us to embrace Christ freely, as He is offered to us in the gospel.

The outward call is God's offer of grace to sinners, inviting them to come and accept of Christ and salvation: "Many be called, but few chosen" (Matthew 20:16). This shows men what they ought to do for salvation and renders them inexcusable in case of disobedience.

The inward call, when God offers grace, works grace. By this call the heart is renewed, and the will is effectually drawn to embrace Christ. The outward call brings men to a profession of Christ; the inward, to a possession of Christ.

Every creature has a voice to call us. The heavens call to us to behold God's glory. Conscience calls to us. God's judgments call us to repent. But every voice does not convert.

Preaching the Word is the sounding of God's silver trumpet in men's ears. God speaks not by an oracle; He calls by His ministers. Perhaps you think it is only the minister who speaks to you in the Word, but it is God Himself who speaks. Therefore Christ is said to speak to us from heaven. How does He speak but by His ministers? As a king speaks by his ambassadors. Know that, in every sermon preached, God calls to you; to refuse the message we bring, is to refuse God Himself.

17

THE HOLY SPIRIT'S CALL

While Peter yet spake these words, the Holy Ghost
fell on all them which heard the word of [God].

ACTS 10:44

The Spirit of God effectually changes men's hearts. Ministers knock at the door of men's hearts, but the Spirit comes with a key, opens the door, and calls them from their ignorance and unbelief. By nature, understanding is enveloped with darkness. God calls men from darkness to light, to behold the light of the sun.

God calls His people from the fire and brimstone of hell and from all those curses to which they were exposed. He calls them out of the world, as Christ called Matthew from the receipt of custom. "They are not of the world" (John 17:16). These are divinely called, not natives, but pilgrims: they do not conform to the world or follow its sinful fashions. They are not of the world; though they live here, yet they trade in the heavenly country. The world is a place where Satan's throne is. It is a stage on which sin every day acts its part. Now such as are called are in the world but not of it.

God calls men to holiness: "God hath not called us to uncleanness, but unto holiness" (1 Thessalonians 4:7). Holiness is a silver star that the godly wear. The called of God are anointed with the consecrating oil of the Spirit: "Ye have an unction from the Holy One" (1 John 2:20).

18

THE EFFECTUAL CALL OF GOD

*For our light affliction, which is but for a moment, worketh
for us a far more exceeding and eternal weight of glory.*

2 CORINTHIANS 4:17

God calls them to glory as if a man were called out of prison to sit upon a throne.

The weight of glory adds to the worth: the weightier gold is worth the most. Glory is permanent, an eternal weight, and better felt than expressed.

God's electing love is the cause of the effectual call: "whom he did predestinate, them he also called" (Romans 8:30). Election is the cause of our vocation. It is not because some are more worthy to partake of the heavenly calling than others, for we were all in our own blood (Ezekiel 16:6). Before effectual calling, we are not only "without strength" (Romans 5:6), but "enemies" (Colossians 1:21). The foundation of vocation is election.

God puts forth infinite power in calling home a sinner to Himself. God rides forth conquering in the chariot of His gospel: He conquers the pride of the heart and makes the will yield and stoop to His grace; He makes the stony heart bleed. It is a mighty call! If God, in conversion, should only morally persuade, that is, set good and evil before men, then He does not put forth so much power in saving men as the devil does in destroying them. The effectual call is mighty and powerful. God puts forth a divine energy, a kind of omnipotence: it is such a powerful call that the will of man has no power effectually to resist.

19

THE HIGH CALLING OF GOD

*I press toward the mark for the prize
of the high calling of God in Christ Jesus.*

PHILIPPIANS 3:14

We are called to high exercises of religion—to be crucified to the world, to live by faith, to do angels' work, to love God, to be living organs of His praise, to hold communion with the Father and the Son.

We are called to high privileges—to justification and adoption, to be kings and priests unto God; to the fellowship of angels; to be co-heirs with Christ (Romans 8:17). Those effectually called are candidates for heaven; they are princes in all lands, though princes in disguise.

It is an immutable call: "the gifts and calling of God are without repentance" (Romans 11:29); those gifts that flow from election are without repentance. God never repents of calling a sinner to be a saint.

We must be called before we are glorified. A man not called can lay claim to nothing in the Bible but warnings: a natural man is not fit for heaven, no more than a man in his rags is fit to come into a king's presence.

Before this effectual call, a humbling work passes upon the soul. A man is convinced he is a sinner; the fallow ground of his heart is broken up. God breaks a sinner's heart and makes it fit to receive the seeds of grace. Such as were never convinced are never called. The Holy Spirit shall convince the world of sin (John 16:8). Conviction is the first step in conversion.

20

ELECTION AND VOCATION

Speak; for thy servant heareth.

1 SAMUEL 3:10

He who is effectually called stops his ears to all other calls that would call him away from God. As God has His call, so there are other contrary calls. Satan calls by temptation; lust calls; evil company calls. But as the adder stops its ear against the voice of the charmer, so he who is effectually called stops his ear against all the charms of the flesh and the devil.

This call proves election: "whom he did predestinate, them he also called" (Romans 8:30). *Election is the cause of our vocation, and vocation is the sign of our election.* Election is the first link of the golden chain of salvation; vocation is the second. He who has the second link of the chain is sure of the first. As by the stream we are led to the fountain, so by vocation we ascend to election. Calling is an earnest and pledge of glory: "God hath from the beginning chosen you to salvation through sanctification of the Spirit and belief of the truth" (2 Thessalonians 2:13). We may read God's predestinating love in the work of grace in our heart.

Let such as are called be thankful to God for that unspeakable blessing. Be thankful to all the persons in the Trinity: the Father's mercy, the Son's merit, the Spirit's worth. To make you thankful, consider, when you had offended God, He called you. When God needed you not, but had millions of glorified saints and angels to praise Him, He called you.

21

JUSTIFICATION: THE PILLAR OF CHRISTIANITY

*Being justified freely by his grace through
the redemption that is in Christ Jesus.*

ROMANS 3:24

Justification is an act of God's free grace whereby He pardons all
our sins and accepts us as righteous in His sight, only for the righteousness of Christ, imputed to us and received by faith alone.

Justification is the pillar of Christianity. Justification by Christ
is a spring of the water of life. To have the poison of corrupt doctrine cast into this spring is damnable.

Justification is a word borrowed from law courts, where a person arraigned is pronounced righteous and is openly absolved.
God, in justifying a person, pronounces him to be righteous and
looks upon him as if he had not sinned.

The source of justification is the free grace of God. The first
wheel that sets all the rest running is the love and favor of God; as a
king freely pardons a delinquent. Justification is a mercy spun out of
the bowels of free grace. God does not justify us because we are worthy, but by justifying us makes us worthy.

The ground of our justification is Christ's satisfaction made to
His Father. How can it stand with God's justice and holiness to pronounce us innocent when we are guilty? The answer is that Christ,
having made satisfaction for our fault, God may, in equity and justice,
pronounce us righteous. It is a just thing for a creditor to discharge a
debtor of the debt when a satisfaction is made by the surety.

As He was man, He suffered; as God, He satisfied. By Christ's
death and merits, God's justice is more abundantly satisfied than if
we had suffered the pains of hell forever.

22

METHODS OF JUSTIFICATION

*This is his name whereby he shall
be called, the LORD our Righteousness.*

JEREMIAH 23:6

This righteousness of Christ, which justifies us, is a better righteousness than the angels', for theirs is the righteousness of creatures; this, of God.

The dignity is not in faith as a grace, but relatively, as it lays hold on Christ's merits.

The cause of our justification is the whole Trinity: All the persons in the blessed Trinity have a hand in the justification of a sinner. God the Father is said to justify. "It is God that justifieth" (Romans 8:33). God the Son is said to justify: "By him all that believe are justified" (Acts 13:39). God the Holy Ghost is said to justify: "But ye are justified . . . by the Spirit of our God" (1 Corinthians 6:11).

The end of our justification is that God may inherit praise: "to the praise of the glory of his grace" (Ephesians 1:6). Hereby God raises the everlasting trophies of His own honor. The justified sinner proclaims the love of God and makes heaven ring with His praises.

The justified person may inherit glory: "whom he justified, them he also glorified" (Romans 8:30). God, in justifying, not only absolves a soul from guilt, but advances him to dignity: as Joseph was not only loosed from prison, but made lord of the kingdom. Justification is crowned with glorification.

23

JUSTIFICATION AND SANCTIFICATION: INSEPARABLE!

But ye are sanctified, but ye are justified in the name
of the Lord Jesus, and by the Spirit of our God.

1 CORINTHIANS 6:2

Whomsoever God justifies, He sanctifies. Righteousness imputed, for justification, and righteousness inherent, for sanctification, are inseparably united. Holiness is not the cause of our justification, but it is the attendant. It is absurd to imagine that God should justify a people and they should still go on in sin. If God should justify a people and not sanctify them, He would justify a people whom He could not glorify. A holy God cannot lay a sinner in His bosom. The metal is first refined before the king's stamp is put upon it; so the soul is first refined with holiness before God puts the royal stamp of justification upon it.

Justification is a fixed permanent thing; it can never be lost. Justified persons may fall from degrees of grace, they may leave their first love, they may lose God's favor for a time, but they will not lose their justification. If they are justified, they are elected; and they cannot fall from their justification or from their election. If one justified person may fall away from Christ, all may; and so Christ would be a head without a body.

There is nothing within us that could justify, but something without us; not any righteousness inherent, but imputed. We may as well look for a star in the earth as for justification in our own righteousness.

Good works are not an usher to go before justification, but a handmaid to follow it.

24

CHRIST'S BLOOD: OUR JUSTIFICATION

By him all that believe are justified.

ACTS 13:39

Adore the infinite wisdom and goodness of God that found a way to justify us by His rich grace and precious blood. We were all involved in guilt; none of us could plead "not guilty." Being guilty, we lay under a sentence of death. That the judge Himself should find a way to justify us, and that the creditor contrive a way to have the debt paid and not distress the debtor, should fill us with wonder and love. The angels admire the mystery of free grace in this new way of justifying and saving lost man—and should not we, who are concerned in it and on whom the benefit is devolved?

Christ laid down His blood for our justification; He offers Himself and all His merits to us, to justify. He invites us to come to Him, and He promised to give His Spirit to enable us to do what is required. Why then, sinners, will we not look after this great privilege of justification? Is the love of Christ to be slighted? Is thy soul, is heaven, worth nothing? Oh, look after justification through Christ's blood!

If we are not justified, we cannot be glorified. He who is outlawed, and all his goods confiscated, must be brought into favor with his prince before he can be restored his former rights and liberties. So, our sins must be forgiven before we enter God's favor by justification, before we can be restored to the liberty of the sons of God, and have a right to that happiness we forfeited in Adam.

25

ADOPTION

As many as received him, to them gave he
power to become the sons of God,
even to them that believe on his name.

JOHN 1:12

The qualification for adoption as God's sons is "as many as received him." Receiving is believing, as is clear: "to them that believe on his name."

The specification of the privilege is "to them gave he power to become the sons of God." He dignified them to become the sons of God.

Christ was the Son of God by eternal generation, but our sonship is by creation: "We are also his offspring" (Acts 17:28). Men may have God for their Father by creation, and yet have the devil for their father.

Our sonship is by adoption: "He gave them power to become the sons of God." Adoption does not discriminate: a first adoption was confined to the people of the Jews, who were grafted into the true olive and dignified with glorious privileges. In the time of the gospel, the charter is enlarged, and believing Gentiles, within the line of communication, have a right to the privilege of adoption as well as the Jews: "In every nation he that feareth [God], and worketh righteousness, is accepted" (Acts 10:35).

Adoption takes both sexes: "[I] will be a father unto you, and ye shall be my sons and daughters" (2 Corinthians 6:18). Adoption is mercy spun out of the bowels of free grace.

26

LIBERTY

Thou art no more a servant, but a son.

GALATIANS 4:7

Adopted sons are free from the dominion of sin, the tyranny of Satan, and the curse of the law. They are free in the manner of worship; they have God's free Spirit; they are "joyful in [my] house of prayer" (Isaiah 56:7).

God makes us heirs of promise, installing us into honor: "Since thou wast precious in my sight, thou hast been honorable" (Isaiah 43:4). The adopted are God's treasure; His jewels; His firstborn. They have angels as guardians, and they are of the royal blood of heaven. The Scripture has set forth their spiritual heraldry: they have a coat of armor; sometimes the lion for courage, sometimes the dove for meekness, and sometimes the eagle for flight.

God adopts all His sons to an inheritance: "It is your Father's good pleasure to give you the kingdom" (Luke 12:32). Adoption ends in coronation. Other kingdoms are corruptible; though they have heads of gold, they have feet of clay. But the kingdom into which the saints are adopted runs parallel with eternity, it is a kingdom that cannot be shaken. The heirs of heaven reign for ever and ever.

Faith interests us in the privilege of adoption: before faith is formed, we are spiritually illegitimate; we have no relation to God as a father. An unbeliever may call God "Judge," but not "Father." Faith is the affiliating grace: it confers upon us the title of sonship and gives us a right to inherit.

27

HEIRS OF THE KINGDOM

*They proceed from evil to evil,
and they know not me, saith the LORD.*

JEREMIAH 9:3

If a man will not adopt his mortal enemy for his heir, that God should adopt us—when we were not only strangers, but enemies—is the wonder of His love. For God to have pardoned His enemies was amazing; to adopt them for His heirs sets the angels in heaven wondering.

Men usually adopt but one heir, but God is resolved to increase His family, so He brings many sons to glory. Had but one been adopted, all of us might have despaired; but He brings many sons to glory, which opens the door of hope.

The more honor God puts upon us in adopting us, the more His love is magnified toward us. What honor that God made us so near in alliance to Him, sons of God the Father, members of God the Son, temples of God the Holy Ghost! He made us as the angels, proclaiming the wonder of God's love in adopting us.

All God's children know their Father, but the wicked do not know Him. God has no dead children; and not being children, they have no right to inherit. Adoption does not come by blood. Many godly parents have wicked sons: Abraham had an Ishmael; Isaac, an Esau. From him who is holy the child springs that is unholy. We are not God's sons as we are born of godly parents, but by adoption and grace.

28

THE OBEDIENCE OF FAITH

To the law and to the testimony: if they speak not
according to this word, it is because there is no light in them.

ISAIAH 8:20

If our obedience be not according to the Word, it is offering up
strange fire. It is *will* worship; and God will say, "Who has required
this at your hand?" The apostle condemns worshiping of angels,
which had a show of humility. The Jews might say that they were
loath to be so bold as to go to God personally; they would be more
humble and prostrate themselves before the angels, desiring them
to be their mediators to God. Here was a show of humility in their
angel worship; but it was abominable, because they had no word of
God to warrant it. Childlike obedience is that which is consonant
to our Father's revealed will.

Obedience must be done from a right principle, from the
noble principle of faith: "the obedience of faith" (Romans 16:26).
A crab tree may bear fruit fair to the eye, but it is sour because it
does not come from a good root. A moral person may give God
outward obedience, which to the eyes of others may seem glorious;
but his obedience is sour because it comes not from the sweet and
pleasant root of faith. A child of God gives Him the obedience of
faith, and that improves and sweetens his services, and makes them
come off with a better relish: "By faith Abel offered unto God a
more excellent sacrifice than Cain" (Hebrews 11:4).

29

THE END OF OBEDIENCE IS GLORIFYING GOD

Though I give my body to be burned, and
have not charity, it profiteth me nothing.

1 CORINTHIANS 13:3

The end determines the value of the deed; the end of obedience is glorifying God. That which spoiled many glorious services is that the end has been wrong: "When thou doest thine alms, do not sound a trumpet before thee, as the hypocrites do . . . that they may have glory of men" (Matthew 6:2). Good works should shine, but not blaze. If I obey so much, and have not a sincere aim, it profits me nothing. True obedience looks at God in all things: that "Christ shall be magnified" (Philippians 1:20).

True childlike obedience is uniform. A child of God makes conscience of every command. All things done for God are done with equal zeal. All God's commands have the same stamp of divine authority upon them; and if I obey one precept because my heavenly Father commands me, by the same rule I must obey all. As the blood runs through all the veins of the body, and the sun in the firmament runs through all the signs of the zodiac, so true childlike obedience runs through the first and second table: "when I have respect unto all thy commandments" (Psalm 119:6). To obey God in some things of religion and not in others shows an unsound heart. Childlike obedience moves toward every command of God. If God calls to duties which are cross to flesh and blood, if we are His children, we shall still obey our Father.

30

SET APART FOR GOD'S SERVICE

For this is the will of God, even your sanctification.

1 THESSALONIANS 4:3

The word *sanctification* signifies "to consecrate and set apart to a holy use." Thus they are sanctified persons who are separated from the world and set apart for God's service. Sanctification has a privative and a positive part.

The privative part of sanctification lies in the purging of sin. Sin is compared to leaven, which sours, and to leprosy, which defiles. Sanctification purges out "the old leaven" (1 Corinthians 5:7). It takes away the love of sin, but leaves life!

A positive part of sanctification is the spiritual refining of the soul, which is called a "renewing of your mind" (Romans 12:2) and "[partaking] of the divine nature" (2 Peter 1:4). The priests in the law were not only washed in the great laver, but adorned with glorious apparel. So sanctification not only washes from sin, but adorns with purity.

Sanctification is a principle of grace savingly fashioned, whereby the heart becomes holy and is made after God's heart. A sanctified person bears not only God's Name, but His image.

Sanctification is a supernatural thing; it is divinely infused. We are naturally polluted, and to cleanse, God takes to be His prerogative: "I the LORD, which sanctify you, am holy" (Leviticus 21:8). Weeds grow by themselves; flowers are planted. Sanctification is a flower of the Spirit's planting, therefore it is called the "sanctification of the Spirit" (1 Peter 1:2).

1

SANCTIFICATION ENGULFS THE WHOLE MAN

Abstain from all appearance of evil.
The God of peace sanctify you wholly.

1 THESSALONIANS 5:23

As original corruption has depraved all the faculties—"the whole head is sick, and the whole heart faint" (Isaiah 1:5), as if all the blood were corrupted—sanctification covers the whole soul. After the Fall, there was ignorance in the mind; but in sanctification, we are "light in the Lord" (Ephesians 5:8). After the Fall, the *will* was depraved; there was not only impotence to good, but obstinacy. After the Fall, the affections were misplaced; in sanctification, they are turned into a sweet order and harmony, the grief placed on sin, the love on God, the joy on heaven. Thus sanctification spreads itself as far as original corruption; it goes over the whole soul: "the God of peace sanctify you wholly." He is not a sanctified person that is good only in some part, but who is sanctified all over. Therefore, in Scripture, grace is called a "new man" not a new eye or a new tongue, but a "new man" (Colossians 3:10). A good Christian, though he be sanctified but in part, yet in every part.

Sanctification is an intense thing: he is holy whose heart boils over in love to God.

Sanctification is a beautiful thing: it makes God and angels fall in love with us.

Sanctification is an abiding thing: one truly sanctified cannot fall from that state.

Sanctification is a progressive thing: it is growing. It is compared to seed which grows: first the blade springs up, then the ear, then the ripe corn in the ear such as are already sanctified may be more sanctified.

2

THE NECESSITY OF SANCTIFICATION

God hath not called us unto uncleanness, but unto holiness.

1 THESSALONIANS 4:7

God has called us to sanctification: He has "called us to glory and virtue" (2 Peter 1:3) to virtue as well as glory. We have no call to sin. We may have a temptation, but no call; no call to be proud or unclean; but we have a call to be holy.

Without sanctification, there is no evidence of justification. Justification and sanctification go together: "But ye are sanctified, but ye are justified" (1 Corinthians 6:11). God "pardoneth iniquity" (Micah 7:18): there is justification. "He will subdue iniquities" (5:19): there is sanctification. "Out of Christ's side came blood and water" (John 19:34): blood for justification; water for sanctification.

Without sanctification, we have no title to the new covenant. The covenant of grace is our charter for heaven. The tenure of the covenant is that God will be our God. Those sanctified are the only ones with an interest in the covenant: "A new heart also will I give you . . . I will put my Spirit within you . . . and I will be your God" (Ezekiel 36:26–28). God makes a will and testament, but it is restrained and limited to such as are sanctified; and it is high presumption for anyone else to lay claim to the will.

Without "holiness, no man shall see the Lord" (Hebrews 12:14). God is a holy God, and He will suffer no unholy creature to come near Him.

3

SIGNS OF SANCTIFICATION (PART ONE)

The Holy Ghost which dwelleth in us.

2 TIMOTHY 1:14

Those sanctified can remember a time when they were unsanctified: we were in our blood, and then God washed us with water and anointed us with oil. Those trees of righteousness that blossom and bear almonds can remember when they were like Aaron's dry rod, not one blossom of holiness growing. A sanctified soul can remember when it was estranged from God through ignorance and vanity, and when free grace planted this flower of holiness in it.

A second sign of sanctification is the indwelling of the Spirit. As the unclean spirit dwells in the wicked and carries them to pride, lust, and revenge, the devil enters into these swine. So the Spirit of God dwells in the elect as their Guide and Comforter. The Spirit possesses the saints. God's Spirit sanctifies the fancy, causing it to mint holy thoughts, and sanctifies the will by putting a new bias upon it, where it is inclined to good. He who is sanctified has the influence of the Spirit, though not the essence.

A third sign of sanctification is an aversion against sin. A hypocrite may leave sin, yet love it; but a sanctified person can say he not only leaves sin, but loathes it. In a sanctified soul there is a holy hostility against sin; and aversions can never be reconciled. Because a man has an aversion against sin, he cannot but oppose it, and seek the destruction of it.

4

SIGNS OF SANCTIFICATION (PART TWO)

Be ye holy in all manner of conversation.

1 PETER 1:15

A fourth sign of sanctification is the spiritual performance of duties, with the heart, and from a principle of love. The sanctified soul prays out of a love for prayer and "call[s] the Sabbath a delight" (Isaiah 58:13). A man may have gifts to admiration; he may speak as an angel dropped out of heaven, yet be carnal in spiritual things; his services may not come from a renewed principle nor be carried upon the wings of delight in duty. A sanctified soul worships God in the Spirit. God judges not our duties by their length, but by the love from which they spring.

A fifth sign of sanctification is a well-ordered life. There is holiness of life where the heart is sanctified; the life will be too. Not only is God's image in the heart, but a superscription of holiness is written in the life. Grace is most beautiful when its light shines that others may see it; this adorns religion and makes proselytes to the faith.

A sixth sign of sanctification is steadfast resolution: he is resolved never to part with His holiness. Let others reproach it, he loves it the more. Let others persecute him for his holiness, and he says, "None of these things move me" (Acts 20:24). He prefers sanctity before safety and had rather keep his conscience pure than his skin whole. The Christian will rather part with his life than his conscience.

5

SANCTIFIED IN AN UNSANCTIFIED WORLD

The whole world lieth in wickedness.

1 JOHN 5:19

Sanctification is our nobility: by it we are born of God and partake of the divine nature. It is our riches, compared to rows of jewels and chains of gold. What evidence have we else to show? Have we knowledge? So has the devil. Do we profess religion? Satan often transforms himself into an angel of light. But our certificate for heaven is sanctification. Sanctification is the first fruits of the Spirit, the only coin that will pass current in the other world. Sanctification is the evidence of God's love. We cannot know God's love by giving us health, riches, success; but by drawing His image of sanctification on us by the pencil of the Holy Ghost, His love is known.

The greatest part of the world remains unsanctified. Many call themselves Christians, but blot out the word *saints*. You may as well call him a man who lacks reason, as him a Christian who lacks grace. Even worse, some are buoyed up to such a height of wickedness that they hate and deride sanctification. It is bad to lack it; it is worse to hate it. They embrace the form of religion, but hate the power. The vulture hates sweet smells, so do they the perfumes of holiness. To ridicule sanctification argues a high degree of atheism and is a black brand of reprobation. Such as scoff at holiness shall be cast out of heaven.

6

ASSURANCE OF GOD'S LOVE

I know whom I have believed.

2 TIMOTHY 1:12

The benefits which flow from sanctification are assurance of God's love, peace of conscience, joy in the Holy Ghost, increase of grace, and perseverance therein to the end.

The first benefit flowing from sanctification is assurance of God's love: "Give diligence to make your calling and election sure" (2 Peter 1:10). Sanctification is the seed, and assurance is the flower which grows out of it: assurance is a consequence of sanctification. The saints of old had it: "We do know that we know him" (1 John 2:3) and "I live by the faith of the Son of God, who loved me" (Galatians 2:20). Here is faith flourishing into assurance.

All sanctified persons have a right to the assurance of God's love, though their comfort may express what they feel. But I dare not affirm that all have assurance in the first moment of their sanctification. Where there is the sanctifying work of the Spirit, He may withhold the sealing work, partly to keep the soul humble; partly to punish our careless walking—as when we neglect our spiritual watch, grow remiss in duty, and walk under a cloud, we quench the graces of the Spirit, and God withholds the comforts; and partly to put a difference between earth and heaven. You may have the water of the Spirit poured on you in sanctification, though not the oil of gladness in assurance. There may be faith of adherence, and not of evidence; there may be life in the root, when there is no fruit in the branches to be seen; so faith in the heart, when no fruit of assurance.

7

TRINITY: THE AUTHOR OF PEACE

Grace unto you, and peace, be multiplied.

1 PETER 1:2

Peace is compared to a river that parts itself into two silver streams. First there is an external peace: peace in a family, peace in the state, or peace in the church. How pleasant it is when the waters of blood begin to ease, and we can see the windows of our ark open, and the dove returning with an olive branch of peace! Peace in the church, like unity in Trinity, is the greatest mystery in heaven. Peace ecclesiastical stands in opposition to division and persecution.

Second there is a spiritual peace or peace with God; and peace within us, or peace with conscience, which is superlative: other peace may be lasting, but this is everlasting. The whole Trinity is its author. God the Father is "the God of peace" (1 Thessalonians 5:23). God the Son is the "Prince of Peace" (Isaiah 9:6). Peace is said to be the "fruit of the Spirit" (Galatians 5:22).

God the Father is the God of peace. As He is the God of order, so He is the God of peace.

God the Son is the purchaser of peace: "having made peace through the blood of his cross" (Colossians 1:20). Christ our high priest, who by His sacrifice pacified His angry Father, made atonement for us. Christ purchased our peace upon hard terms; for His soul was in agony while He was travailing to bring forth peace to the world.

The Spirit clears up the work of grace in the heart, from whence arises peace.

The Father decrees peace, the Son purchases it, and the Holy Ghost applies it.

8

SPIRITUAL JOY

The fruit of the Spirit is . . . joy.

GALATIANS 5:22

Joy is setting the soul upon the top of a pinnacle; it is the cream of the sincere milk of the Word. Spiritual joy is a sweet and delightful passion, arising from the apprehension and feeling of some good, whereby the soul is supported under present troubles and fenced against future fear.

Spiritual joy is a delightful passion. It is contrary to sorrow, which is a perturbation of mind that, when not dealt with, may cause the heart to be perplexed and cast down. Joy is a sweet and pleasant affection that eases the mind, exhilarates and comforts the spirits.

Joy is not a fancy or conceit; but it is rational, and arises from the feeling of some good, as the sense of God's love and favor. Joy is so real a thing that it makes a sudden change in a person and turns mourning into melody. As in the springtime, when the sun comes to our horizon, it makes a sudden alteration in the face of the universe—birds sing, flowers appear, the fig tree puts forth her green figs; everything seems to rejoice and put off its mourning, as being revived with the sweet influence of the sun. So, when the Sun of Righteousness arises on the soul, it makes a sudden alteration, and the soul is infinitely rejoiced with the golden beams of God's love.

Joy swallows up troubles; it carries the heart above them, as oil swims above the water.

9

JOY: A CORDIAL AND AN ANTIDOTE

I will fear no evil: for thou art with me;
thy rod and thy staff they comfort me.

PSALM 23:4

Joy is a cordial, providing relief to the spirits when they are sad; and an antidote, fencing off fear of approaching danger.

This joy arises partly from the promise. As the bee lies at the breast of the flower, and sucks out its sweetness, so faith lies at the breast of a promise, and sucks out the essence of joy. "Thy comforts delight my soul" (Psalm 94:19); that is, the comforts that distill from the promises. The *Comforter* drops this golden oil of joy into the soul; the Spirit whispers remission of his sin and sheds God's love abroad in the heart, whence flows infinite joy and delight.

There are five seasons in which God gives His people divine joys. First, sometimes at the Lord's Supper the soul comes weeping after Christ in the Sacrament, and God sends it away weeping for joy. There are two grand ends of this Sacrament: the strengthening of faith and the flourishing of joy. In this ordinance, God displays the *banner of His Love*; believers taste not only sacramental bread, but hidden manna. Not that God always meets the soul with joy. He may give increase of grace when not increase of joy; but oftentimes He pours in the oil of gladness and gives the soul a private seal of His love; as Christ made Himself known in the breaking of bread.

Growth in Grace

But grow in grace.

2 Peter 3:18

True grace is progressive, of a spreading and growing nature. It is with grace as with light: first, there is the daybreak; then it shines brighter to the full meridian. A good Christian is like the crocodile: he never stops growing. The saints are not only compared to stars for their light, but to trees for their growth. A good Christian is not like Hezekiah's sun that went backwards, nor Joshua's sun that stood still, but is always advancing in holiness and increasing with the increase of God.

A Christian grows in the exercise of grace. His lamp is burning and shining: therefore he has a lively hope. Here is the activity of grace. The church prays for the blowing of the Spirit, that her spices might flow forth.

A Christian grows in the degree of grace: he goes from strength to strength, from one degree of grace to another. A saint goes from faith to faith, and his love abounds more and more.

A Christian is humbled: "I am a worm, and no man" (Psalm 22:6). The sight of corruption and ignorance makes a Christian grow to dislike himself; he vanishes in his own eyes. Job abhorred himself in the dust.

The right manner of growth is to grow proportionately, to grow in one grace as well as another. As the beauty of the body consists in symmetry of parts, in which not only the head grows, but the arms and breast, so spiritual growth is most beautiful when there is symmetry and proportion, when every grace thrives.

11

PERSEVERANCE IN GRACE

*Who are kept by the power
of God through faith unto salvation.*

1 PETER 1:5

The last fruit of sanctification is perseverance in grace. The heavenly inheritance is kept for the saints, and they are kept to the inheritance (1 Peter 1:4–5). The apostle asserts a saint's stability and permanence in grace. The saint's perseverance is much opposed; but it is not any less true.

A Christian's main comfort depends upon this doctrine of perseverance. Take this away, and you prejudice religion and cut cheerful endeavors.

Believers persevere, but such as are so only in profession may fall away. "Demas hath forsaken me" (2 Timothy 4:10). Blazing comets soon evaporate. A building on sand will fall. Seeming grace may be lost, and hypocrites are only tied on Christ by an external profession; they are not ingrafted. Whoever thought artificial motions would hold long?

Some of the angels, who were stars full of light and glory, actually lost their grace; and if those pure angels fell from grace, much more would the godly, who have so much sin to betray them, if they were not upheld by a superior power.

Although true believers do not fall away actually, and lose all their grace, yet their grace may fail in degree, and they may make a great breach upon their sanctification. Grace may be dying, but not dead. "Strengthen the things which remain, that are ready to die" (Revelation 3:2). Grace may be like fire in the embers: though not quenched, yet the flame is gone out. This is a decay of grace.

12

To Live is Christ

For to me to live is Christ . . .

PHILIPPIANS 1:21

Paul was a great admirer of Christ. He desired to know nothing but Christ, and Him crucified (1 Corinthians 2:2). "For me to live is Christ": that is, Christ is my life, or my life is made up of Christ. As a wicked man's life is made up of sin, so Paul's life was made up of Christ: he was full of Christ.

"For me to live is Christ": Christ is to be the principle of my life. As the branch gets its sap from the root, Christians get their life from Christ: "Christ liveth in me" (Galatians 2:20). Jesus Christ is a head of influence; He sends forth life and spirits into me, to quicken me to every holy action. Thus, "for to me to live is Christ": Christ is the principle of my life; from His fullness I live, as the vine branch lives from the root.

"For me to live is Christ": Christ is the end of my life; I live not to myself but to Christ: all my living is to do service to Christ. "Whether we live, we live unto the Lord, and whether we die, we die unto the Lord" (Romans 14:8). When we lay out ourselves wholly for Christ, we trade for Christ's interest: we propagate His gospel; the design of our life is to exalt Christ and make the crown upon His head flourish. It may then be said, for to us to live is Christ. Our whole life is a living to Christ.

13

A BELIEVER'S STATE AT DEATH

To die, is gain.

PHILIPPIANS 1:21

Christians rejoice in Christ's righteousness, and they can rejoice in Christ when worldly joys are gone. When relations die, saints rejoice in Christ, the pearl of price. In this sense, "For me to live is Christ." He is the joy of my life; if Christ were gone, my life would be death to me.

Christ is the principle of my life, the end of my life, the joy of my life. If we can say, "For me to live is Christ," we may comfortably conclude that to die shall be gain. To a believer, death is great gain. A saint can tell what his losses for Christ are here, but he cannot tell how great his gains are at death. Death to a believer is the day-break of eternal brightness. To show fully what a believer's gains are at death was a task too great for an angel; all obvious exaggeration fall short of it; the reward of glory exceeds our very faith.

Believers at death shall gain a written order of ease from all sins and troubles; they shall be in a state of excellence: sin expires with their life. I think sometimes what a happy state that will be, never to have another sinful thought, and to have a release from all troubles in this life!

14

A Believer's Privilege at Death

To die is gain.

PHILIPPIANS 1:21

Hope is a Christian's anchor, which he casts within the veil. A Christian's hope is not in this life, but "the righteous hath hope in his death" (Proverbs 14:32). A saint's comfort begins when his life ends; but the wicked have all their heaven here. "Woe unto you that are rich! for ye have received your consolation" (Luke 6:24). You may make your acquittance and write *Received in Full*. "Son, remember that thou in thy lifetime receivedst thy good things" (Luke 16:25). But a saint's happiness is in reversion: God keeps the best wine till last: "The day of death [is better] than the day of one's birth" (Ecclesiastes 7:1).

The saints, at death, have great immunities and freedoms: when life is over, they are made free! There are in the best the remnants of sin, some remainders and relics of corruption. "O wretched man that I am! who shall deliver me from the body of this death?" (Romans 7:24). It may well be called a *body* for its weightiness, and a body of *death* for its repulsion. It weighs us down: "The good that I would I do not" (Romans 7:19). He is like a ship under sail, and at anchor! Grace would sail forward, but sin is the anchor that holds it back.

15

SIN BINDS

The evil which I would not, that I do.

ROMANS 7:19

Sin is more active in its sphere than grace. How stirring was the lust in David when his grace lay dormant! Sin sometimes gets the mastery and leads a saint captive. "The evil which I would not, that I do": Paul was like a man carried down the stream and could not bear up against it. How often is a child of God overpowered with pride and passion! Therefore Paul calls sin a law in his members (Romans 7:24). It binds as a law; it has jurisdiction over the soul.

Sin defiles the soul; like a stain to beauty, it turns the soul's azure brightness into sable. Sin debilitates us, disarms us of our strength. "I am this day weak" (2 Samuel 3:39). Though a saint be crowned with grace and anointed a spiritual king, he is weak. Sin is ever restless: "the flesh lusteth against the spirit" (Galatians 5:17). Sin adheres to us; we cannot get rid of it. Sin mingles with our duties and graces. It makes a child of God weary of his life, and makes him weep to think sin is so strong, and he often offends the God he loves. This made Paul cry out, "O wretched man that I am!" (Romans 7:24). He did not cry out for his affliction, or his prison chains, but for the body of sin. Now a believer at death is freed from sin: he is not taken away in, but from his sins; he shall never have a vain, proud thought more; he shall never grieve the Spirit of God anymore.

16

A Believer's Death is Freeing

The spirits of just men made perfect.

HEBREWS 12:23

Sin brought death into the world, and death shall carry sin out of the world. Death smites a believer, as the angel did Peter and made his chains fall off. Believers at death are made perfect in holiness. At death the souls of believers recover their virgin purity: without spot or wrinkle; to be purer than the sunbeams; to be as free from sin as the angels! This makes a believer desirous to have his passport and to be gone; he would live in that pure air where no black vapors of sin arise.

At death the saints shall be freed from this life's trouble. Life and trouble are married together. There is more in life to wean us than to tempt us. Man is heir to trouble, and it is his birthright; you may as well separate weight from lead as trouble from the life of man. There is a far greater proportion of bitterness than pleasure in this life. "I have perfumed my bed with myrrh, aloes, and cinnamon" (Proverbs 7:17). For one sweet ingredient there were two bitter.

A man's grace will not exempt him from troubles. "Few and evil have the days of the years of my life been" (Genesis 47:9). There are many things to embitter life and cause trouble, but death will free a child of God from all.

17

A Believer's Death is the Only Cure

*Blessed are the dead which die in
the Lord . . . they rest from their labors.*

REVELATION 14:13

There are many things to embitter life and cause trouble, but death frees us from all. The mind is full of perplexed thoughts, how to bring about such a design; how to prevent such an evil. Care excruciates the mind; wastes the spirits. Care is a spiritual canker that eats out the comfort of life. Death is its only cure.

Fear is the fever of the soul, which sets it shaking. "Fear hath torment" (1 John 4:18). There is a mistrustful fear, a fear of want; and a distracting fear, a fear of danger; and a discouraging fear, a fear God does not love us. These fears leave sad impressions upon the mind. At death a believer is freed from these torturing fears; he is as far from fear as the damned are from hope. The grave buries a Christian's fear.

God has made a law: "In the sweat of thy face shalt thou eat bread" (Genesis 3:19). But death takes a believer off from his day labor. Who needs work, when they have their reward? Who needs fighting, when the crown is set on their head?

Believers are as the dove among birds of prey. The wicked have an aversion to them, and secret hatred will break forth into open violence: "He that was born after the flesh, persecuted him that was born after the Spirit" (Galatians 4:29). But at death the godly shall be freed from the molestations of the wicked; Death does to a believer, as Joseph of Arimathaea did to Christ: it takes him down from the cross and gives him a writ of ease. Death gives the soul the wings of an eagle to fly above all the venomous serpents here below.

DECEMBER

18

A Believer's Death is Gain

To die is gain.

Philippians 1:21

Though Satan is a conquered enemy, yet he is restless (1 Peter 5:8). It is no small trouble to be continually followed with temptations, but death will free a child of God from temptation, so that he shall never be vexed more with the old serpent. After death has shot its dart, the devil will be done shooting his. Grace puts a believer out of the devil's possession, but death only frees him from the devil's temptation.

A cloud of sorrow often gathers in the heart and drops into tears. "My life is spent with grief, and my years with sighing" (Psalm 31:10). It was part of the curse: "In sorrow thou shalt bring forth children" (Genesis 3:16). Sorrow is the evil spirit that haunts us. We spend our years with sighing: it is a valley of tears; but death is the funeral of all our sorrows. "And God shall wipe away all tears" (Revelation 7:17). Then Christ's spouse puts off her mourning; for how can the children of the bride chamber mourn when the bridegroom is with them? Death gives a believer release, freeing him from sin and trouble. Though the apostle calls death the last enemy, yet it is the best friend. "To me . . . to die is gain."

19

FAITH ANCHORS THE SOUL TO CHRIST

*Which hope we have as an anchor
of the soul, both sure and stedfast . . .*

HEBREWS 6:19

"To me," says Paul, "to die is gain" (Philippians 1:21); to me insofar as I am a believer. Faith is operative: with secret virtue in it; it anchors the soul to Christ. It has both a justifying and sanctifying virtue, removing blood from Christ's side to pardon and water out of His side to purge. Faith works by love; it constrains to duty; it makes us learn of Christ, confess Him, and work for Him.

I have read of a father who had three sons and left in his will all his estate to that son who could find his ring with the jewel that had a healing virtue. The case was brought before the judges: the two elder sons counterfeited a ring, but the younger son brought the true ring, which was proved by its virtue, so his father's estate went to him. To this ring, compare faith. There is a counterfeit faith in the world: but if we can find this ring of faith that has the healing virtue to purify the heart, it is the true faith that gives an interest in Christ, entitling us to all these privileges at death, to be freed from sin and sorrow and to have our bodies united to Christ

At death the souls of believers pass into glory. Death brings the removal of all evils, and the attainment of all things; it is the day-break of eternal brightness.

20

CELESTIAL GLORY

We shall see him as he is.

1 JOHN 3:2

Glory is a state made perfect by the gathering together of everything good; it is a perfect state of bliss, which consists in the accumulation and heaping together all the good things of which immortal souls are capable. And truly here I am at a loss, for all I can say falls short of the celestial glory. We shall never understand glory fully until we are in heaven.

A sublime part of the glory of heaven is the full and sweet realization of God: the very essence of happiness is the enjoyment and realization of God. God is an infinite, inexhaustible fountain of joy; and to have Him, is to have all.

The enjoyment of God implies several things. It implies our seeing God, and we shall see Him intellectually with the eyes of the mind. We shall have a full knowledge of God, though not know Him fully. We will not know Him fully until we get to heaven, thus the sight of God will be very glorious.

We shall corporally behold the glorified body of Jesus Christ. How blessed a sight will it be to behold the Sun of Righteousness sitting in glory above the angels! Surely the eyes of saints will be satisfied with seeing that orient brightness that shall shine from the beautiful body of Christ!

It must be satisfying, because through Christ's flesh some rays and beams of the Godhead will gloriously display themselves. God's excellent majesty would overwhelm us; but through the veil of Christ's flesh, we shall behold the divine glory.

21

TRANSFORMED

We shall be like him.

1 JOHN 3:2

Saints will be in some measure changed into His image, being always in God's presence. Once in heaven, the saints shall so see God, as that sight shall transform them into His likeness: "When I awake, I shall be satisfied with thy likeness" (Psalm 17:15). Not that the saints shall partake of God's essence; for as the iron in the fire is made fiery, it is still iron. So the saints, by beholding God's majesty, shall be made glorious creatures, but are creatures still.

The saints will never be weary of seeing God; for, God being infinite, there shall be, every moment new, and fresh delight springing from Him into their souls.

In heaven saints shall be like the seraphims, burning with divine love. Love is a pleasant affection and has joy in it. To love beauty is delightful. God's amazing beauty will attract the saints' love, and it will be their heaven to love Him.

Were there glory in God, yet if there were not love, it would much eclipse the joys of heaven; but "God is love" (1 John 4:16). The saints glorified cannot love so much as they are loved. What is their love to God's? What is their star to this Sun? God loves His people on earth when they are black as well as comely. If now they have their imperfections, oh, how entirely will He love them when they are without spot or wrinkle (Ephesians 5:27).

22

DEATH'S GLORIOUS BENEFITS

And I John saw the holy city, new Jerusalem,
coming down from God out of heaven,
prepared as a bride adorned for her husband.

REVELATION 21:2

See what little cause believers have to fear death when it brings such glorious benefits. Is it not a blessed thing to see God, to love God, and to lie forever in the bosom of divine love? Is it not a blessed thing to meet our godly relations in heaven? Why should the saints be afraid of their blessings? What hurt does death, but take us from among fiery serpents and place us among angels? What hurt does it do, but to clothe us with a robe of immortality? Has he any wrong done him that has his sackcloth pulled off and has cloth of gold put upon him? Fear not dying, you who cannot live but by dying.

You, whose hearts are purified by faith, spend much time in musing upon those glorious benefits which you shall have by Christ at death. We should contemplate the celestial glory, when we shall see God face to face! A true saint every day takes a turn in heaven: his thoughts and desires are like cherubim flying up to paradise. Can men of the world delight in looking upon their bags of gold and fields of corn, and shall not the heirs of heaven take more delight in contemplating their glory in reversion? Could we send forth faith as a spy and every day view the glory of the Jerusalem above, how would we rejoice, as it does the heir good to think of the inheritance to be in his hand shortly?

23

THE RESURRECTION

*Marvel not at this: for the hour is coming, in which all that are
in the graves shall hear his voice, and shall come forth; they
that have done good, unto the resurrection of life; and they
that have done evil, unto the resurrection of damnation.*

JOHN 5:28–29

At the resurrection, believers will have their bodies raised up to
glory, they will be openly acquitted at the day of judgment, and they
shall be made perfectly blessed in the full enjoyment of God to all
eternity.

The doctrine of the resurrection is a fundamental article of our
faith; the apostle puts it among the first principles of the doctrine
of Christ (Hebrews 6:2). The body shall rise again. Some hold that
the soul shall be clothed with a new body; but then it would not be
a resurrection, it would be rather a creation. "Though . . . worms
destroy this body, yet in my flesh shall I see God" (Job 19:26). Not
in another flesh, but in my flesh.

Scripture proves the resurrection: "I will raise him up at the
last day" (John 6:44) and "He will swallow up death in victory"
(Isaiah 25:8). Christ is risen, therefore the bodies of saints must
rise. Christ rose from the dead as the head of the church; and the
head being raised, the rest of the body shall not always lie in the
grave. Christ's rising is a pledge of our resurrection: "Knowing that
he which raised up the Lord Jesus shall raise up us also by Jesus" (2
Corinthians 4:14).

24

THE FIRST RESURRECTION

Awake and sing, ye that dwell in the dust.

ISAIAH 26:19

The saints' bodies shall rise out of their graves triumphal; the bodies of the wicked, with trembling. Some are about to receive their fatal doom; the others, awake from the dust too, shall sing for joy. When the archangel's trumpet sounds, the bodies of believers shall come out of the grave, as the chief butler came out of the prison and was restored to his dignity in the court, to be happy, but the bodies of the wicked shall come out of the grave, as the chief baker out of prison, to be executed (Genesis 40:21–22).

The same body that dies shall rise again, and with the soul be crowned. Without this belief, every religion will fall to the ground. If the dead rise not, then Christ is not risen, and our faith is in vain (1 Corinthians 15:14).

The body is sensitive to joy, as well as the soul; and indeed, we shall not be in our glory until our bodies are reunited to our souls. The grave is your long home, but not your last home. Though at death all our strength and beauty be taken away, at the resurrection God will restore all again in a more glorious manner. "Blessed and holy is he that hath a part in the first resurrection" (Revelation 20:6). The body of he who lies buried in sin shall be raised, but not in glory. This is the first resurrection; and if your souls are thus spiritually raised, your bodies shall be gloriously raised, and shall shine as stars in the kingdom of heaven.

25

No More Death

Glorify God in your body.

1 CORINTHIANS 6:20

God will glorify our bodies if our bodies glorify Him.

God will not leave us in the grave, for we will be united to Christ. The dust of a believer is part of Christ's spiritual body.

The soul does not sleep in the body, but "shall return unto God who gave it" (Ecclesiastes 12:7). When God's time is come, the graves shall deliver up their dead (Revelation 20:13). Though the bodies of the saints shall rot and be repugnant in the grave, yet afterwards they shall be made illustrious and glorious. Therefore the resurrection is called a time of restoring things. The bodies of the saints shall be made like Christ's glorious body, and "they shall hunger no more" (Revelation 7:16).

At the resurrection the saints' bodies will be immortal: "This mortal must put on immortality" (1 Corinthians 15:53). Our bodies shall run parallel with eternity. "Neither can they die any more" (Luke 20:36).

Believers' bodies shall be raised up to glory and shall be openly acquitted on judgment day: "For we must all appear before the judgment seat of Christ" (2 Corinthians 5:10).

By the testimony of Scripture that there will be a day of judgment: "For God shall bring every work into judgment, with every secret thing" (Ecclesiastes 12:14) and "For he cometh, for he cometh to judge the earth" (Psalm 96:13). Reduplication denotes the certainty.

"I beheld till the thrones were cast down, and the Ancient of days did sit, whose garment was white as snow. . . . The judgment was set, and the books were opened" (Daniel 7:9–10).

26

CHRIST THE JUDGE

The Father . . . hath committed all judgment to the Son.

JOHN 5:22

There will be a day of retribution, in which God renders to everyone according to his work. Things seem to be carried unequally in the world: the wicked to prosper, as if they were rewarded for doing evil; and the godly to suffer, as if they were punished for being good. Therefore, for vindicating the justice of God, there must be a day wherein there shall be a righteous distribution of punishments and rewards to men, according to their actions.

The Lord Jesus Christ will be the judge (John 5:22). It is an article of our creed that Christ shall come "to judge the quick and the dead" (1 Peter 4:5). It is a great honor put upon Christ: He who was Himself judged shall be judge; He who once hung upon the cross shall sit upon the throne of judgment. He is fit to be judge, as He partakes of both the manhood and Godhead.

Being clothed with the human nature, Jesus may be visibly seen of all. It is requisite the judge should be seen: "Behold, he cometh with clouds; and every eye shall see him" (Revelation 1:7). As He partakes of the Godhead, Jesus is of infinite knowledge to understand all causes brought before Him and of infinite power to execute offenders. He is described with seven eyes (Zechariah 3:9) to denote His wisdom; and a rod of iron (Psalm 2:9) to denote His power. He is so wise that He cannot be deluded and so strong that He cannot be resisted.

27

THE GREAT JUDGMENT

Of that day and hour knoweth no man, no,
not the angels of heaven, but my Father only.

MATTHEW 24:36

One great sign of the approach of the day of judgment is that "iniquity shall abound" (Matthew 24:12). Sure then that day is near at hand, for iniquity never more abounded than in this age, in which lust grows hot and love grows cold. When the elect are all converted, then Christ will come to judgment. As he that rows a ferryboat stays till all the passengers are taken in and then rows away, so Christ stays till all the elect are gathered in, and then He will hasten away to judgment.

The dead and the living will be cited. Men, when they die, avoid the censure of the law courts, but at the last day, they are cited to God's tribunal. "I saw the dead, small and great, stand before God" (Revelation 20:12). This citing of men will be by the sound of a trumpet. This trumpet will sound so loud it will raise men from their graves. Those who don't hear the trumpet of the gospel sound, "Repent and believe!", will hear the trumpet of the archangel sounding, "Arise, and be judged."

The approach of the judge to the tribunal will be terrible to the wicked. How will sinners tremble when they shall see Christ come to judgment! Christ is described, sitting in judgment, with a fiery stream issuing from Him. The Lamb of God will then be turned into a lion!

28

STANDING BEFORE THE JUDGE

Against thee, thee only, have I sinned.

PSALM 51:4

Christ will come in splendor and great glory to administer justice on the last day. He was like a prince in disguise at His first coming; but His second coming will be illustrious: He shall come in the glory of His Father. What a bright day, when a vast number of angels, those morning stars, appear in the air, and Christ the Sun of Righteousness shall shine in splendor above the brightest cherub! He will come as a friend: He who loves the saints, and prayed for them, is their judge. They need not fear.

The trial will fall heavy on the wicked when the judge is set and the books opened. The sinners' charges being read, their sins laid open, Christ will say, "What can you plead for yourselves, that the sentence of death should not pass?" Then, convicted, the dismal sentence: "Depart from me, ye cursed, into everlasting fire, prepared for the devil and his angels" (Matthew 25:41). He that said to God, "Depart from us" (Job 21:14) and to religion, "Depart from me," will hear his judge say, "Depart from me": a dreadful, but a righteous, sentence. The sinner himself shall cry, "Guilty!" When once the sentence is passed, it is irreversible; there is no appealing to a higher court.

The trial has also a light side: it will increase the joy and happiness of the righteous. The day of judgment will be a day of jubilee to the saints.

29

CHRIST WILL OWN THE SAINTS BY NAME

He shall bring forth thy righteousness as the light.

PSALM 37:6

Those whom the world scorned, Christ will take by the hand and openly acknowledge as His, openly acknowledging them to be precious in His eyes.

Christ is judge and advocate, sitting on the bench and pleading at the day of judgment. Christ will plead His own blood: "These persons I have purchased. They are the travail of My soul. They have sinned, but My soul was made an offering for their sin." Christ will vindicate them and clear their innocence. He will wipe their tears and absolve His people before men and angels, saying of the elect, "I find no fault in them. I pronounce them righteous." Then, "Come, ye blessed of my Father, inherit the kingdom" (Matthew 25:34).

Christ will mention before men and angels all the good deeds the saints have done. Christ will take notice of it at the last day and say, "Well done, thou good and faithful servant" (Matthew 25:21). The saints shall sit with Christ in judgment as justices of peace, applauding Christ's righteous sentence on the wicked. As it is a great honor to the saints, so it adds to the sorrows of the wicked, to see those whom they once hated and ridiculed sit as judges upon them.

The saints shall be fully crowned with the enjoyment of God forever; they shall be in His sweet presence forever. The banner of God's love will be eternally displayed. The joys of heaven shall be without intermission and expiration, "and so shall we ever be with the Lord" (1 Thessalonians 4:17).

30

THE LAST DAY

The Lord himself shall descend from heaven with a shout,
with the voice of the archangel, and the trump of God . . .
wherefore comfort one another with these words.

1 THESSALONIANS 4:16, 18

The day of judgment comforts in respect of weakness of grace. At the last day, if Christ finds only a measure of true grace, it shall be accepted. If thine be true gold, though it is many grains too light, Christ will put His merits into the scales and make it pass current.

What a comfort is it to the saints who have met unrighteous judgment in the world, who have been wronged of their wealth in lawsuits or had their lives taken away by an unrighteous sentence: Christ will judge things again and will give a righteous sentence. If your wealth has been taken away wrongfully, you shall be restored a thousandfold at the day of judgment. If you have lost your life for Christ, you shall not lose your crown; you shall wear a garland made of the flowers of paradise, which fade not away.

The meditation of this last day should make us very sincere. We should labor to approve our hearts to God, the great Judge of the world. God sees what the heart is and will accordingly pass His verdict.

Christ's coming to judge us should also keep us from judging our brethren. "Who art thou that judgest another?" (James 4:12). You that passest a rash sentence upon another, you must come shortly to be judged, and then perhaps he may be acquitted and you condemned.

So demean and carry yourself that, at the last day of judgment, you may be sure to be acquitted and have the glorious privileges with which the saints shall be crowned.

31

THE VOICE OF GOD

*Herein do I exercise myself, to have always a
conscience void to offence toward God, and toward men.*

ACTS 24:16

Be careful, holy, and just. Have hearts without false aims, and hands without false weights.

Keep conscience as clear as your eye. They that sin against conscience will be shy of their judge. Christian, your conscience will be opened at the last day, and Christ will search to see what sins, what prohibited goods, thou hast taken in; then He proceeds to judgment. The voice of conscience is the voice of God. If conscience, upon just grounds, acquits us, God will acquit us. "If our heart condemn us not, then have we confidence toward God" (1 John 3:21).

If you would stand acquitted at the last day, trade with your talents for God's glory; honor Him with your substance; relieve Christ's members, that you may be acquitted.

If you would stand acquitted at the day of judgment, get a sincere love to the saints.

Love is the truest touchstone of sincerity. To love grace for grace shows the spirit of God to be in a man. Does conscience witness for you? Are you perfumed with this sweet spice of love? Do you delight most in those in whom the image of God shines? Do you reverence their graces? Do you bear with their infirmities? One blessed evidence that you shall be acquitted in the day of judgment: "We know that we have passed from death unto life, because we love the brethren" (1 John 3:14). Hallelujah!

DEDICATION

It is with deep respect, honor, and love that I dedicate this book to my dear late husband Rev. Donald R. Hummel, Sr., who introduced me to the works of mighty men of God like Thomas Watson. Without Don's devotion to Christ and his commitment to sharing the truths that he learned, this new devotional work taken from Watson's *A Body of Divinity* would not be a reality. Don lived his life the same way Watson did, determined that Christ would be glorified in and through him.

Also, to Tiffany, Devan-Marie, Donnie, Leigh, Mia, Dan & Kathy, who, in their unique and special way, offer much to my life every day.

THANK YOU

When a work requires as much research as *Glorifying God*, many people are needed to pull it together, making certain the original intention is also the final product. It is with a grateful heart that I thank Mark Gilroy, who believed in this project from the beginning; Lisa Stilwell who embraced it with genuine commitment to see it become what was intended from the beginning and that the voice of Thomas Watson would not be lost—that the Biblical message would remain at the forefront. I am also thankful to each person at Thomas Nelson Publishers, who worked tirelessly to make this book the beautiful example of quality and solid message that it is.

Thank you to Lisa Guest, who spent hours working with me on the final edit.

How does one thank a man like Pastor Byron Yawn, who wrote the Introduction for this work by Thomas Watson that touched his life many years ago? Pastor, I am indeed grateful for your continuous encouragement, support, and prayers as I completed this manuscript. Your life is an inspiration to me because, like Watson, you desire to bring glory to God every day.

Thank you to Dr. J. Robertson McQuilken, Dr. D. Jeffrey Bingham, Pastor Doug Searle, and Dr. Jim and Mrs. Joyce Carpenter for encouraging me as you reviewed the manuscript, offered advice and guidance, and endorsed Watson's work.

And thank you, readers. It is my prayer that your life will be enriched and brought closer to Christ as you read from the heart of a man who spent his adult life in the study of the Word of God, learning how to express, and expressing, the joy of *Glorifying God*!